瑷珲海关
历史档案辑要

监管征税（下）
（第四卷）

黑龙江省档案馆　编译

社会科学文献出版社
SOCIAL SCIENCES ACADEMIC PRESS (CHINA)

目 录

专题三

邮寄包裹

1. 为要求对往来满洲商埠的邮寄包裹实行统一征税办法事

Postal Parcel : taxation of in Manchurian trade marts.
uniform procedure desirable. Report in re requested.

C O P Y.

N No. 2367/80,428

Inspectorate General of Customs,

Peking, 29th Sept. 1920.

Sir,

    I am directed by the Inspector General to say that reports received from Antung, Dairen and Newchwang show that there is a great divergence among these ports in the duty and transit dues treatment of postal parcels sent to, or arriving from, Manchurian Trade Marts. The Inspector General considers that it would be desirable to have a uniform procedure for all Manchurian Custom Houses and that the correct procedure would be to follow the duty treatment accorded to ordinary cargo. Before introducing any changes in your office practice, however, I am to request you to report how such a change would affect your office and if any local difficulties would arise in carrying it out.

    You are further requested to submit a comparative table - vide appendix - showing differences in the present duty and transit dues treatment between postal parcels and ordinary cargo passing through, destined for, or originating from, a Manchurian Trade Mart.

    If necessary you may consult the Commissioners of the other Manchurian Customs to whom a similar despatch is being addressed in this matter, before despatching your reply

        I am, etc.

        (Signed) J. W. Richardson,

        Chief Secretary.

The Commissioner of Customs,

    H A R B I N.

        True Copy,

        2nd Clerk, D.

APPENDIX.

Duty treatment of Postal Parcels and ordinary goods by Tahuiho & Aigun Customs Houses.

Route	Foreign or Native	Present Duty Treatment of Postal Parcels	Present Duty Treatment of ordinary Goods
Port – Mart	Foreign	Full Import	Free Import
	Native	" Export	" Export
Mart – Port	Foreign	" Import	" Import
	Native	" Export	" Export
Mart – Port – Inland	Foreign	Free	" Import
	Native	Free	" Export
Inland – Port – Mart	Foreign	Free	" Import
	Native	Free	" Export
Mart – Port – Port	Foreign	Free	" Import
	Native	Free	" Export
Port – Port – Mart	Foreign	Full Import	" Import
	Native	Full Export	" Export
Inland – Mart – Port	Foreign	Full Import	" Import
	Native	Full Export	" Export
Port – Mart – Inland	Foreign	Full Import	" Import
	Native	Full Export	" Export
Inland – Mart – Port – Inland	Foreign	Free	" Import
	Native	Free	" Export

NOTE : For purposes of this table, any open mart at the frontier is to be considered as a port.

True Copy,

2nd Clerk, D.

Custom House,
Aigun/Tahuiho, 26. Oct. 70

2° Ant-g.

致哈尔滨关第 2367/80428 号令　　　　海关总税务司署（北京）1920 年 9 月 29 日

尊敬的哈尔滨关税务司：

　　奉总税务司命令，特此告知，据安东关、大连关及牛庄关呈文所示，该几处口岸对往来满洲商埠的邮政包裹所采取的关税及子口半税征收办法存在较大差异。总税务司认为满洲各关应统一征收手续，最好依照普通货物的征税办法办理。然在做出调整之前，请先汇报说明调整后会对哈尔滨关有何影响，执行过程是否会有何困难。

　　另请呈交对照表一份（参阅附录），以示哈尔滨关对往来满洲商埠的邮政包裹及普通货物所采取的关税及子口半税征收标准有何不同。

　　此令亦已发送至满洲其他各关，如有必要，回复之前可与其他税务司商议。

　　　　　　　　　　　　　　　　　　　　您忠诚的仆人

　　　　　　　　　　　　　　　　　李家森（J. W. Richardson）

　　　　　　　　　　　　　　　　　　　总务科税务司

该抄件内容真实有效，特此证明：

录事：二等同文供事副后班

附录

大黑河及瑷珲口岸对往来满洲商埠的邮政包裹及普通货物所采取的征税办法

运输路线	洋货／土货	邮政包裹	普通货物
口岸－商埠	洋货	进口正税	进口正税
	土货	出口正税	出口正税
商埠－口岸	洋货	进口正税	进口正税
	土货	出口正税	出口正税
商埠－口岸－内地	洋货	免税	进口正税
	土货	免税	出口正税
内地－口岸－商埠	洋货	免税	进口正税
	土货	免税	出口正税
商埠－口岸－口岸	洋货	免税	进口正税
	土货	免税	出口正税
口岸－口岸－商埠	洋货	进口正税	进口正税
	土货	出口正税	出口正税
内地－商埠－口岸	洋货	进口正税	进口正税
	土货	出口正税	出口正税
口岸－商埠－内地	洋货	进口正税	进口正税
	土货	出口正税	出口正税
内地－商埠－口岸－内地	洋货	免税	进口正税
	土货	免税	出口正税

注：对于上表所列，凡边境沿线开放之商埠一律视作口岸。

2. 为指示满洲出入境邮递包裹何时征收子口税及修订征税办法事

[4.—29]

No. 5　COMMRS.

Aigun　No. 86,519

INSPECTORATE GENERAL OF CUSTOMS,

PEKING, 1st November, 1921.

Sir,

With reference to the Collection of Duty and Transit Dues on Postal Parcels to and from the interior of Manchuria, I am directed by the Inspector General to instruct you as follows :

1. Postal Parcels containing foreign or native goods, arriving at your port from the interior posted at a place which is not a Manchurian trade mart, are on arrival to be charged Transit Dues, no matter whether they are intended for local consumption or for transmission to a foreign country, a Chinese treaty port, a Manchurian trade mart or a place in the interior of Manchuria which is not a trade mart.

2. Postal Parcels containing foreign or native goods, arriving at your port from the interior, posted a trade mart, are to be passed free of Transit

Dues

The Commissioner of Customs,

　AIGUN.

Dues if they are intended for local consumption or for transmission to a foreign country, a Chinese treaty port or a Manchurian trade mart. If they are intended for transmission to a place in the interior of Manchuria which is not a trade mart they are to be charged Transit Dues.

3. Postal Parcels containing foreign or native goods arriving at your port from a foreign country or Chinese treaty port, are to be charged Transit Dues if they are intended for transmission to a place in the interior which is not a trade mart. If they are intended for transmission to a Manchurian trade mart they are to be passed free of Transit Dues.

4. Postal Parcels containing foreign or native goods, posted at your port and sent by land, to a Manchurian trade mart are to be passed free of all dues and duties: if sent by land to an inland place in Manchuria, that is not a trade mart, they are to be charged Transit Dues only.

5.

5. In the case of foreign goods arriving from a foreign country for transmission to the interior and native goods arriving from the interior for transmission to a foreign country the Transit Dues collected are to be carried to Revenue Account. In all other cases the Transit Dues collected by you under the above instructions are to be placed in a separate account and held pending further instructions which will be issued by Circular.

I am,

Sir,

Your obedient Servant,

Cecil a. v. Browne

Chief Secretary.

N.

I. G.

Aigun / Taheiho 19th November, 21.

Sir,

In reply to Circular No. 3220, II :

Collection of likin, or transit dues in
lieu of likin, on postal parcels :
procedure re, and disposal of, etc.:

I have the honour to report that so far no likin
or transit dues have been collected by this Office
on postal parcels.

I have the honour to be,

Sir,

Your obedient Servant,

Acting Commissioner.

The Inspector General of Customs,

PEKING.

9.

I. G.

Aigun / Taheiho, 21st November, 1921.

Sir,

I have the honour to acknowledge the
receipt of your Despatch No. 5/86,519 :

Postal Parcels : to and from interior
of Manchuria : Transit Dues on, when to
be collected, instructions re :

and to ask for further instructions with regard

to duty treatment of Postal Parcels.

1.　　　The present practice of this Office may be

briefly summarised as follows :

A. Parcels originating at another Treaty Port

are passed without examination and without charging

duty, if sealed by the Custom House at place of

origin.

B. Parcels from one Inland place to another,

whether

The Inspector General of Customs,

PEKING.

- whether they pass through one Treaty Port or several - are not examined, and are passed free of all duties here, following the instructions of the last paragraph of Circular No. 2397.

C. All other parcels, irrespective of the origin or destination, and of the nature of the goods, are charged one full duty at the rate of 5 % _ad valorem_; if the value is under ¥ 15, they are passed free. Duty thus collected is carried to account under "Import", in the case of incoming parcels, and under "Export", in the case of outgoing parcels.

2.   Port practice requires certain readjustments to fall in line with the instructions just received; I have therefore the honour to request your ruling on the following points :

1. Shall this Office in future collect duty on parcels passing Aigun _en route_ between two inland places, as indicated in par. 2 of your Despatch ? Such course requires, I believe, a special working agreement with the C. P. O., which must collect duty at destination on behalf of the Customs, or pay duty first and recover the amount

afterwards

afterwards from the consignees.- I would also like to know what arrangements have been made with the Post Office by other open Ports (Shanghai, etc), for parcels posted at a place in the Interior for transmission to a Foreign Country, (par. 2) and for parcels from a Foreign Country for transmission to a place in the Interior. - Parcels from abroad destined to another Treaty Port may be more conveniently left to pay at destination, of course.

2. Are goods arriving from - or destined to - a Trade Mart wich is also an open Port (Harbin, Hunchun), to be passed free of all dues and duties when carried by parcel ? (par. 4).

3. Shall this Office re-examine - and collect additional duty on, if due - parcels originating at an open Port, if they are properly stamped by the Customs and are presented intact here ? . This course seems indicated by the words (par. 3) :"from "a foreign country or Chinese Treaty Port, are to "be charged Transit Dues if they are intended for "transmission to a place in the interior". A heavy additional burden would be thrown on our very

short-handed

short-handed Examiners' Staff and on the General
Office if we had to adopt such a procedure.

4. Shall we go on collecting one full duty
only on parcels to or from China proper, or
shall we

a) collect Coast Trade Duty on native goods
passing through more than one Treaty Port outside
of Manchuria, and

b) collect Transit Dues on parcels originating
from - or destined to - a place in the interior
of China, so as not to discriminate against
parcels moved within Manchuria ?

5. Taheiho (a barrier of Aigun) is considered
as a Trade Mart and an open Port for duty
paying purposes: what is the status - for the
purpose of duty treatment of postal parcels, and
eventually of issue of Manchurian Special Exemption
Certificates - of Suifenho (not a Trade Mart, but
empowered to issue Manchurian Special E. C.),
Lahasusu (which has been recently changed from a
Barrier to a Station) and Lungchints'un (which,
although opened to Trade together with three other

places

places by the Chientao agreement, and a branch Office of the Hunchun Customs, is nevertheless not enumerated amongst the Trade Marts) ?

3.   Pending receipt of further instructions, I have notified the Public of the new ruling for collection of Transit Dues on Postal Parcels, and asked the C. P.O. to present for examination and payment of duties all parcels, including those en route from an inland place to another. But I will not be very strict on the latter point, which is still open to the objections set forth in your Circular No. 2397.

Concerning my question No. 2, I gave orders to continue collecting one full duty on parcels to Treaty Ports which are also Trade Marts, and generally to go on with the old practice for the time being.

I have the honour to be,

Sir,

Your obedient Servant,

Acting Commissioner.

[A.—29]

No. 14   COMMRS.

Aigun   No. 87,199

INSPECTORATE GENERAL OF CUSTOMS,

PEKING, 17th December, 1921.

Sir,

In reply to your despatch No. 9 :

Postal Parcels: duty treatment of : Aigun practice reported, and instructions on collection of Transit Dues and on other points, solicited;

the Inspector General directs me to state that

1. The rules concerning the duty treatment of Postal Parcels are given in the Handbook of Customs Procedure at Shanghai page 138, etc. These rules apply equally to Manchuria. In § 357 of that book, sections 2 and 4, there ought not to be a comma before " which can be reached ".

2. For the present you need not collect dues or duties on a parcel going from one inland place to another.

3.

The Commissioner of Customs,

    AIGUN.

3. For this purpose a Trade Mart where there is no Custom House is to be treated as an inland place.

4. A Trade Mart where there is a Custom House, e.g. Lahasusu, Suifenho and Lungchingts'un, is to be treated as a treaty port.

5. Parcels from Aigun to Taheiho, or from Taheiho to Aigun, are to be treated for duty paying purposes in the same way as goods shipped from the one place to the other.

6. A parcel sent to Harbin or Hunchun is to be charged duty if it contains dutiable goods.

7. Parcels arriving at, or passing through, your port that were originally posted at a treaty port must be considered to have paid all the dues and duties due on them when they were posted.

I am,

Sir,

Your obedient Servant,

Chief Secretary.

No. 18

Aigun

COMMRS.

No. 87,308

INSPECTORATE GENERAL OF CUSTOMS,

PEKING,   28th December, 1921.

Sir,

1.   With reference to my despatch No. 5/86,519:

Postal Parcels to and from interior of
Manchuria: Transit Dues on, when to be
collected;

the Inspector General directs me to inform you that,

in deference to the wishes of the Co-Director

General of Posts, he has agreed for the present not

to collect dues or duties on parcels passing through

your port sent from one inland place to another,

and for this purpose to consider as an inland

place a trade mart where there is no Custom House.

2.   In the case of parcels from the interior,

passing through your port on their way to another

treaty port, the transit dues on them can be

collected at the second port, if this is more

convenient.

3.

The Commissioner of Customs,

A I G U N.

3.　　　　　　The instructions of § 4 of that despatch
are also to be modified.　A trade mart where
no Custom House has been opened is to be treated
for all Customs purposes as an inland place,
except that if goods that are entitled to a
Special Manchurian Exemption Certificate apply for
such a Certificate and are sent under it to a
trade mart they must of course be passed free.
If they do not take out a Special Manchurian
Exemption Certificate and are sent by parcel post
from your port to a mart where there is no
Custom House, they are to be charged transit dues
in lieu of likin and they are to be treated
in the same way if they arrive at your port
from such a trade mart.　On the other hand a
trade mart where a Custom House has been opened
is to be treated as a treaty port.　Parcels
sent to it are to be charged the same duties
as if they were sent to Tientsin or any other

Chinese

Chinese treaty port, unless of course they are
entitled to, and covered by, Special Exemption
Certificate.

> I am,
>
> Sir,
>
> Your obedient Servant,

Chief Secretary.

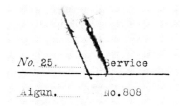

No. 25.   Service

Aigun.   No.808

CUSTOM HOUSE,

HARBIN, 3rd November, 1922.

Sir,

1.   The Harbin Authorities having raised the question of the treatment of Postal Parcels as compared with the treatment of goods sent as freight, pointing out that the former were at a disticnct disadvantage as compared with the latter, the question was referred to the Inspector General for decision.

2.   As the Inspector General's subsequent instructions affect the whole of North Manchuria, including your district, I beg to hand you, herewith enclosed, copies of the correspondence which has taken place, namely:

Harbin Despatch to I.G. of 2nd August, 1922, No.2683.

I.G. Despatch to Harbin of 7th September, 1922, No.2936/90,993.

Harbin Despatch to I.G. of 26th October, 1922, No.2740.

3.   On the strength of the Inspector General's instructions, Harbin Practice Order No. 119 has been issued, and of this, also, I enclose a copy for your information.

I am,

Sir,

Your obedient Servant,

Commissioner.

To

The Commissioner of Customs,

AIGUN.

COPY.

2683.

I.G.   Harbin, 2nd August, 1922.

       Sir,

1.   A very important Postal Parcels Traffic is
       developing in this district, which will assume still
       greater proportions as soon as the negotiations now
       taking place between China on one part and Soviet
       Russia and the Far Eastern Republic on the other,
       have been concluded. In this connection, Mr, Ritchie,
       Postal Commissioner for North Manchuria, is very
       anxious to obtain as many facilities as possible
       from the Customs with regards to the duty treatment
       and simplification of formalities. The following
       points have been raised by Mr. Ritchie, some of which
       I have been able to settle locally, others which
       require reference to the Inspectorate General before
       a definite reply can be given.

2.   The Postal Commissioner for North Manchuria
       and the Chief of Posts and Telegraphs of the
       Priamur District (Vladivostock) having concluded an
       agreement relative to the re-posting at Suifenho of
       Parcels from the Priamur destined for places in
       North Manchuria, I was requested by the former to
       assist in the development of this postal traffic by
       facilitating the Customs formalities at the frontier
       station.

             I have acceded to this request   and the
       following procedure has been established at Suifenho:

                                        1). Parcels
To
   the Inspector General of Customs

      P E K I N G.

1). Parcels from the Priamur for North Manchurian places, on arrival at Suifenho, are escorted from the train to the Chinese Post Office by Customs Officers, and their handing over to the Chinese Post Office is duly supervised.

2). Duty on parcels for Suifenho or for places between Suifenho and Harbin is assessed at Suifenho and parcels held there pending collection from the addressees by the Postal Authorities.

3). For parcels destined for Harbin or beyond in North Manchuria, duty payment is arranged for at the last Custom House passed before parcels reach the destination. Such parcels are stamped by the Customs Officer on duty at the Chinese Post Office at Suifenho "From abroad: To Pay".

3.　　　The second request from the Postal Commissioner is relative to the exchange of mail bags between Harbin and Vladivostock and _vice versa_. These mail bags were originally handed over à découvert, thus involving a day's delay in transit. The new agreement concluded between the Chinese Post Office and the Priamur Post Office provides for direct closed mails between Harbin and Vladivostock and _vice versa_, and for the examination of these mail bags by the Customs at the frontier station of Suifenho in the mail vans. The Postal Commissioner explains that the mail vans which are controlled and paid for by the Chinese Post Office are allowed to run through to Vladivostock

as

as a matter of courtesy and convenience to the Priamur Post Office. The closed mails will in no case contain parcels. I have requested to facilitate the transit of these closed mails so that no delay takes place at the frontier.

This question presents no difficulty and I have replied to the Postal Commisioner that closed mail bags bearing the seals of the Chinese Post Office when going outwards, and those arriving inwards and handed over to the Chinese Post Office at the frontier, will not be intefered with or delayed in transit, that we reserve the right of searching the mail vans for contraband, etc., and that we rely on the Chinese Post Office to see that closed bags to and from Vladivostok for and from North Manchuria contain no parcels.

4.   The third request from the Postal Commissioner concerns the discriminatory duty treatment of Postal Parcels in North Manchuria. Mr. Ritchie complains that:

1) Coast Trade duty is levied on postal parcels while goods moving by rail or river are exempted from this levy, and that

2) while goods transported on the Chinese Eastern Railway pay duty at the tariff rate reduced by one-third, Postal Parcels are charged the full import or export duty.

I replied to Mr. Ritchie that while every effort was being made to accord the same duty treatment to postal

postal parcels as is given to freight, yet in some
instances, of which the levy of Coast Trade duty
within North Manchuria is one, it was not possible
for this office to change its present practice
which is based on instructions from the Inspectorate.

5.   With regard to the levy of duty at the full
tariff rates on parcels transported on the Chinese
Eastern Railway instead of at reduced rate as paid
by freight, this matter can be adjusted by applying
the ruling of Article 67 of the Provisional Regulations
for the working of Chinese Custom House at Suifenho
and Manchouli, which reads as follow: "All regulations
relative to duty payment at reduced rate or exemption
from duty are equally applicable to articles sent by
postal parcels from within, or into, the station areas".
Previous to the closing of the Russian Post Offices
in 1920 all the postal parcels traffic was handled .
by the Russian Post Office at the reduced tariff rates.
There is no reason therefore why the same preferential
treatment should not be applied to parcels now
handled by the Chinese Post Office, and I propose
with your authorization to alter our practice forthwith
of charging full tariff.

6.   The levy of transit dues __in lieu__ of likin
(by the Customs for the account of the Likin
Authorities) is another source of anxiety and
irritation for the Postal Commissioner. I have
explained to Mr. Ritchie that the withdrawal of this
levy by the Customs would surely bring forth the
opening of likin offices at the doors of the
Chinese Post office at inland places, which was very
undesirable.

                                        7.   Mr.

7.   Mr. Ritchie has also brought up the question
of Customs treatment of (a) postal parcels to and
from the Priamur from and to places in China and
(b) of postal parcels from the Priamur for Foreign
countries in transit through Manchuria and Shanghai.
(1) Question (a): concerning parcels between China
and the Priamur and vice versa can be settled
without any difficulty. The exchange will take
place at Suifenho; the parcels from the Priamur
arriving at Suifenho will be escorted to the
Chinese Post Office by Customs Officers and their
handing over to the Chinese Post Office duly
supervised. The Customs duty treatment of parcels
destined for Suifenho, Harbin and beyond in North
Manchuria will be explained in paragraph 2 of
this despatch. For parcels destined for places in
China duty will be assessed at destination if there
is a Custom House at the place, otherwise at the
last Custom House before reaching destination. This
procedure is in accordance with actual practice
for parcels from Foreign Countries. The following
stamp will appear on each parcel: "From Abroad :
To Pay".
(2) For parcels emanating from the Priamur destined
for Foreign Countries and sent in transit through
Manchuria to Shanghai for shipment abroad through
the Chinese Post Office, the Customs duty treatment
cannot be settled without previous reference to the
Inspectorate. Two courses are open:
a) to charge import duty at Suifenho on arrival
from the Priamur and release the parcels for export
abroad in transit through Shanghai and the use of
a special stamp to show that duty has been paid
                                                    at

at Suifenho; or

b) to exempt these parcels from duty, plumb the postal
bags, baskets, etc., with Customs plumbs, which will be
removed by the Shanghai Customs at time of
exportation, the Post Office to supply all necessary
proof of re-exportation abroad.

On one hand I would recommend taking advantage of
the present situation - the absence of Postal Parcels
arrangement between the Far Eastern Republic and other
countries - to consider these parcels from the Priamur
as importations and charge duty; on the other hand
this arrangement with the Priamur Postal Authorities
will be of great benefit to the sister Service and
to the Chinese Government and the less burden and
formalities we place on this traffic the more benefit
will accrue to the Chinese Government. We must
however, take what securities are necessary to assure
ourselves that the parcels passing in transit through C
China actually leave for abroad.

                    I have etc.,
              Signed: R. d'Anjou.
              Commissioner.

True Copy:

3rd Assistant A.

<u>COPY.</u>

No.2.936. Commrs.   INSPECTORATE GENERAL OF CUSTOMS,

Harbin.   No.90,993.   PEKING, 7th September, 1922.

Sir,

       I am directed by the Inspector General to acknowledge receipt of your Despatch No.2,683:

       Postal Parcels: development in North Manchuria Arrangements for exchange of mails and parcels between Chinese Post Office and Maritime Provinces and in future with Soviet Russia and Far Eastern Republic: Postal Commissioner requests change in duty treatment of parcels and facilities for fostering parcel traffic:

and, in reply, to state as follows:

1. <u>Parcels from the Priamur for North Manchurian Places:</u>

       The proposed procedure is approved, provided that the arrangement for duty payment at the last Custom House passed before the parcels reach their destinations referred to in § 2 (3) is such as to ensure that the parcels will be duly presented for Customs examination and payment of duty before proceeding to their destinations. You are requested to state the details of this arrangement.

2. <u>Exchange of Mail Bags between Harbin and Vladivostock and vice-versa:</u>

       This arrangement is approved provided that
                                     you

The Commissioner of Customs,

    H A R B I N.

you have an assurance in writing from the Postal
Commissioner that these closed bags will contain no
parcels, but that should any parcels be discovered
in them, the parcels will be detained by the Post
Office and the fact at once communicated to the
Customs.

3. Coast Trade Duty on Postal Parcels moving
   within North Manchuria:

    The principle to be followed here is that
which is laid down in the first paragraph of I. G.
despatch 2739/87,007, namely parcels shall be treated
as nearly as possible in the same way as ordinary
goods conveyed through the Customs. Coast Trade
Duty on Postal Parcels transported to or from a
Trade Mart in North Manchuria where there is a
Collecting Custom House need not therefore be
charged in future if goods otherwise conveyed throug
the Customs are exempt. But Transit Dues in lieu
of Likin are to continue to be charged, in
accordance with the instructions of I. G. despatch
No.2762/87,307, on parcels (not under, or entitled to
a Special Manchurian Exemption Certificate) to and
from Trade Marts where there are no Custom House.

4. Levy of Duty at Full Tariff Rates on Parcels
   Transported on the Chinese Eastern Railway:

    The reduced import and export tariff rates
may be applied to parcels transported on the
Chinese Eastern Railway to or from places in
North Manchuria in the same manner as they are
applied to cargo carried as freight on this
Railway to and from such places for so long a
time as freight cargo continues to enjoy this
                                    privilege.

privilege.

5. <u>The levy of Transit Dues in lieu of Likin:</u>

Parcels on which the Customs levy Transit Dues in lieu of Likin are rightly subject to Likin which must be paid, and the present method of collecting it is undoubtdly less inconvenient than any other ~~other~~ both to the Post Office and to the public.

6. <u>Parcels to and from the Priamur from and to places in China:</u>

This procedure is approved provided that the arrangement - with regard to which you are requested to report, as under (2) above - made for examination and payment of duty at the last Custom House passed before the parcels reach their destination is satisfactory.

7. <u>Parcels from the Priamur for Foreign Countries in transit through Manchuria and Shanghai:</u>

I am to enquire if it would not be possible to come to an arrangement with the Post Office with regard to these parcels similar to that authorised by I. G, despatch No.2779/87,573 whereby, in the case of Postal Parcels imported by rail from Siberia into Manchuli and transported thence through the Chinese Post Office to Shanghai for re-export abroad, drawbacks may be issued on definite proof of re-export being furnished to the Harbin Customs by the Chinese Post Office.

I am, etc.,

Signed: C. Bowra.

Chief Secretary.

True Copy:

3rd Assistant A.

2740

I. G.

Harbin, 26th October, 1922.

Sir,

1.   I have the honour to acknowledge receipt of I. G. Despatch No.2936/90,993 (in reply to Harbin Despatch No.2683):

relative to the development in North Manchuria of Postal Traffic, arrangements for the exchange of mails between the Chinese Post Office and the Maritime Provinces and in futur with Soviet Russia and the Far Eastern Republic and to certain concessions in the duty treatment of postal parcels granted by the Inspectorate at the request of the Postal Commissioner.

2.   In reply to the various queries made by the Inspectorate General in the body of that despatch I beg to report as follows, seriatim.

1. Parcels from the Priamur for North Manchurian Places.

The arrangement for duty payment at the last Custom House passed before the parcels reach destination will be on the lines of I.G. Circular No.1073 Postal No.60 (e) for International Parcels addressed direct to Inland places. Duty will be assessed by the Customs at the last Custom House passed and collected by the Chinese Post Office.

2. Exchange

To

The Inspector General of Customs.

I.

PEKING.

2. Exchange of Mail bags between Harbin and Vladivostok
and vice-versa.

I have the assurance in writing from the
Postal Commissioner that these closed mails will contain
no parcels, but that should any parcels be discovered
in them, the parcels will be detained by the Post
Office and the fact at once communicated to the
Customs.

3. Coast Trade Duty on Postal Parcels moving within North
Manchuria.

In this respect I am following instructions of
I.G. Despatches Nos.2739/87,007 and 2762/87,307 and those
of the I.G. Despatch under reply. I beg to remark that
part of the quotation under brackets made in I.G.
Despatch No.2936 e.g. (" or entitled to") is not in
agreement with the terms as laid down in I.G, despatch
No.2762 referred to and that I am not giving effect
to this interpretation. The Despatch referred to ｛
(No.2762) distinctly says: "If they do not take out a
Special Manchurian Exemption Certificate and are sent by
Parcel Post from your Port to a Mart where there is
no Custom House they are to be charged Transit Dues
in lieu of Likin and they are to be treated in the
same way if they arrive at your Port from such a
Trade Mart".

4. Levy of Duty at Full Tariff Rates on Parcels
transported on the Chinese Eastern Railway.

According to your instructions the reduced import
and export tariff rates are now being applied to
parcels transported on the Chinese Eastern Railway to
and from places in North Manchuria in the same manner
as they are applied to cargo carried as freight on
this

this railway to and from such places for so long a
time as freight cargo continues to enjoy this privilege.

5. The Levy of Transit Dues in lieu of Likin is
being continued according to your instructions.

6. Parcels to and from the Priamur from and to
places in China.

The same procedure will apply as now applies to
International Parcels sent direct to places Inland as
laid down in your Circular No.1073 Postal No.60 (e).

7. Parcels from the Priamur for Foreign Countries in
transit through Manchuria and Shanghai.

Recommandations as to the treatment of these parcels
will be made in good time.

8.   Copy of Despatch No.308 from the Postal Commissioner
relative to these matters is appended for your
information.

I have etc.,
Signed: R. d'Anjou.
Commissioner.

True Copy:

3rd Assistant A.

COPY.

No. 308   Postal   POST OFFICE.
General   No. -   Harbin, 27th September, 1922.

Sir,

I have the honour to acknowledge receipt of your despatch No.1400 of 21. September:

> Notifying the abolition of Coast Trade Duty on Postal Parcels moving within the North Manchuria and the reduction of Customs charges on parcels transported by the Chinese Eastern Railway

and to thank you for this additional proof of your interest in postal development in this territory.

<u>Coast Trade Duty and Reduction of Tariff Rate on Chinese Eastern Railway.</u> Information regarding the date on which the changes take effect is requested.

<u>Parcels from Priamuria to places in China.</u>

My despatch No.268 of 1. August last, gives the information desired by the Inspector General. As arrangements are not yet in force by which Priamursky postage stamps frank parcels in China, reposting at Suifenho with Chinese stamps is necessary. Parcels, actually originating at Suifenho, would under existing Customs rules have all Customs levies paid by the senders, but this is obviously not practicable in the case of goods by post from places in Priamuria. The application of the Customs procedure - collection of duty from the addressees at the last Treaty Port passed - in force for parcels from America, Great Britain etc., to China would meet all requirements. A parcel from Vladivostok to Chengtu would therefore, pay Duty at Chungking, and the Customs Revenue

would

The Commissioner of Customs,
    H A R B I N.

would be safeguarded for the small traffic expected from
Vladivostok in the ᴬsame way as at present for the enormous
import by parcel post from the United States.

Parcels from places in China to Priamuria. Here no
change in existing Customs procedure is asked for.
Parcels would pay duty at the Treaty Port of origin ;
if from an inland place, the first treaty port passed
would assess the Customs charges, the Post Office
retaining the parcel till revenue requirements were
satisfied. This is the practice for export parcels from
China to America etc.,

Exchange of mail bags, Harbin-Vladivostok and vice-versa
Harbin Despatch No.260 of 27. July last states that
"the arrangement therein outlined in no way concerns
parcels", and it is in this respect analogous to the
thousands of closed letter mails exchanged daily
between Post Offices in China, and to the frequent
letter mails between countries of the Postal Union
and China. The assurance asked for, however - that these
closed bags will contain no parcels, but that, should
any parcels be discovered in them, the parcels will
be detained, and the fact at once reported to the
Customs - is placed on record.

Parcels from Priamuria for Foreign Countries in
Transit through Manchuria and Shanghai. The arrangement
for drawbacks outlined by the Inspector General would
be welcomed by the Post Office, and the same safeguards
as are now applied, to the satisfaction of the Customs,
for fur parcels from the Far Eastern Republic, posted
at Manchuli Chinese Post Office for the United States,
could be successfully adopted for the traffic from
Priamuria.   Proposed

<u>Proposed levy of a Customs fee on drawback parcels.</u>

The Parcel Agreement between China and the Far Eastern Republic is still at the stage of discussion, but it does not in any case provide for the transmission by China of parcels from the Far Eastern Republic for foreign/countries. No increase of drawback work will therefore accrue, and the matter of a special levy per parcel to cover Customs expenses need not, it is suggested, arise at present.

I have etc.,

Signed: W.W. Ritchie,

Postal Commissioner.

True copy:

3rd Assistant <u>A</u>.

PRACTICE ORDER No. 119.

Harbin, 27th October, 1922.

POSTAL PARCELS: DUTY TREATMENT OF & GENERAL INSTRUCTIONS:

In accordance with the instructions of I.G. Desps.
Nos.2702/86,518, 2739/87,007, 2762/87,307 and 2936/90,993,
the duty treatment of Postal Parcels is henceforth to be
as follows.   This Order supersedes Practice Order No.77
but, it will be noted, includes the instructions of Practice
Order No.112 which, in accordance with I.G. Despatch No.
2936/90,993, directs that parcels containing native goods,
moved within North Manchuria, be exempt from Coast Trade
Duty, and that the 2/3rd duty treatment (and duty-free list)
privileges in existence for cargo moved on the Chinese
Eastern Railway, be extended to Postal Parcels.

From Abroad via Manchouli or Suifenho:

For Manchouli or Suifenho:	2/3rd Import Duty.
" Harbin :	2/3rd Import Duty.
" Chinese Eastern Railway Stations at which there is no Custom House:	2/3rd Import Duty.
" Trade Mart in North Manchuria at which there is a Custom House, not on the Chinese Eastern Railway:	Full Import Duty.
" Interior or a Trade Mart in North Manchuria at which there is no Custom House, not on the Chinese Eastern Railway:	2/3rd Import Duty and Transit Dues.
" Treaty Port in China Proper or South Manchuria:	Full Import Duty.
" Interior of China Proper or South Manchuria:	Full Import Duty and Transit Dues.
" Dairen :	Full Import Duty.

From

<u>From Abroad via Kwanchengtzu:</u>

For Trade Mart at which there   Full Import Duty.
    is a Custom House:

  " Interior or a Trade Mart   Full Import Duty and
    at which there is no   Transit Dues.
    Custom House:

       <u>From Manchouli or Suifenho:</u>

for abroad via Kwangchengtze:
Foreign: free
Native: Full Export Duty.

For Abroad via Manchouli or
    Suifenho:
        Foreign: Free.
        Native: 2/3rd Export Duty.

  " Chinese Eastern Railway
    Stations:
        Foreign: 2/3rd Import Duty.
        Native: Free.

  " Trade Mart <u>in North Manchuria</u>
    at which there is a Custom
    House, <u>not</u> on the Chinese
    Eastern Railway:
        Foreign: Full Import Duty.
        Native: Full Export Duty.

  " Interior or a Trade Mart <u>in</u>
    <u>North Manchuria</u> at which
    there is no Custom House,
    not on the Chinese Eastern
    Railway:
        Foreign: 2/3rd Import Duty and
                                Transit Dues.

        Native:
          Direct: Transit Dues in lieu of
                                Likin.

         <u>via</u> another Trade Mart   Full Export Duty and
         at which there is a   Transit Dues in lieu of
         Custom House: Likin.

  " Treaty Port <u>in China Proper</u>
    <u>or South Manchuria:</u>
        Foreign: Full Import Duty.
        Native: Full and ½ Export Duty.

  " Interior of <u>China Proper</u>
    or South Manchuria:
        Foreign :   Full Import Duty and
                                  Transit Dues.
        Native :   Full and ½ Export Duty and
                                  Transit Dues in lieu of
                                  Likin.

  " Dairen:
        Foreign: Full Import Duty.
        Native :   Full Export Duty.

                                          From Harbin

From Harbin:

For Abroad via Manchouli or Suifenho:
    Foreign: Free.
    Native: 2/3rd Export Duty.

" Chinese Eastern Railway Stations: Free.

" Trade Mart in North Manchuria
at which there is a Custom
House, not on the Chinese
Eastern Railway:
    Foreign: Full Import Duty.
    Native: Full Export Duty.

" Interior or a Trade Mart in
North Manchuria at which
there is no Custom House, not
on the Chinese Eastern Railway:
    Foreign: Full Import Duty and
                              Transit Dues.
    Native:
        Direct: Transit Dues in lieu of
                              Likin.
        via another Trade   Export Duty and Transit
        Mart at which there Dues in lieu of Likin.
        is a Custom House:

" Treaty Port in China Proper
or South Manchuria:
    Foreign: Full Import Duty.
    Native: Full and ½ Export Duty.

" Interior of China Proper
or South Manchuria:
    Foreign: Full Import Duty and
                              Transit Dues.
    Native:
        Direct: Transit Dues in lieu of
                              Likin.
        via another Trade   Full and ½ Export Duty
        Mart at which there and Transit Dues in lieu
        is a Custom House: of Likin.

" Dairen:
    Foreign: Full Import Duty.
    Native: Full Export Duty.

" Abroad via Kwanchengtze:
    Foreign: Free.
    Native: Full Export Duty.

From Trade Mart in North Manchuria at which there is
a Custom House, not on the Chinese Eastern Railway:

For Abroad:
    Foreign: Free.
    Native: Full Export Duty.

                                          For Trade

For Interior or a Trade Mart in
        Underline North Manchuria at which there
is no Custom House:
    Foreign: Full Import Duty and
                          Transit Dues.

    Native:
      Direct: Transit Dues in lieu of
                         Likin.
      <u>via</u> another Trade Mart Full Export Duty and
      at which there is a   Transit Dues in lieu of
      Custom House: Likin.

  " Treaty Port in <u>China Proper</u>
     <u>or South Manchuria</u>:
        Foreign: Full Import Duty.
        Native: Full and $\frac{1}{2}$ Export Duty.

  " Interior of <u>China Proper or</u>
     South Manchuria:
        Foreign: Full Import Duty and
                         Transit Dues.
        Native: Full and $\frac{1}{2}$ Export Duty and
                         Transit Dues in lieu of
                         Likin.

  " Dairen <u>via</u> Harbin:
        Foreign: Full Import Duty.
        Native: Full Export Duty.

     <u>From Chinese Eastern Railway Stations at which</u>
     <u>there is no Custom House</u>:

For Abroad <u>via</u> Manchouli or
     Suifenho:
        Foreign: Free.   X
        Native: 2/3rd Export Duty.

  " Chinese Eastern Railway   Free.
     Stations:

  " Trade Mart <u>in North Manchuria</u>
     at which there is a Custom
     House, not on the Chinese
     Eastern Railway:
        Foreign: Full Import Duty.   X ?
        Native: Full Export Duty and
                         Transit Dues in lieu of X ?
                         Likin.

  " Interior or a Trade Mart <u>in</u> Free.
     <u>North Manchuria</u> at which
     there is no Custom House, not
     on the Chinese Eastern Railway:

  " Treaty Port in <u>China Proper or</u>
     <u>South Manchuria</u>:
        Foreign: Full Import Duty.   X
        Native: Full and $\frac{1}{2}$ Export Duty and
                         Transit Dues in lieu of
                         Likin.

                              For

249.
(Page e).

For Interior of <u>China Proper</u>
<u>or South Manchuria</u>:   Free.

" Dairen:
    Foreign :   Full Import Duty.
    Native: Full Export Duty and Transit
                       Dues.

" Abroad <u>via</u> Kwanchengtzu:
    Foreign: Free.
    Native: Full Export Duty and
                       Transit Dues.

<u>From Interior or a Trade Mart in North Manchuria</u>
<u>at which there is no Custom House, not on the</u>
<u>Chinese Eastern Railway</u>:

For Abroad: _← via Kwangchangtze_
    Foreign: Free.
    Native: Full Export Duty and
                       Transit Dues.

" Trade Mart <u>in North Manchuria</u>
    <u>at which there is a Custom</u>
    <u>House</u>:
    Foreign: Full Import Duty.
    Native:
        Direct: Transit Dues in lieu of
                       Likin.
        via Trade Mart at   Full Export Duty and Transit
        which there is a   Dues in lieu of Likin.
        Custom House:

" Interior or a Trade Mart <u>in</u> Free.
    <u>North Manchuria</u> at which
    there is no Custom House:

" Treaty Port in <u>China Proper</u>
    <u>or South Manchuria</u>:
        Foreign: Full Import Duty.
        Native: Full and ½ Export Duty
                       and Transit Dues in lieu of
                       Likin.

" Interior of <u>China Proper</u>   Free.
    <u>or South Manchuria</u>:

" Dairen:
        Foreign: Full Import Duty.
        Native: Full Export Duty and
                       Transit Dues.

<u>From a Treaty Port in China Proper or South</u>
<u>Manchuria</u>:

For Abroad <u>via</u> Manchouli or
    Suifenho:
        Foreign: Free.
        Native: Full Export Duty.

                                 For Trade

250.
(Page f).

For Trade Mart in North Manchuria
at which there is a Custom
House, ~~not on the Chinese~~
~~Eastern Railway~~:

  Foreign: Full Import Duty.
  Native: Full and ½ Export Duty.

 " Interior or a Trade Mart in
  North Manchuria at which
  there is no Custom House:
   Foreign: Full Import Duty and
             Transit Dues.

   Native:
    Direct: Transit Dues in lieu of
            Likin.

    via Trade Mart at Full and ½ Export Duty and
    which there is a   Transit Dues in lieu of
    Custom House: Likin.

FROM Interior of China Proper or South Manchuria:

For Abroad via Manchouli or
 Suifenho:
  Foreign: Free.
  Native :   Full Export Duty and
             Transit Dues.

 " Trade Mart in North Manchuria
  at which there is a Custom
  House:
   Foreign: Full Import Duty.
   Native:
    Direct: Transit Dues in lieu of
            Likin.

    via a Treaty Port: Full and ½ Export Duty and
             Transit Dues in lieu of
             Likin.

 " Interior or a Trade Mart Free
  in North Manchuria at
  which there is no Custom
  House:

NOTES:

1.- Parcels from the Interior to a Treaty Port outside the
  Harbin District, or to a Trade Mart at which there is a
  Custom House may be passed for duty collection at
  destination.
  (The foregoing does not apply to parcels for Dairen, the
  duty on which must be paid at Harbin).

2.- A Trade Mart at which there is a Custom House is, for
  Customs purposes, treated as a Treaty Port.

3.- A Trade Mart at which there is no Custom House is treated
  as a place in the Interior.

4.- Transit Dues on parcels from abroad for places in the
  Interior and vice versa are to be brought to account in
  Revenue Account.

5.- Transit Dues collected on other parcels are to be treated
  as in lieu of Likin and are to be kept in a separate account.

6.- Parcels sent by river during the navigation season are to
                 receive

receive the same duty treatment as cargo sent by river,
i.e. one full export duty is to be collected.

7.- There is no duty differentiation between parcels posted
at Pristan or Fuchiatien and at the New Town, Harbin,
Post Office.

8.- In all cases of incoming Postal Parcels the absence of
proof of previous duty payment should be ascertained.

9.- At Manchouli and Suifenho only such goods as are of
undoubted local origin are to be treated as Native.

GENERAL INSTRUCTIONS:

1.-   Duty receipts will be issued, upon written indent, to
the Officers stationed at Postal Parcel Offices by the
Commissioner's Secretary, at Harbin, and by the Senior
Assistants at Manchouli, Suifenho and Lahasusu.   These
Assistants will keep a record of such issues and will,
personally, supervise the numbering of the receipts.

2.-   Duty Receipts should, as far as possible, show full
particulars.   While the face of these Receipts do not
allow of lengthy entries, fuller particulars should appear
on the back of the carbon copy.   The term "various" for
furs exported is inadmissible, except on the face of the
Receipt, and full details should appear on the back of the
carbon copy.   The terms "sundries", "Haberdashery",
"Piece goods", etc., are only admissible in the instances
where parcels contain such a conglomeration of different
articles as to make detailed entries on the back of Receipts
impracticable.   Carbon copies of Duty Receipts, supported
by Parcel lists, Export Way Bills and cleared Import Way
Bills, are to be sent to the Assistant in Charge of Returns
Office, at Harbin, and the Senior Assistants at Sub-offices,
on the first day of every month.

3.-   The Officer will keep a Duty Record Book showing the
following particulars; Date, Post Office Parcel Receipt Nos.
number of Parcels, Duty Receipt No. and Duty (Import, Export,
Coast Trade, Transit, and Transit in lieu of Likin).   The
Officer

Officer will further keep two Parcel Records, one for
incoming and one for outgoing parcels, showing date, Post
Office Parcel Receipt Nos., number of parcels and, if
dutiable, No. of Duty Receipt, or, if free, the word "Free",
- for all parcels passed by him.

4.   For incoming parcels Officers stationed at Postal
Parcel Offices will be supplied with a locally compiled
list of parcels by the Post Office and will, in addition,
be shown all incoming Parcel Way Bills.   The Officer will
check the former with the latter, satisfy himself that the
Nos. of the Way Bills are consecutive, stamp, date and initial
the latter and return them to the Post Office.   In addition
to the above the Officer will receive, stamp, date and retain
duplicate Parcel Way Bills from Shanghai and the Harbin
Station Parcel Office.

5.   For outgoing parcels two carbon copies of outgoing
Parcel Way Bills will be handed to the Officer by the Post
Office, either on the day of despatch of parcels or on the
next working day.   The Officer will check these with his
Duty collection and outgoing Parcel Record, date, stamp and
initial both copies, return one copy to the Post Office and
retain the other in support of his Duty Collection Record.
The Officer will further satisfy himself that the Nos. of
these Way Bills are consecutive.   Parcels are exchanged
by the Harbin Head Office and the Wutaoshieh Sub-Office as
follows:-

HEAD OFFICE		WUTAOCHIEH SUB-OFFICE	
Receives direct parcel mails from following Offices.	Closes direct parcel mails on following Offices.	Receives direct parcel mails from following Offices.	Closes direct parcel mails on following Offices.
Seattle	Shanghai (Union)	Shanghai	Tientsin
San Francisco	Shanghai	Tientsin	Chefoo
New York	Moukden Station	Chinkiang	Moukden
Shanghai	Towtaokow	Chefoo	Suifenho
Harbin Station Office(i.e. all Chinese Offices except Shanghai)	Tientsin	Hulan	Siaosuifen
	Peking,Kalgan	Sansing	Taheiho
	Manchouli	Harbin Station Offices (i.e. all Chinese Offices except those mentioned above.	Manchouli
	Suifenho		Kiamusze
	Tsitsihar		Hailar
	Hailar		Tingchow.
	Taheiho,Hankow		
	Chinkiang		
	Nanking		
	Harbin Station Office.		

(signed) René   d'Anjou,

Commissioner.

True copy:

[signature]

Unclassed Assistant.

致瑷珲关第 5/86519 号令　　　　　　海关总税务司署（北京）1921 年 11 月 1 日

尊敬的瑷珲关税务司：

　　根据满洲《出入境包裹关税和内地子口税征收办法》，奉总税务司命令，特作出如下指示：

　　1. 凡从满洲境内的非满洲交易市场邮寄，并抵达瑷珲关的洋货或土货邮递包裹，无论是拟供本地消费，还是拟运至其他国家/地区、中国通商口岸、满洲交易市场或者满洲境内非交易市场等场所，包裹抵达港口后，一律征收子口税。

　　2. 凡从满洲境内的交易市场邮寄，并抵达瑷珲关的洋货或土货邮递包裹，若包裹拟供本地消费，或拟运至其他国家/地区、中国通商口岸或满洲交易市场，则免征子口税予以放行。若包裹拟运至满洲境内非交易市场场所，则需征收子口税后予以放行。

　　3. 凡从外国或中国通商口岸邮寄，并抵达瑷珲关的洋货或土货邮递包裹，若包裹拟运至满洲境内非交易市场场所，则需征收子口税后予以放行。若包裹拟运至满洲交易市场，则免征子口税予以放行。

　　4. 凡从瑷珲关邮寄并通过陆运发送的洋货或土货邮递包裹，若包裹拟运至满洲交易市场，则一律免税放行；若通过陆运发送，拟运至满洲内陆非交易市场场所，则需征收子口税后予以放行。

　　5. 凡从国外运至满洲境内的洋货以及从满洲境内运至国外的土货，则所征收的子口税记入税收账户。对于其他情形，瑷珲关根据上述指示征收的子口税应存放在单独账户，并静候发布通令的进一步指示。

您忠诚的仆人

包罗（C. A. V.Bowra）

总务科税务司

呈海关总税务司署 <u>8</u> 号文　　　　　　　瑷珲关 / 大黑河 1921 年 11 月 19 日

尊敬的海关总税务司（北京）：

根据海关总税务司署第 3220 通令（第二辑）：

"对邮政包裹征收厘金或代征厘金的子口税的相关手续与处理办法等。"

兹报告，本关尚未对邮政包裹征收厘金或子口税。

您忠诚的仆人

包安济（G. Boezi）

瑷珲关署理税务司

呈海关总税务司署 <u>9</u> 号文　　　　　瑷珲关 / 大黑河 1921 年 11 月 21 日

尊敬的海关总税务司（北京）:

根据海关总税务司署第 5/86519 号令:

"邮政包裹: 关于对往来满洲境内之包裹征收子口税的相关指示。"

烦请对邮政包裹的征税办法予以进一步指示。

1. 瑷珲关目前征税办法扼要如下:

（1）凡包裹经其他通商口岸邮寄, 且经原邮寄地海关签印者, 瑷珲关均免税放行, 不予查验。

（2）凡包裹于内陆各地间邮寄者, 无论所经通商口岸多少, 瑷珲关均照海关总税务司署第 2397 号通令指示免税放行, 不予查验。

（3）其余包裹, 无论邮寄地与目的地及货物种类, 均按值百抽五之税率征收一次正税; 凡价值低于 15 银圆者, 均免税。凡对运入瑷珲关之包裹所征之税款, 均记入"进口"项下, 凡对运出瑷珲关之包裹所征之税款, 均计入"出口"项下。

2. 然若照贵署最新指令办理, 本口惯例则须做出一定调整, 遂请对以下几点予以进一步指示:

（1）根据海关总税务司署第 5/86519 号令第 2 段指示, 今后瑷珲关是否须对内陆各地间邮寄之包裹征税? 兹以为, 若如此, 则需与中国邮政局签订特别协议, 协定由其代表海关于包裹目的地征税, 或由其预付税金, 然后再向收货人征收此款项。此外, 关于该项指示, 烦请告知其他通商口岸（江海关等）对于往来内陆及外国的包裹是如何与中国邮政局协定征税办法的? 当然, 由外国邮寄至各通商口岸之包裹若可于目的地缴税, 应更为方便。

（2）根据海关总税务司署第 5/86519 号令第 4 段指示, 瑷珲关是否须对往来既为贸易市场又为通商口岸之地（哈尔滨, 珲春）的货物包裹免税放行?

（3）根据海关总税务司署第 5/86519 号令第 3 段指示"凡包裹自外国或中国通商口岸邮寄者, 若拟运至内陆某地, 则须征收子口税", 瑷珲关是否须对所有此类包裹征税? 若包裹原封未动且印有原邮寄地海关之签印, 瑷珲关是否仍须重新予以检查并征税? 瑷珲关验货员人数本就不足, 若如此, 负担恐会更重, 征税汇办处的负担亦会加重。

（4）对于往来中国内陆各地之包裹, 瑷珲关是否应仅征一次正税, 或:

① 对在满洲以外通商口岸中转超过一次之土货包裹征收复进口半税, 并

② 对寄自或寄至中国内陆各地之包裹征收子口税，以示对满洲以内邮寄之包裹的公平对待？

（5）鉴于大黑河（瑷珲关分关驻地）既为贸易市场亦为征税通商口岸，因此对于邮政包裹征税办法及满洲特别免重征执照签发之事，还望告知绥芬河（非贸易市场，但有权签发满洲特别免重征执照）、拉哈苏苏（已于近期由分卡改为分关）及龙井村（虽已照《中日图门江满韩定界条款》之规定与其他三处一并成为通商之地，且亦为珲春关之分关，但仍为归为贸易市场之行列）三处分关之状况。

3. 在等待海关总税务司署进一步指示期间，本署已公布对包裹征收子口税之新规定，并请中国邮政局出示所有包裹，包括内陆各地间邮寄之包裹，以供海关检查征税。但对于内陆各地间邮寄之包裹，本署将不会完全遵照海关总税务司署第 2397 号通令指示办理。此外，本署已暂令继续按照现行惯例对往来既为贸易市场又为通商口岸之地的货物包裹征收一次正税。

您忠诚的仆人

包安济（G. Boezi）

瑷珲关署理税务司

致瑷珲关第 <u>14/87199</u> 号令　　　　海关总税务司署（北京）1921 年 12 月 17 日

尊敬的瑷珲关税务司：

第 9 号呈收悉：

"包裹征税办法：汇报瑷珲关现行办法，并请示子口税征收及其他方面的指示。"

奉总税务司命令，现批复如下：

1. 关于包裹征税办法的准则，见《海关实务手册》第 138 页。这些准则同样适用于满洲。在该手册第 357 章第 2 节和第 4 节，在 "which can be reached（可达到）" 文字前不应有逗号。

2. 目前对内陆地点之间邮递的包裹，瑷珲关无须征收关税。

3. 为此，拟将无税关的交易市场视为内陆地点。

4. 将具有税关的交易市场（如拉哈苏苏、绥芬河和龙井村）视为通商口岸。

5. 凡瑷珲与大黑河两地往来的包裹，视同于两地之间往来的货物，一律征收关税。

6. 凡发往哈尔滨关或珲春关的包裹，若包含应征税货物，应予以征税。

7. 凡最初在通商口岸邮寄、之后抵达瑷珲关或从瑷珲关中转的包裹，必须视为在邮寄之时已缴清所有应缴税费。

您忠诚的仆人

包罗（C. A. V.Bowra）

总务科税务司

致瑷珲关第 <u>18/87308</u> 号令　　　　海关总税务司署（北京）1921 年 12 月 28 日

尊敬的瑷珲关税务司：

1. 根据我签发的第 5/86519 号令：

"满洲出入境包裹子口税：何时征收。"

奉总税务司命令，现批复如下：为了尊重总邮政司的意愿，总税务司同意目前对经由瑷珲关往来内陆地点的过关包裹暂不征收税捐，因此，应将其视作交易市场无税关的内陆地点。

2. 凡发自满洲境内、经由瑷珲关运往其他通商口岸的包裹，为了便利起见，子口税可以在第二个通商口岸予以征收。

3. 该令文第 4 条指示也有更正。为了所有海关方便起见，无税关设立的交易市场应视为内陆地点，但以下情况除外：凡有资格获得满洲特别免重征执照的货物、申请获得上述证明并依照此证运送到某交易市场，则对此类货物必须予以免税放行。凡没有办理满洲特别免重征执照并通过邮包自瑷珲关寄往无税关的交易市场的货物，一律征收子口税，原厘金不再征收。凡发自上述交易市场并抵达瑷珲关的货物，按照与前一条同样的方法进行征税。另一方面，开设有税关的贸易市场应视为通商口岸。凡寄往此处的包裹，其关税征收与寄往天津或中国其他通商口岸的情况相同，但此类包裹有资格获取满洲特别免重征执照或在满洲特别免重征执照的涵盖范围之内的情况除外。

您忠诚的仆人

包罗（C. A. V.Bowra）

总务科税务司

致瑷珲关第 25/808 号函　　　　　　　哈尔滨关 1922 年 11 月 3 日

尊敬的瑷珲关税务司：

　　1. 关于哈尔滨政府提出邮政包裹之征税办法与普通货物相比有明显不公一事，已请总税务司示下。

　　2. 鉴于海关总税务司之指示涉及北满洲全境，瑷珲关区亦在此列，故此附上相关来往信函抄件，如下：

　　1922 年 8 月 2 日哈尔滨关致海关总税务司署第 2683 号呈；

　　1922 年 9 月 7 日海关总税务司署致哈尔滨关第 2936/90993 号令；

　　1922 年 10 月 26 日哈尔滨关致海关总税务司署第 2740 号呈；

　　3. 本署已照总税务司指示颁布哈尔滨关第 119 号办法；随附该办法抄件，以供参考。

您忠诚的仆人

（签字）覃书（R. C. L. d' Anjou）

哈尔滨关税务司

录事：三等帮办前班

哈尔滨关致瑷珲关第 25 号函附件 1

哈尔滨关致海关总税务司署第 2683 号呈抄件

呈海关总税务司署 2683 号文 　　　　　　哈尔滨关 1922 年 8 月 2 日

尊敬的海关总税务司（北京）：

　　1. 目前，哈尔滨关区有一条非常重要的邮政包裹运输路线，待中国与苏俄及远东共和国协商结束后，该条运输路线或将承载更大的运输份额。北满邮务长李齐先生希望海关可在征税方面为之提供更大的便利，尽量简化海关手续。关于李齐先生所提请求，凡可于本地解决者，本署已酌情办理，余者还须贵署指示。

　　2. 北满邮务管理局已与俄符拉迪沃斯托克（Vladivostok①）地区［邮电司（Chief of Posts and Telegraphs）就自黑龙江沿岸地区运往北满洲各地之包裹于绥芬河的转运办法达成协议，希望本署可简化绥芬河这一边境分关的办事手续，以便该条运输路线能够顺利开展。

　　本署已同意该项请求，并于绥芬河分关做出如下安排。

　　（1）凡包裹自黑龙江沿岸各地运往北满洲各地者，运抵绥芬河后，均须由海关关员自火车站护送至中国邮政局，移交过程亦须在海关关员监督下完成。

　　（2）凡此等包裹运往绥芬河或绥芬河与哈尔滨之间各地者，均由绥芬河海关估税留置，待邮局向收件人征收税款后，再予放行。

　　（3）凡此等包裹运往哈尔滨或北满洲以外各地者，均须于抵达目的地之前，在沿途最后一处海关关卡完纳关税。此类包裹均会由在绥芬河中国邮政局当职的海关关员加盖印章，注明"自国外：待支付"。

　　3. 中国邮政局亦与黑龙江沿岸地区邮政局就在哈尔滨和俄符拉迪沃斯托克两地之间直接运送的装成总包（closed mail）达成新协议，协定由绥芬河海关关员在邮政货车上对此类包裹进行检查。邮务长李齐先生希望本署可简化检查手续，避免包裹在边境运输过程中遭到延误，并称邮政货车皆由中国邮政局出资管理，海关允许其通过边境驶入俄符拉迪沃斯托克地区，亦是对黑龙江沿岸地区邮政局的礼遇。

---

　　① 即海参崴。

该项请求并非难事,本署已向邮务长说明,凡（装成总包 closed mail）出境时于邮袋上印有中国邮政局印章者,以及入境时于边境直接交予中国邮政局者,海关均不会阻扰或延误运输,但仍有于邮政货车上搜查违禁品之权利。此外,还需由中国邮政局确保往来俄符拉迪沃斯托克和北满洲之间的装成总包中未夹杂其他包裹。

4. 邮务长[李齐先生另对北满洲邮政包裹的征税办法提出异议：

（1）海关对邮政包裹征收复进口半税,却对由火车或船只运送的货物免征此税；

（2）海关对由中东铁路运送之邮政包裹征收进口正税或出口正税,却对普通货物减征三分之一的税。

本署对此回复,海关已尽力使邮政包裹与普通货物享有同等待遇,且北满洲境内之普通货物有时亦须交纳复进口半税,然本关现行惯例乃依照海关总税务司指示而设,不可自行变更。

5. 至于对由中东铁路运送之邮政包裹征收正税,而未如普通货物一般减征三分之一关税一事,其实绥芬河分关和满洲里分关临时章程第 67 条已有规定："凡与减免关税有关之规定,均适用于关区内以邮政包裹运送之货物。"此外,1920 年俄国邮政局关闭以前,邮政包裹运输均由之管控,概享减税待遇。既如此,何以中国邮政局接管邮政包裹后不可继续享此待遇,故此申请批准立即更改本关征收正税之惯例。

6. 此外,邮务长李齐先生对海关（为厘捐局）征收代征厘金的子口税一事,颇有意见。本署已向其说明,一旦海关停止征收此税,厘捐局便会于内陆各地有中国邮政局之地开设分卡,此绝非其想要之结果。

7. 关于邮政包裹（1）往来黑龙江沿岸各地与中国各地之间者,及（2）自黑龙江沿岸各地经由满洲和上海转运至外国各地者的征税办法,李齐先生亦有疑问。

（1）黑龙江沿岸各地与中国各地之间往来邮政包裹的征税问题较易解决,可于绥芬河进行转运。包裹自阿穆尔沿岸地区运抵绥芬河后,由海关关员护送至中国邮政局,移交过程亦在海关关员监督下完成。至于运往绥芬河、哈尔滨及北满洲以外各地之邮政包裹的征税办法,参见本呈第二部分。对于运往中国内陆各地之邮政包裹,若目的地设有税关,则于目的地税关估税,若目的地未设税关,则于抵达目的地之前,于沿途最后一个税关估税；手续均照运往外国包裹的实际惯例办理；每件包裹上皆需加盖印章,注明"自国外：待支付"。

（2）关于自黑龙江沿岸各地经由满洲和上海通过中国邮政局转运至外国各地之邮政包裹的征税办法,须请总税务司示下。有两种办法可供参考：

① 包裹自黑龙江沿岸各地运抵绥芬河后，由当地海关征收进口税并放行其经由上海转运至外国，另于包裹上加盖特殊印章，以示包裹已于绥芬河海关完纳关税；

② 对此类包裹免征关税，仅于邮袋等外包装上加盖海关铅印，待包裹于上海出口时，再由江海关拆除铅印，唯邮政局须提供复出口所需一应证明。

鉴于远东共和国目前尚未与其他国家协定邮政包裹征税办法，故建议将自黑龙江沿岸各地运来之包裹视作进口货物，征收关税；不过，北满邮务管理局与黑龙江沿岸地区邮政局所定安排，于相关机构及中国政府而言，均颇有裨益。当然，海关对邮政包裹运输所加负担越轻，中国政府便获益越多，只是海关须采取必要措施，确保包裹进入中国后，最终确系转运至外国。

您忠诚的仆人

（签字）覃书（R. C. L. d'Anjou）

哈尔滨关税务司

该抄件内容真实有效，特此证明：

录事：三等帮办前班

海关总税务司署致哈尔滨关第 2936 号令抄件

致哈尔滨关第 <u>2936/90993</u> 号令　　　　海关总税务司署（北京）1922 年 9 月 7 日

尊敬的哈尔滨关税务司：

　　哈尔滨关致海关总税务司署第 2683 号呈收悉：

　　　　"邮政包裹：汇报为北满洲邮政包裹运输路线之发展，海关与中国邮政局已就日后与苏俄及远东共和国往来信件及包裹在北满洲境内转运事商定办法：邮政司希望海关变更邮政包裹征税办法，以利便包裹运输。"

　　奉总税务司命令，现批复如下。

　　1. 自黑龙江沿岸地区运至北满洲各地之邮政包裹：

　　若贵署呈文第二部分 3）所拟征税办法，即包裹须于抵达目的地之前在沿途最后一处海关关卡完纳关税，可确保包裹于前往目的地之前会至海关接受查验并纳税，则可予以批准。请详述此办法。

　　2. 往来哈尔滨和俄符拉迪沃斯托克（Vladivostok）之间的装成总包（closed mail）：

　　批准拟议办法，唯须邮政司以书面形式保证此等装成总包中不会夹杂其他包裹；一旦查有夹杂包裹，邮政局应即行扣留，并立即告知海关。

　　3. 对北满洲境内运送之邮政包裹征税复进口半税：

　　海关总税务司署第 2739/87007 号令（第一段）已说明，邮政包裹的征税办法应尽可能与海关对普通货物的征税办法保持一致。因此，凡邮政包裹往来北满洲设有税关的贸易市场者，复进口/复出口半税的征收办法均与以其他方式运输之货物相同；但若包裹（未持有或无权持有满洲特别免重征执照）往来未设有税关的贸易市场，则应继续照海关总税务司署第 2762/87307 号令指示征收代征厘金的子口税。

　　4. 对由中东铁路运输之邮政包裹征收正税：

　　只要通过中东铁路往来北满洲境内各地之普通货物享有减税特权，则以相同方式运往相同区域之邮政包裹亦享有同等减税待遇。

　　5. 征收代征厘金的子口税：

　　凡邮政包裹被海关征收代征厘金的子口税者，均为须缴纳厘金者；现行办法于邮政局和民众而言，皆更为便利。

6. 黑龙江沿岸各地与中国各地之间往来之邮政包裹：

若可确保包裹于前往目的地之前会至沿途最后一处海关关卡接受查验并纳税，则可予以批准。另请详述此办法。

7. 自黑龙江沿岸各地经由满洲和上海转运至外国之包裹：

对于此类包裹，能否与中国邮政局协定类似于海关总税务司署第 2779/87573 号令所批准之办法；由此，对于通过铁路自西伯利亚运入满洲里，再通过中国邮政局运至上海复出口之邮政包裹，哈尔滨关便可根据中国邮政局提供之复出口凭证为包裹签发退税存票。

您忠诚的仆人

（签字）包罗（C. A. V. Bowra）

总务科税务司

该抄件内容真实有效，特此证明：

录事：三等帮办前班

哈尔滨关致海关总税务司署第 2740 号呈抄件

呈海关总税务司署 <u>2740</u> 号文　　　　　　哈尔滨关 1922 年 10 月 26 日

尊敬的海关总税务司（北京）：

　　1. 根据总税务司第 2936/90993 号令（回复哈尔滨关致海关总税务司署第 2683 号呈）：

　　　　"邮政包裹：关于为发展北满洲邮政包裹运输路线，海关与中国邮政局就日后与苏俄及远东共和国往来信件及包裹在北满洲境内转运事所定之办法，总税务司批准按照邮政司之要求，在邮政包裹征税办法上做出让步。"

　　2. 对于总税务司之问题，兹汇报如下。

　　（1）自黑龙江沿岸地区运至北满洲各地之邮政包裹：

　　关于包裹于前往目的地之前至沿途最后一处海关关卡完纳关税之办法，将照海关总税务司署第 1073 号通令关于外国包裹直接运往中国内陆各地之指示办理；税费将由沿途最后一处海关关卡估算，并由中国邮政局征收。

　　（2）往来哈尔滨和俄符拉迪沃斯托克（Vladivostok）之间的装成总包（closed mail）：

　　邮政司已以书面形式保证此等装成总包中不会夹杂包裹，一旦发现夹有其他包裹，邮政局将即行扣押，并立即告知海关。

　　（3）对北满洲境内运送之邮政包裹征收复进口半税：

　　已照海关总税务司署第 2739/87007 号、2762/87307 号及现下回复之 2936/90993 号令指示办理。

　　然海关总税务司署第 2936 号令所载（"或无权持有"）之指示与第 2762 号令所载不符，故无法遵照执行。海关总税务司署第 2762 号令载明："凡包裹未持有满洲特别免重征执照者，若往来未设有税关的贸易市场，则征收代征厘金的子口税。"

　　（4）对由中东铁路运输之邮政包裹征收正税：

　　已照贵署指示，只要通过中东铁路往来北满洲境内各地之普通货物享有减税特权，则对以相同方式运往相同区域之邮政包裹施行同等减税办法。

　　（5）征收代征厘金的子口税：

　　继续遵照执行。

　　（6）黑龙江沿岸各地与中国各地之间往来之邮政包裹：

将照海关总税务司署第 1073 号通令关于外国包裹直接运往中国内陆各地之指示办理。

（7）自黑龙江沿岸各地经由满洲和上海转运至外国之包裹：

将择机向邮政司建议此类包裹的征税办法。

3. 兹附哈尔滨邮政局第 308 号函抄件，以供参考。

您忠诚的仆人

（签字）覃书（R. C. L. d' Anjou）

哈尔滨关税务司

该抄件内容真实有效，特此证明：

录事： 三等帮办前班

哈尔滨吉黑邮务管理局致哈尔滨关第 308 号函抄件

致哈尔滨关第 <u>308</u> 号函　　　　　哈尔滨吉黑邮务管理政局 1922 年 9 月 27 日

尊敬的哈尔滨关税务司：

9 月 21 日哈尔滨关第 1400 号函收悉：

"通知：日后于北满洲境内往来之邮政包裹免纳复进口半税，由中东铁路运输之邮政包裹享减税待遇。"

感谢贵署对北满洲邮政发展的支持。

1. 关于由中东铁路运送之邮政包裹的复进口半税及减税办法：

烦请告知免征复进口半税及减税办法将自何日起生效。

2. 自黑龙江沿岸地区运至中国各地之邮政包裹：

海关总税务司所需信息可见于 1921 年 8 月 1 日哈尔滨邮政局致哈尔滨关第 268 号函。然因关于黑龙江沿岸地区邮票可为于中国境内运输之包裹加盖免付邮资印记之协定尚未生效，故自黑龙江沿岸地区运来之包裹须于绥芬河重新粘贴中国邮票。按照现行海关惯例，凡于绥芬河发出之包裹，均由寄件人交税，但该惯例并不适用于自黑龙江沿岸地区运来之包裹，相对来说，自美英等国运入中国之包裹的征税办法更为适用，即由收件人于沿途最后一处通商口岸交税。如此，自俄符拉迪沃斯托克（Vladivostok）运往成都之包裹便可于重庆关交税，海关税收亦可有所保障。目前自美国运入之包裹数量巨大，而自俄符拉迪沃斯托克运入之包裹数量还相对较小。

3. 自中国各地运至黑龙江沿岸地区之邮政包裹：

对于此类包裹，海关现行办事手续暂无变更之需要。包裹于始发通商口岸交税，若自内陆某地运出，则由沿途首个通商口岸估税，包裹完税以前均由邮政局保管。此为自中国运往美国等地之邮政包裹的现行征税办法。

4. 往来哈尔滨和俄符拉迪沃斯托克之间的装成总包（closed mail）：

1921 年 7 月 27 日哈尔滨关第 260 号函载明 "所定办法与邮政包裹无关"，如此，中国各地邮政局每日运送之大量装成总包，以及中国与已入邮会各国之间频繁运送之信件亦不在办法规定之列。另按照要求于此声明，兹保证装成总包中不会夹杂其他包裹，一旦查有夹杂包裹，即行扣留，并立即告知海关。

5. 自黑龙江沿岸各地经由满洲和上海转运至外国之包裹：

对于海关总税务司所定签发退税存票之办法，邮政局欣然接受。目前，自远东共和国运出经由满洲里中国邮政局转运至美国之皮货包裹已开始使用该办法，且已获海关认同，相信亦会成功适用于自黑龙江沿岸地区运来之包裹。

6. 对退税包裹拟征海关费用：

中国与远东共和国关于邮政包裹之协议尚在讨论阶段，但议项中并未涉及自远东共和国运往外国之包裹在中国的转运办法，因此与邮政包裹相关的退税工作并无增加之可能，故此建议，暂且不对包裹征收特别海关费用。

您忠诚的仆人

（签字）李齐（W. W. Ritchie）

北满邮务长

该抄件内容真实有效，特此证明

录事：三等帮办前班

哈尔滨关致瑷珲关第 25 号函附件 2

哈尔滨关第 119 号办法

哈尔滨关 1922 年 10 月 27 日

为邮政包裹征收办法及相关指令事：

根据海关总税务司署第 2702/86518 号、2739/87007 号、2762/87307 号及 2936/90993 号令指示，邮政包裹最新征税办法如下。

第 77 号办法将由本办法取而代之，但第 112 号办法继续有效，即根据海关总税务司署致哈尔滨关第 2936/90993 号令指示，凡装有土货的邮政包裹于北满洲境内运输者，均免征复进口半税，凡邮政包裹通过中东铁路运输者，均与以相同方式运输之普通货物同享减税（仅征 2/3 关税）（及免税名单）特权。

1. 自外国寄发经由满洲里或绥芬河之邮政包裹	
运至满洲里或绥芬河	征收 2/3 进口正税
运往哈尔滨	征收 2/3 进口正税
运往中东铁路沿线未设税关之地	征收 2/3 进口正税
运往北满洲设有税关的贸易市场（不在中东铁路沿线）	征收进口正税
运往北满洲未设税关的内陆地区或贸易市场（不在中东铁路沿线）	征收 2/3 进口正税及内地子口税
运往中国内地或南满洲的通商口岸	征收进口正税
运往中国内地或南满洲的内陆地区	征收进口正税及内地子口税
运往大连	征收进口正税
2. 自外国寄发经由宽城子之邮政包裹	
运往设有税关的贸易市场	征收进口正税
运往内地或未设税关的贸易市场	征收进口正税及内地子口税
3. 自满洲里或绥芬河寄发之邮政包裹	
经由满洲里或绥芬河运往外国	

洋货	免税
土货	征收 2/3 出口正税
运往中东铁路沿线	
洋货	征收 2/3 进口正税
土货	免税
运往北满洲设有税关的贸易市场（不在中东铁路沿线）	
洋货	征收进口征税
土货	征收出口正税
运往北满洲未设税关的内陆地区或贸易市场（不在中东铁路沿线）	
洋货	征收 2/3 进口正税及内地子口税
土货	
（1）直达	征收代征厘金的子口税
（2）途经设有税关的贸易市场	征收出口正税及代征厘金的子口税
运往中国内地或南满洲的通商口岸	
洋货	征收进口正税
土货	征收一倍半出口正税
运往中国内地或南满洲的内陆地区	
洋货	征收进口正税及内地子口税
土货	征收一倍半出口正税及内地子口税
运往大连	
洋货	征收进口正税
土货	征收出口正税
4.自哈尔滨寄发之邮政包裹	
经由满洲里或绥芬河运往外国	
洋货	免税
土货	征收 2/3 出口正税

运往中东铁路沿线	免税
运往北满洲设有税关的贸易市场（不在中东铁路沿线）	
洋货	征收进口正税
土货	征收出口正税
运往北满洲未设税关的内陆地区或贸易市场（不在中东铁路沿线）	
洋货	征收进口正税及内地子口税
土货	
（1）直达	征收代征厘金的子口税
（2）途经设有税关的贸易市场	征收出口正税及代征厘金的子口税
运往中国内地或南满洲的通商口岸	
洋货	征收进口正税
土货	征收一倍半出口正税
运往中国内地或南满洲的内陆地区	
洋货	征收进口正税及内地子口税
土货	
（1）直达	征收代征厘金的子口税
（2）途经设有税关的贸易市场	征收一倍半出口正税及代征厘金的子口税
运往大连	
洋货	征收进口正税
土货	征收出口正税
经由宽城子运往外国	
洋货	免税
土货	征收出口正税

5.自北满洲设有税关的贸易市场（不在中东铁路沿线）寄发之邮政包裹

运往外国	
洋货	免税

土货	征收出口正税
运往北满洲未设税关的内陆地区或贸易市场（不在中东铁路沿线）	
洋货	征收进口正税及内地子口税
土货	
（1）直达	征收代征厘金的子口税
（2）途经设有税关的贸易市场	征收出口正税及代征厘金的子口税
运往中国内地或南满洲的通商口岸	
洋货	征收进口正税
土货	征收一倍半出口正税
运往中国内地或南满洲的内陆地区	
洋货	征收进口正税及内地子口税
土货	征收一倍半出口正税及代征厘金的子口税
经由哈尔滨运往大连	
洋货	征收进口正税
土货	征收出口正税

6.自中东铁路沿线未设税关之地寄发之邮政包裹

经由满洲里或绥芬河运往外国	
洋货	免税
土货	征收2/3出口正税
运往中东铁路沿线	免税
运往北满洲设有税关的贸易市场（不在中东铁路沿线）	
洋货	征收进口正税
土货	征收出口正税及代征厘金的子口税
运往北满洲未设税关的内陆地区或贸易市场（不在中东铁路沿线）	免税
运往中国内地或南满洲的通商口岸	
洋货	征收进口正税

土货	征收一倍半出口正税及代征厘金的子口税
运往中国内地或南满洲的内陆地区	免税
运往大连	
洋货	征收进口正税
土货	征收出口正税及内地子口税
经由宽城子运往外国	
洋货	免税
土货	征收出口正税及内地子口税

7. 自北满洲未设税关的内路地区或贸易市场（不在中东铁路沿线）寄发之邮政包裹

经由宽城子运往外国	
洋货	免税
土货	征收出口正税及内地子口税
经由满洲里或绥芬河运往外国	
洋货	免税
土货	征收 2/3 出口正税及内地子口税
运往北满洲设有税关的贸易市场	
洋货	征收进口正税
土货	
（1）直达	征收代征厘金的子口税
（2）途经设有税关的贸易市场	征收出口正税和代征厘金的子口税
运往北满洲未设税关的内陆地区或贸易市场	免税
运往中国内地或南满洲的通商口岸	
洋货	征收进口正税
土货	征收一倍半出口正税及代征厘金的子口税
运往中国内地或南满洲的内陆地区	免税
运往大连	
洋货	征收进口正税
土货	征收出口正税及内地子口税

8. 自中国内地或南满洲的通商口岸寄发之邮政包裹

经由满洲里或绥芬河运往外国	
洋货	免税
土货	征收出口正税
运往北满洲设有税关的贸易市场	
洋货	征收进口正税
土货	征收一倍半出口正税
运往北满洲未设税关的内陆地区或贸易市场	
洋货	征收进口正税及内地子口税
土货	
（1）直达	征收代征厘金的子口税
（2）途经设有税关的贸易市场	征收一倍半出口正税及代征厘金的子口税

9. 自中国内地或南满洲的内陆地区寄发之邮政包裹

经由满洲里或绥芬河运往外国	
洋货	免税
土货	征收出口正税及内地子口税
运往北满洲设有税关的贸易市场	
洋货	征收进口正税
土货	
（1）直达	征收代征厘金的子口税
（2）途经设有税关的贸易市场	征收一倍半出口正税及代征厘金的子口税
运往北满洲未设税关的内陆地区或贸易市场	免税

注：

1. 凡包裹自内陆地区运往哈尔滨关区以外某通商口岸或设有税关的贸易市场者，或可于目的地缴纳关税。

（凡包裹运往大连者，概不适用此条，均须于哈尔滨关缴纳关税。）

2. 凡贸易市场设有税关者，一律视为通商口岸。

3. 凡贸易市场未设税关者，一律视为内陆地区。

4. 凡对往来于外国和内陆各地之间的包裹所征收之内地子口税，均计入税收账户。

5. 凡对其它包裹所征收之内地子口税,均为代征厘金的子口税,单独入账。

6. 凡于航运季期间由海路运送之包裹,均与由海路运送之普通货物享受同等对待,即仅征一次出口正税。

7. 自哈尔滨埠头 ① 或傅家甸 ② 以及新市街 ③ 邮政局寄出之包裹,征税办法相同。

8. 凡运入本埠之邮政包裹,均须查明是否持有完税凭证。

9. 满洲里和绥芬河海关仅将确系土产之货物视为土货。

相关指令

1. 完税收据将由哈尔滨关税务司文案及满洲里、绥芬河和拉哈苏苏三处分关的超等帮办根据书面凭单开具并发给海关邮包处关员。超等帮办将负责完税收据的签发登记及编号管理事项。

2. 完税收据所载各项应尽量详实,但不得于正面载入过多记项,详细信息均应载于抄本背面。凡出口皮货之完税收据,除正面外,均不得出现"各类"之字样,详细信息应载于抄本背面。凡"杂货"、"男子服饰用品"及"按件货物"等字样,仅可于包裹内之物品种类过多以致无法于收据抄本背面载明所有详细信息时使用。完税收据之抄本,并附包裹清单、出口运搬凭单及结关进口运搬凭单,将于每月首日送交哈尔滨关统计课负责帮办及各分关超等帮办处。

3. 海关邮包处关员须于关税登记簿上载明:日期、邮政局收包执据号数、包裹数量、完税收据号数及关税种类(进口正税、出口正税、复进口半税、内地子口税及代征厘金的子口税);另须为其经手之寄人及寄出之包裹分别登记,载明日期、邮政局收包执据号数、包裹数量,若为应税包裹,则登记完税收据号数,若为免税包裹,则注明"免税"。

4. 关于寄人之包裹,海关邮包处关员在收到邮政局提供的当地汇编包裹清单后,需将之与寄人包裹运搬凭单进行核对,在确定运搬凭单之号数为连续后,需于运搬凭单上加盖戳记,注明日期,以姓名首字母签字,并返还邮政局。除此之外,海关邮包处关员亦将收到由上海及哈尔滨海关邮包处提供的包裹运搬凭单副本,收到后须为之加盖戳记,注明日期并留存。

5. 关于寄出之包裹,海关邮包处关员在(包裹派发当日或下一工作日)收到由邮政局

---

① 经查为今哈尔滨道里区,因当时此处被开辟为码头,故被称"埠头","布里斯坦"为其俄文名称的音译。

② 经查为今哈尔滨道外区。

③ 经查为今哈尔滨南岗部分区域,当时亦称秦家岗。

提供的两份寄出包裹运搬凭单抄本后,需将之与其征税记录和寄出包裹记录进行核对,并为两份抄本注明日期,加盖戳记,以姓名首字母签字,最后将其中一份抄本返还邮政局,另一份留存以作征税记录之佐证,此外还需确定搬凭单号数皆为连续。由哈尔滨海关邮包总处及五道街海关邮包分处①转运之包裹如下。

哈尔滨海关邮包总处		五道街海关邮包分处	
从下列各处接收之直达邮包:	结关发往下列各处之直达邮包:	从下列各处接收之达邮包:	结关发往下列各处之直达邮包:
西雅图	上海（工会）	上海	天津
旧金山	上海	天津	芝罘（烟台）
纽约	奉天海关邮包处	镇江	奉天
上海	头道沟	芝罘（烟台）	绥芬河
哈尔滨海关邮包处（即除上海以外之所有中国海关邮包处）	天津	呼兰	小绥芬
	北京、张家口	三姓	大黑河
	满洲里	哈尔滨海关邮包处（即除上述各处以外之所有中国海关邮包处）	满洲里
	绥芬河		佳木斯
	齐齐哈尔		海拉尔
	海拉尔		汀州
	大黑河、汉口		
	镇江		
	南京		
	哈尔滨海关邮包处		

（签字）覃书（R. C. L. d'Anjou）

哈尔滨关税务司

---

① 原文为 Parcels are exchanged by the Harbin Head Office and the Wutaochieh Sub-Office, 因与海关邮包处 Parcels Office（参阅由陈诗启和孙修福先生主编之《中国近代海关常用词语宝典》）相关,故译为哈尔滨海关邮包总处及五道街海关邮包分处。

3. 为北满境内以邮递包裹及以普通方式运送之土货的征税办法事

83.

I. G.   Aigun/Tahsiho 29th November, 2

Sir,

1.   In your despatch No. 14/87,199 :

          Duty Treatment of Postal Parcels ;

you instructed me to follow the rules given in the

"Handbook of Customs Procedure at Shanghai"; this Office

accordingly started collection of Coast Trade Duty on

all Native Goods conveyed in Postal Parcels moved

between two or more Treaty Ports, or Trade Marts

where there is a Custom House. - Again, in your

despatch No. 18/87.308, you ruled that parcels sent

to a Trade Mart where a Custom House has been ope-

ned "are to be charged the same duties as if they

"were sent to Tientsin or any other Chinese Treaty

"Port".

2.   A short while ago, however, I was informed

by the Postal Commissioner for North Manchuria that

                                                      the

The Inspector General of Customs,

       PEKING.

the rules for levy of Coast Trade Duty on Postal Parcels moved within his District was being modified; and, quite recently, the Harbin Commissioner transmitted copy of the correspondence exchanged with the Inspectorate on this question. - Your despatch No.29 6/90,993 directs that parcels should be treated as nearly as possible in the same way as ordinary goods conveyed through the Customs, and that Coast Trade Duty on Postal Parcels transported to or from "a Trade Mart "in North Manchuria where there is a collecting Custom "House" need not be charged in future, if goods otherwise conveyed through the Customs are exempt.

3.   At the same time I have been approached by delegates of the local Chamber of Commerce, who contend that Native Goods conveyed by the overland (Liangchiat'un), route in Postal Parcels should be free of duty, in the same way as when they are conveyed by carts. - This contention can only be considered with respect to parcels moved between this place and Harbin, Manchouli, Suifenho and inland places in North Manchuria beyond that, because a) beyond these limits full duty becomes payable without doubt, as in the case of ordinary goods moved south of Harbin; b)

this

this side of Harbin or Manchouli, parcels do not pass a second Treaty Port or Mart with a Custom House, and therefore only Transit Dues are charged. - But even thus restricted, the contention that goods sent by Postal Parcel must be treated always in the same way as ordinary goods should, in my opinion, be taken cum grano salis : it may be noted that Postal Parcels enjoy many privileges over ordinary goods (exemption from Inland Taxation, examination only at one place, etc) which may justify a uniform duty treatment for the whole of China; and, if that principle was to be strictly applied, it may mean, e.g., that parcels between Mengtsz and Szemao should be passed free of duty, or that, supposed an interruption of traffic between Shanghai and Ningpo by steamer (due, say, to a strike), Native Customs Duty should be charged on parcels which the C.P.O. may send by Junk.

4.   I have the honour to submit the various questions referred to, to your decision, and to solicit, on the following points, your definite instruction in order to avoid misunderstanding and frequent change in practice, detrimental to the Public and to us :

1. Shall this Office, following the lead of the
Harbin

Harbin Office, cease collecting Coast Trade Duty on parcels moved within North Manchuria (although such Duty would be payable on Manchurian Special N.Gs)?

2. Which are the limits of North Manchuria for the above purpose? Do they include, besides Aigun, Harbin, Manchouli, Suifenho, Lahasusu and Sansing, also Hunchun and Jungchingtsun?

3. What is the status of Mukden, where there is no "collecting" Custom House? Is Export and Coast Trade Duty to be collected on parcels between Aigun and Mukden? or Export Duty and Transit Dues? or Export Duty only?

4. Is Coast Trade Duty to be charged on parcels between this Port and Dairen?

5. Am I to take as correct the contention of the Chamber of Commerce, and treat parcels sent by the Jungchist'un route in the same way as ordinary goods? In this case, should such parcels (containing native goods)

a) be exempt from payment of Export duty altogether, or

b) 1) if sent to or received from Harbin, Manchouli or Suifenho, pay 2/3rds Export Duty for the part of the journey effected on the Chinese Eastern Railway, and

b) 2) if sent to, or received from Inland places on the C.E.R., or in North Manchuria via the C.E.R., pay 2/3rds Export Duty, plus Transit Dues?

I have the honour to be, Sir,

Your obedient Servant,

Acting Commissioner.

[1—29]

99   **COMMRS.**   INSPECTORATE GENERAL OF CUSTOMS,

igun   No. 92,424   PEKING, 19th December, 1922.

          Sir,

1.   With reference to your despatch No. 83 :

                Postal Parcels: duty treatment of
                Native Goods conveyed in, within
                North Manchuria; instructions in re
                soliciting;

I am directed by the Inspector General to forward for your information and guidance copy of his despatch No. 2809/88,114 to Harbin, in § 3 of which are laid down the general principles by which the Customs should be guided in the duty treatment of native goods in Manchuria. You will observe that the principle is laid down that the taxation of native trade in Manchuria is a matter for the Chinese (i.e. Provincial) Authorities; and that we are concerned solely with the collection of duties on trade crossing the frontier.

2.   With regard to Postal Parcels there are two

                                   principles

The Commissioner of Customs,

    A I G U N.

principles to be kept in mind :

(1) Postal Parcels pay as far as possible to the

Customs in Manchuria the same duties as goods

moved as ordinary freight, i.e. in Manchuria,

where special conditions prevail;

(2) The levy of Coast Trade Duty on inter-trade-

mart trade is, in the Inspector General's

opinion, incorrect.

3.   With regard to the points on which you

have asked for definite instructions under

Queries (1), (2) and (3-1st paragraph):

Coast Trade Duty should not in future

be levied on Postal Parcels transported to or from

a Trade Mart where there is a collecting Custom

House if goods otherwise conveyed through the

Customs to or from the same Marts are exempt.

But Transit Dues in lieu of Likin are to be

continue to be charged, in accordance with the

instructions of I.G. despatch No.18/87,308 to Aigun,

on Parcels (not under S.M.E.C.) to and from Trade

Marts

Marts where there are no collecting Custom Houses.
In this respect, Moukden, not being a collecting
Custom House, parcels to and from Moukden should
be treated in accordance with the above rule.

These instructions should be given effect
to at once as they are already in force at
Harbin.

With regard to the queries under (3-remaining
paragraphs), (4) and (5), your queries and remarks,
especially those concerning export duty, give rise
to doubt as to the correctness of your procedure
with regard to the duty treatment of goods moved
as ordinary freight, and before issuing instructions
with regard to the duty treatment of such parcels
as are referred to, the Inspector General wishes
you to submit, in as concise a form as possible,
a report on the duty treatment of native goods,
moved as ordinary freight, between Aigun and
(1) Trade Marts in Manchuria (_vide_ Circulars _re_
Special Manchurian Exemption Certificate),

(a)

(a) where there is a collecting Custom House

(e.g. Harbin, etc.),

(b) where there is no collecting Custom House -

with special reference to Moukden;

(2) places in Manchuria which are not Trade Marts

(3) Treaty Ports in Manchuria (e.g. Newchwang,Dairen);

(4) Treaty Ports in China proper (i.e. if goods

are so declared.).

With regard to your remark under Query (1):

"Although such duty (Coast Trade Duty) would

be payable on Manchurian Special Exemption

Certificates", it is not clear under what

circumstances you would issue a Special

Manchurian Exemption Certificate to Native

Goods moving from Aigun to another Trade Mart.

If such certificates are issued by your office,

what duties do you levy ?

A copy of this despatch as well as of

your despatch under reply is being sent to the

Harbin Commissioner with whom you should consult

with

with regard to the duty treatment of goods moved
as ordinary freight in Manchuria, as uniformity
of procedure is essential.　　A copy of your reply
to this despatch should also be sent to the
Harbin Commissioner for the same reason.

　　　　　　　　I am,

　　　　　　　　　　Sir,

　　　　　Your obedient Servant,

　　　　　　Cecil A. V. Bowra,

　　　　　　　Chief Secretary.

Appendix.

The Inspector General to the Harbin Commissioner.

No.2809   Commrs.   Peking,   25th February, 1922.
Harbin   No. 88,114.

Sir,

1.   I have to acknowledge the receipt of your
despatch No. 2599 :

                    duty treatment of, and documents issued to,
                    all goods from and to Harbin district:
                    further remarks and suggestions in re;
and, in reply, to thank you for bringing out so
clearly the various points which the instructions
you have received in connection with the re-organisation
of the Harbin Customs district have brought to the
front.

2.   The chief points are those which you
enumerate under the headings 1,2,3 and though
as you state they are to a certain extent
interdependent I propose to deal with them
comprehensively in connection with the question of
Kwanchengtze.

3.   The principal object I have in view in
opening a Customs station at Kwanchengtze is
to obtain a footing at the point on the Railway
system of Manchuria where break of gauge
necessitates transference of cargo from one
system to another.   We are committed to
opening at least a Checking Station there and
have authority to do so : the question whether
the opening should be postponed or should
immediately take place is the only one on which

                                        there

there is room for difference of opinion.

You urge very strongly the view that we should proceed to open at once and you give reasons the cogency of which I am bound to admit, backed as they are, by experience and knowledge of your district and its administrative needs. In instructing you that the office is not to be opened until an Agreement has been reached with the Administrations of the various railway systems I have been influenced by the following considerations.

The opening up and development of Manchuria are forcing to the front questions of transportation which unless we can secure Customs control of cargo throughout the railway systems connecting Manchuria with foreign countries, the sea and China proper, will cause increasing difficulty as time goes on.

When Manchuria was thrown open to foreign trade by treaties under the Trade Mart system, the question arose how the Customs could best meet the new responsibilities which these treaties forced upon the Service. The system decided upon was, broadly speaking, to keep out of the interior of Manchuria and to confine ourselves to the frontiers, whether those frontiers were between Chinese and foreign territory or between what may be called China proper and Manchuria. I think it was intended that we should tax trans-frontier trade, and that we should keep our fiscal hands off native trade

within

within the three Eastern Provinces altogether.
This intention, it appears to me, was evident
in the arrangement made for protecting from
provincial taxation goods entering Manchuria and
destined for a specified Trade Mart.   The
Special Manchurian Exemption Certificates issued
to cover both foreign and native Customs duty
paid goods are free Transit Passes.   Like
Transit Passes they cover the goods and not
the means of conveyance over which they imply
no measure of control and are merely a proof
to Inland Tax Stations that the goods they
purport to cover have fulfilled Maritime Customs
requirements.   The system originally introduced
has I believe on the whole met trade requirements
it has certainly done what from the Customs
administrative point of view it was intended
to accomplish, namely to obviate the necessity
of opening Maritime Customs establishments at a
large number of towns in Manchuria.   And, while
foreign interests have been satisfied and have
not pressed for such opening, the fact that
the Chinese authorities have raised no question
of the taxation by the Customs of inter trade
mart trade seems to support the view that such
an extension of the Customs fiscal sphere was
never contemplated.   Nevertheless certain
features of the situation would appear to have
escaped notice at the outset. Harbin opened
as a Trade Mart very soon owing to its
command of both a railway and river frontier

soon

soon assumed very much the status of an ordinary
Treaty Port and to a certain extent the same is
true of the Harbin ex-sub-station Aigun and the
frontier Marts Hunchun and Lungchingts'un.   In
framing regulations for all these places treaty
port principles were wrongly, I think, made the
basis, and this has caused a certain amount of
confusion.   At Harbin it has led to a
control of Sungari River trade which has become
firmly established, at Aigun and Hunchun, it
has produced friction with native authorities
and traders, and for a considerable time
resulted in the payment of all duties under
protest supported by the Russian and Japanese
representatives in China.   From the foreign
merchants point of view our position, confused
as I believe it has been by our own application
of principles which were never meant to apply,
has never been understood.   Accustomed to
Treaty Port trade and regulations foreign
merchants have considered that on passing goods
over the frontier and paying the Maritime
Customs duties leviable they are entitled to
the same protection, facilities and procedure
that they would receive at any of the Treaty
Ports in China.   Politically they recognise no
sub-frontier at Shanhaikuan and the fact that
the Customs are established at the sea-doors
of Manchuria, Antung, Dairen and Newchwang, gives
them in their view the right to demand ordinary
Customs treatment for their goods whether

proceeding

proceeding from Russia to China or abroad on the
one hand, or from China, or abroad to Russia on
the other hand. Improvement in inter-railway
traffic arrangements encouraged trade between Russia
and China and between Russia and Japan via
Dairen and already before the War it was
seen that the merchants demand, reasonable in
itself, would have to be met. Attempts to
meet it were made by the local practice of
issuing Exemption Certificates and Cargo
Certificates at Manchouli, a procedure not
authorised, and by the authority of the Shui-wu
Ch'u conveyed in I.G. despatch No. 352/28,493 for
the treatment of foreign goods under Through
Bill of Lading to Dairen. During the War
the question remained in abeyance, but it has
once more arisen, and were it not for the
disorganisation in Siberia, it would have assumed
far greater prominence.

My view is that we were putting the
cart before the horse in attempting to apply
Treaty Port principles and procedure without
an understanding with all the railway systems
traversing Manchuria that would give us control
of cargo carried from the frontier to destination,
whether sea port in Manchuria or China Proper.
And I think that when the arrangements were
made for opening Harbin and Antung some
procedure analogous to that of the Special
Manchurian Exemption Certificate should have
been adopted to protect goods entering or leaving
China by the northern frontier from inland

taxation

taxation when in transit through Manchuria, the
right to re-export privileges with issue of
drawbacks to be dependent on arrangements to be
made with the railways for adequate control
of the cargo carried on their systems. It is
difficult to retrace our steps because we have
to a considerable extent given our case away,
but so strongly do I feel that, until we
obtain these arrangements, our difficulties under
foreign pressure will only increase, that I have
been reluctant to give the word to go ahead at
Kwanchengtze until our object is attained, lest
by doing so we deprive ourselves of the benefit
of that pressure which might otherwise be exerted
on our behalf. The main reason for not
establishing ourselves at Kwanchengtze at present
is not that the Government is afraid of opposition
to the Customs right to collect duty on goods
moved between Treaty Port and Treaty Port. As
I have explained I believe that there was never
any intention that we should collect duty on
inter-trade mart trade or in any way tax the free
movement of native goods in Manchuria. We are
concerned solely with the collection of duties
on trade crossing the frontier; the taxation of
native trade in Manchuria is a matter for the
Chinese Authorities. Moreover a movement is in
progress that must sooner or later, possibly sooner
lead to the abolition of Export and Coast Trade
duties and it is not desirable that we should
inaugurate a system leading in the opposite

direction

direction. My object in establishing ourselves at Kwanchengtze is to provide a link in a chain of control that I foresee is indispensable to the carrying out of our proper duties in Manchuria. If I were assured that establishing ourselves there now would not retard the attainment of my object I would be prepared to go ahead, but, in any case, the station would be a Checking Station only and would not collect duty unless that duty were properly payable at Harbin, e.g. balance of 1/3rd duties payable after 1st April next.

4.   What precedes covers in the main the points you raise. Instructions have been issued to the Tientsin Commissioner not to issue Sanlientan for the districts of Manchouli and Suifenho and it is hoped that this will lessen the difficulty you foresee.

In regard to the control in Harbin Railway Station I do not wish you to assume control over cargo coming from or going to South Manchuria, nor of cargo to and from places in North Manchuria exempt Manchouli and Suifenho. Our objects in establishing ourselves in the Harbin Railway Station are to concentrate railway and river Customs work on one spot as far as possible and to enable cargo loaded at Harbin for export to Russian territory to be examined at Harbin instead of when crossing the frontier and similarly to enable cargo arriving from Russian territory to be examined at Harbin or bonded if that is more convenient to the merchants.

5.

5.　　　　　What is now wanted appears to me to be an arrangement with the three Railways concerned which will make it possible for cargo passing through Manchuria under Through Bill of Lading to be accompanied by Cargo Certificates or Exemption Certificates, to destination, i.e. terminal points on the borders of Manchuria, and in the case of the Peking-Moukden Railway, Tientsin.

　　　　　　　　I am,
　　　　　　　　　Sir,
　　　　　　　Your obedient Servant,
　　　　　　　(Signed) F.A.Aglen,
　　　　　　　　Inspector General.

True copy :

[signature]

Acting Assistant Secretary.

90.

J. G.   Aigun/Taheiho 5th January, 1923.

Sir,

1.   I have the honour to acknowledge the

receipt of your despatch No. 99/92,424 :

          concerning duty treatment of native
          goods conveyed in postal parcels within
          North Manchuria, and calling for a
          report on duty treatment of native
          goods moved as ordinary freight ;

and, in reply, to say that your instructions have

been carried out without delay : the levy of coast

trade duty within the limits of North Manchuria

has been stopped ; Moukden is treated as an inland

place ; and I have taken North Manchuria to include

the Provinces of Kirin and Heilungchiang.

2.   Thus the Aigun practice is now as follows:

          Parcels moved within North Manchuria, not passing

en route another Trade Mart with a collecting Custom

House (e.g. to or from Moho, Tsitsihar, Hailar) pay

                                                    only

The Inspector General of Customs,

          PEKING.

only Transit Dues *in lieu* of likin.

Parcels to or from another Trade Mart in North Manchuria, at which there is a collecting Custom House, pay export duty.

Parcels to or from the interior of North Manchuria passing *en route* two of the Marts with a collecting Custom House, pay export duty and transit dues *in lieu* of likin.

Parcels to Antung, Newchwang, Dairen, Tientsin, or beyond,(and from such places) pay export and coast trade duty ; and transit dues *in lieu* of likin, if the origins or destination is an Inland place.

This procedure is in accordance with that in force at Harbin, except on one point : Harbin does not collect coast trade duty on parcels to or from Dairen.

3.   As regards your querries, the Aigun procedure in levying duty on native goods conveyed as ordinary freight within China may be summed up as follows :

1. No Manchurian Special Exemption Certificates were ever issued by this Office.

2. Other Documents are issued within the following limits : the Amur, the Argun, and the Sungari up to Harbin, for river-borne cargo ; the Liangchiat'un Barrier, for overland cargo.

3. Native cargo to or from places on the Chinese
                                          side

side of the Amur and Argun is free, although the Iahasusu Office taxes the same cargo (as reported in Aigun despatch No. 37)

4. Native cargo passing the Liangchiat'un Barrier is also free of duty, since 1st November, 1922.

5. Native cargo for of from points on the Sungari pays full export duty.

This Office has therefore no control of goods beyond Harbin or Liangchiat'un, while control of Postal Parcels extends without interruption over the whole of China; consequently the duty treatment of native goods sent in Postal Parcels can hardly *by this Office* be based on the duty treatment of ordinary goods — the only criterium being this, that, if Manchurian *Exemption* Special Certificates were issued, they should be issued, in the owrds of Circular No. 1472, to "export "and coast-trade duty-paid native goods".

4.   I am consulting with the Harbin Commissioner with regard to the duty treatment of ordinary goods moved south of Harbin, especially to and from Dairen and Moukden.

Copy of this despatch is forwarded to the Harbin Commissioner.

I have , etc.

Acting Commissioner.

[A—28]

No. 115   Commrs.   INSPECTORATE GENERAL OF CUSTOMS,

Aigun   No. 94,145   PEKING, 21st April 1923.

Sir,

       With reference to your despatch No. 90:

       Postal Parcels: duty treatment of native
       goods conveyed in, within Northern Manchuria;
       submitting a report on the duty treatment
       by the Aigun office of ordinary goods
       moved in North Manchuria;

I am directed by the Inspector General to say that

your procedure with regard to the duty treatment of

postal parcels, as reported, is now in accordance with

the rules laid down, except that, following the

Harbin practice, coast-trade duty should not be charged

on parcels to or from Dairen, for the reasons stated

by the Harbin Commissioner in his despatch No.32/820

to Aigun.

       A copy of this despatch is being sent to

the Harbin Commissioner.

             I am,

                Sir,

            Your obedient Servant,

The Commissioner of Customs,

    AIGUN.   Chief Secretary Officiating.

呈海关总税务司署 <u>83</u> 号文　　　　　　　　瑷珲关／大黑河 1922 年 11 月 29 日

尊敬的海关总税务司（北京）：

　　1. 兹汇报，本署此前已照海关总税务司署第 14/87199 号令关于邮政包裹征税办法的指示，参照《江海关海关手续手册》对通过邮政包裹往来两个或两个以上通商口岸或者设有税关的贸易市场之土货征收复进口／复出口半税，随后海关总税务司署第 18/87308 号令又指示，凡邮政包裹寄往设有税关的贸易市场者，其征税办法与寄往天津或中国其他通商口岸者相同。

　　2. 然本署近日从北满邮务管理局处得知，北满洲地区内运送之邮政包裹的复进口／复出口半税征收办法已开始修订；另自哈尔滨关税务司处收到海关总税务司署致哈尔滨关第 2936/90993 号令的抄件，令文指示，邮政包裹的征税办法应尽可能与海关对普通运输货物的征税办法保持一致，凡邮政包裹往来"北满洲设有税关的贸易市场"者，复进口／复出口半税的征收办法均与以其他方式运输之货物相同。

　　3. 同时，本地商会代表向本署提出，凡土货通过邮政包裹经陆路（梁家屯分卡）运输者，均应与通过货车运输者同享免税待遇。兹认为，若考虑此提议，亦应仅限于瑷珲关区与哈尔滨、满洲里、绥芬河及其他北满洲内陆地区间运输之包裹，因为 1）超出此等范围运输之包裹，自然应与在哈尔滨以南各地运输的普通货物一样缴纳正税；2）包裹自哈尔滨或满洲里运入瑷珲关区的途中不会通过其他通商口岸或设有税关的贸易市场，因此只征收子口税。但即便如此限制，本署依然认为，对于通过邮政包裹运送之货物应与普通货物享受同等待遇之主张，不应全盘接受，毕竟与普通货物相比，邮政包裹享有诸多特权，比如免纳内地统捐及仅于一处验货等。实际上，最好可于中国境内对邮政包裹施行统一的征税办法。例如：凡邮政包裹在蒙自关和思茅关之间运输者，均应免税放行；若上海与宁波之间的轮船运输中断（比如，由于罢工），中国邮政局通过民船运送之包裹则应交纳常关税。

　　4. 为避免误解，避免频繁更改征税办法为公众及海关带来不利影响，特此提出以下问题，望贵署予以指示：

　　（1）瑷珲关是否应效法哈尔滨关，对北满洲内运输之包裹停止征收复进口半税（但目前持有满洲特别免重征执照者须纳此税）？

　　（2）于上述办法而言，北满洲内之地区除瑷珲关区以外，是否还包括哈尔滨、满洲里、绥芬河、拉哈苏苏及三姓，珲春与六道沟（龙井村）是否亦在此列？

（3）鉴于奉天未设"征税"海关，对于往来于瑷珲关区与奉天之间的包裹应如何征税？是应征收出口税及复出口／复进口半税？或是出口税及子口税？或是仅征收出口税？

（4）对于往来于瑷珲关区与大连之间的包裹，是否应征收复出口／复进口半税？

（5）本地商会之主张是否可取？经梁家屯路线运送之邮政包裹是否可与普通货物享受同等征税待遇？若可以，此类包裹（装有土货）：

① 是否应免交出口税？

②（A）若往来于瑷珲关区与哈尔滨、满洲里或者绥芬河之间，是否应仅支付 2/3 的出口税，毕竟其中一部分路程由中东铁路运输？

（B）若由中东铁路运输往来内陆地区或北满洲内各地区，是否应支付 2/3 的出口税及子口税？

您忠诚的仆人

包安济（G. Boezi）

瑷珲关署理税务司

致瑷珲关第 <u>99/92424</u> 号令　　　　　海关总税务司署 1922 年 12 月 19 日,北京

尊敬的瑷珲关税务司：

根据第 83 号呈：

1. "北满洲境内用邮递包裹运送的土货征税办法；请求指示。"

奉总税务司命令,随附海关总税务司署致哈尔滨关第 2809/88144 号令副本,以供参考。该令副本第 3 款规定了海关在满洲土货征税方面应遵循的通则。通则中显示,对满洲境内本土贸易的征税由中国地方政府（即省政府）负责；海关只负责过境贸易的税款征收。

2. 至于邮递包裹,应牢记两条原则：

（1）若无特殊条款条件,邮递包裹应尽量与普通货运货物征税方法相同；

（2）总税务司认为,不应对贸易市场间贸易征收土货复进口半税。

3. 对于贵署在问题（1）、（2）及（3）第一条中要求明确指示的几点问题。

凡设有税关的贸易市场,倘若以其他运送方式往来该市场并经海关查验的货物属于免税货物,那么将来同样的货物采用邮递包裹往来该市场,不得对邮递包裹征收土货复进口半税。但根据海关总税务司署致瑷珲关第 18/87308 号令的指示,子口税取代厘金,往来未设立税关的贸易市场的包裹（未持有满洲特别免重征执照）需继续征收子口税。从此角度来讲,奉天（沈阳）未设立税关,故往来奉天的包裹应依照上述规则执行。

这些指示已在哈尔滨关实施,瑷珲关也应当立即执行。

至于贵署问题（3）的剩余部分、问题（4）以及问题（5）,尤其是关于出口税的问题与意见,让我们怀疑贵署对普通货运运输货物的征税方法是否正确。在针对上文所述的包裹做出征税办法指示前,总税务司希望贵署上呈一份报告,尽可能简明扼要地介绍按照普通货运方式运输的土货在往来瑷珲关与其他下列地方之间的征税办法：

（1）满洲境内贸易市场（参见有关满洲特别免重征执照的通令）；

① 当地设有税关（如哈尔滨关等）；

② 当地未设有税关（如奉天）；

（2）满洲境内非贸易市场地区；

（3）满洲境内通商口岸（如牛庄关、大连关）；

（4）中国本土通商口岸（若货物按此申报）。

至于贵署在问题（1）下的备注："尽管持满洲特别免重征执照需要缴纳此种税款（土

货复进口半税）"，但尚未明确贵署在何种情况下向从瑷珲关运向另一个贸易市场的土货开具满洲特别免重征执照。若贵署开具此类证明，贵署还征什么税？

　　此令副本与贵署呈文已抄送给哈尔滨关税务司，贵署应征求哈尔滨关税务司对满洲普通货运货物征税办法的意见，保持各关操作规程一致至关重要。同时基于同样原因，贵署回复此令的副本也应抄送哈尔滨关税务司。

您忠诚的仆人

包罗（C. A. V. Bowra）

总务科税务司

附件

海关总税务司致哈尔滨关税务司令

致哈尔滨关第 <u>2809/88114</u> 号令　　　海关总税务司署（北京）1922 年 2 月 25 日

尊敬的哈尔滨关税务司：

1. 第 2559 号呈收悉：

"所有往来哈尔滨关关区货物的凭证开具及征税办法；更多意见与建议。"

现批复如下：贵署在收到哈尔滨关关区改制指示后，非常明确地提出几点建议，感谢贵署给出的重要意见。

2. 最关键的建议是贵署在标题 1、2、3 下罗列的几点。尽管贵署称这几点之间没有确切联系，但我建议结合宽城子（现长春）问题，综合处理。

3. 在宽城子新建一个分关的主要考量是想在满洲铁路网上取得一个立足点，由于铁路归属和管理分属不同势力，轨距存在差异，货物往往需要从一个铁路系统转运至另一个铁路系统。我们现已得到授权，可以在此地设立至少一个检查分卡，但设立时间是即刻执行还是延后进行还有待商榷。

贵署强烈建议立即着手建立分关，并且必须承认，从贵关区的经验和见识，还有行政需求方面给出的理由令人信服。但出于以下几点考虑，请在与各铁路系统管理部门达成协议之前，不得设立新分关。

满洲的开放发展必会触及运输问题，除非我们海关能确保对经由（将满洲与外国、公海和中国内陆连通的）铁路系统运输的货物实施全面控制，否则随着时间的推移，该问题会越来越严重。

满洲根据条约规定采取贸易市场体制开展对外贸易，随之产生了一个问题：海关如何恰当应对这些条约赋予的新责任。泛言之，选定的制度要求海关不插手满洲内部贸易，将自身约束在过境贸易上，无论是经过中国与其他国家之间的边境，还是所谓的中国本土内陆地区与满洲之间的边境。本署认为，此举意图是使海关只对过境贸易征税，不插手东三省境内本土贸易。在本署看来，这种意图在为了货物在运入满洲并拟运往特定贸易市场时免纳省税而订立的协议中显露无疑。所开具的满洲特别免重征执照载有洋关和常关完税货物信息，实际上是一种免税入内地验单。就像入内地验单一样，执照记载的是货物内容，但不包含货物运输方式，对此没有任何控制措施。并且此执照对于内陆税局来说仅仅是他们声称所载货物满足海关要求的凭证。最初提议的制度，兹以为，大体上可以满足贸易需求。从海关管理角度来看，此制度已达到预期，换而言之，已无须在满洲各个城镇中建立海关。并且国外利益已得到满足，不再催促分关建立，而中国政府对贸易市场间贸易税款可由海关征收一事也从未提出疑问，这似乎证明了一直以来中国政府其实并未考虑扩大海关财务权力。不过，刚开始的确很难察觉这种情况的某些特征。哈尔滨之所以能作为贸易市场迅速建立，是因为哈尔滨掌控一条铁路和一条界河，可以推断它很快就会成为一个普通通商口岸，扩张几成定局。这样的情况对哈尔滨关的前分关瑷珲关，还有边境市场珲春和龙井村同样适用。本署认为，设计这些地方法规时所参照的通商口岸准则是错误的，很容易引起困惑。在哈尔滨，海关已完全控制松花江沿江贸易，而在瑷珲和珲春，海关与当地政府及商人都有摩擦，导致有大量时间都在处理受日俄驻中国代表支持的缴税抵制事件。在洋商看来，海关的地位很让人困惑。本署认为原因在于我们参照的准则不正确，导致难以让人理解。习惯于通商口岸贸易及章程的洋商认为，在运输货物过境，向海关缴纳应缴税额后，洋商便能享受与中国其他通商口岸相同的保障、便利和办法。政治上他们承认在山海关不存在边界，而在满洲、安东、大连和牛庄的海上门户设立海关，这让他们觉得，无论是从俄国运送至中国或其他国家的货物，还是从中国或其他国家运送至俄国的货物，都有权要求海关按常例平等对待。铁路交通运输协定的改善，加强了俄罗斯与中国的贸易，还促进了俄罗斯经大连中转与日本的贸易。在战争开始之前就已经有商人提出类似要求。要求合理，应予以解决。开始海关打算依照当地惯例，在满洲里签发免征执照、货单这种未经授权的办法来解决此类问题，抑或通过海关总税务司署第352/28493号令中传达税务处授权允许对洋货按照联运提单方式抵达大连关采用的处理办法来解决此类问题。战争期间，此问题一直处于搁置状态，但现在又被提起来了，此次要不是西伯利亚政府瓦解，可以推断将来问题会越来越严重。

本署认为，在没有与所有遍布满洲的铁路网之间达成谅解之前，企图实施通商口岸准则和办法，有些本末倒置了。我们只有达成谅解，才可以对从边境运入满洲海港或中国内陆本土等目的地的货物实现控制。本署认为，在签署开放哈尔滨和安东的协议时，应实施办法来保护从北方边境进出中国的货物，类似开具满洲特别免重征执照，避免在满洲转运时再次缴纳内地统捐。要通过退还税款来维护复出口特权，需与铁路系统签署协议，进而充分控制铁路系统承运的货物。我们很难重来一次，因为在很大程度上，是海关自己放弃了时机。但我有强烈预感，如果海关不签署这样的协议，在其他国家的重压下，我们遇到的问题只会越来越多。在达到我们的目的之前，对于宽城子问题，我迟迟不愿意松口继续前行，以免这些压力以其他方式强加在我们身上，失去这些压力所带来的利益。目前，海关尚未在宽城子建立分关，其主要原因不是因为政府害怕此举与海关对往来各通商口岸间的货物征收税款的权利相悖。正如之前的解释，兹以为当局从未想让海关负责贸易市场间的贸易税收，也不想让海关负责满洲境内自由流动的土货的税收。海关只负责过境贸易的税款征收；满洲境内本土贸易的税款征收由中国政府负责。此外，有项动作正在进行中，迟早，大概很快就要废除出口税和土货复进口半税，值此时机，我们制定一个与此相悖的系统的做法并不可取。我提议在宽城子建立分关目的是想在控制链中增加一环，可以预见，该环节对于海关能够在满洲履行相应职责有不可或缺的作用。若能得到保证，现于宽城子建立分关不会妨碍我的目标，即着手准备设关工作。但不管怎样，该分关仅仅是一个检查关卡无法收税，除非是在哈尔滨关缴纳部分税款，例如，在次年4月1日后缴纳剩余税款的三分之一。

4. 以上是对贵署所提几点建议的回复。已指示津海关税务司不要向满洲里和绥芬河地区的货物发放三联单，希望可以减少贵署所遇见的难题。

至于哈尔滨火车站的货物管控，希望贵署不要管控往来南满洲以及往来北满洲（除满洲里和绥芬河以外）地区的货物。海关在哈尔滨火车站建立分关，目的是为了将铁路和水路海关工作尽可能集合在一地，让自哈尔滨装载并出口至俄罗斯地区的货物能够在哈尔滨验货，不需要在过境时验货，同样如果商人觉得更方便，也可以让运自俄罗斯地区的货物能够在哈尔滨验货或保税。

5. 在本署看来，目前海关最需要的是与三条铁路之间签订协议，让用联运提单运输的货物可以领取货单或免征执照，经由满洲中转运往目的地，即满洲边境上的目的地，比如北京 – 奉天的火车，目的地就是天津。

您忠诚的仆人

（签字）安格联（F. A. Aglen）

海关总税务司

此副本内容真实有效，特此证明。

确认人签字：福贝士（A. H. Forbes）

呈海关总税务司署 <u>90</u> 号文　　　　　　瑷珲关／大黑河 1923 年 1 月 5 日

尊敬的海关总税务司（北京）：

　　1. 根据海关总税务司署第 99/92424 号令：

　　　"指示北满洲境内以邮政包裹运送之土货的征税办法，另请汇报以普通方式运送之土货的征税办法。"

　　兹汇报，已照贵署指示，立即停止对北满洲限定范围内以邮政包裹运送之土货征收复进口／复出口半税，另将奉天视作内陆地区，将吉林省与黑龙江省均视作北满洲境内之地。

　　2. 瑷珲关邮政包裹现行征税办法如下：

　　凡包裹于北满洲境内运输者，若沿途未经另一设有税关的贸易市场（如往来于瑷珲关区与漠河／齐齐哈尔／海拉尔之间），则仅交纳代征厘金的子口税。

　　凡包裹往来于瑷珲关区与北满洲境内另一设有税关的贸易市场之间者，均交纳出口税。

　　凡包裹于北满洲境内运输者，若沿途经过两个设有税关的贸易市场，则交纳出口税及代征厘金的子口税。

　　凡包裹往来于瑷珲关区与安东关、牛庄关、大连关、天津关或他其他各地之间者，均交纳出口税及复进口／复出口半税；凡包裹往来于瑷珲关区与内陆各地之间者，仅交纳代征厘金的子口税。

　　此征税办法与哈尔滨关征税办法总体一致，唯哈尔滨关不对往来哈尔滨关与大连关之间的包裹征收复进口／复出口半税。

　　3. 瑷珲关对于中国境内以普通方式运送之土货实施以下征税办法：

　　（1）未曾签发过满洲特别免重征执照；

　　（2）签发的其他海关凭证有效范围仅限于：水运货物——黑龙江、额尔古纳河及松花江（至哈尔滨关），陆路货物——梁家屯分卡；

　　（3）凡土货往来黑龙江及额尔古纳河华岸各地者，均免税放行，不过拉哈苏苏海关对此类货物均予征税（参阅瑷珲关第 37 号呈）；

　　（4）凡土货经由梁家屯分卡者，自 1922 年 11 月 1 日起，均免税放行；

　　（5）凡土货往来于松花江沿岸各地者，均交纳出口正税。

　　由此可见，哈尔滨关或梁家屯分卡以外之土货均不在瑷珲关管辖之列，但中国境内各地往来于本埠的邮政包裹一直都在；因此于瑷珲关而言，以邮政包裹运送之土货的征税办法难以根据普通货物的征税办法而定。此外，若瑷珲关签发满洲特别免重征执照，亦应仅发给海关总税务司署第 1472 号通令所述之"已完纳出口税及复进口半税之土货"。

4. 本署已向哈尔滨关税务司询问有关哈尔滨以南各地普通货物的征税办法，尤其是往来于哈尔滨关与大连关及奉天关之间的货物。

此抄件已发送至哈尔滨关税务司。

您忠诚的仆人

包安济（G. Boezi）

瑷珲关署理税务司

致瑷珲关第 <u>115/94145</u> 号令　　　　海关总税务司署 1923 年 4 月 21 日，北京

尊敬的瑷珲关税务司：

　　根据第 90 号呈：

　　　"邮寄包裹：北满洲境内土货征税办法；呈交关于瑷珲关对运至北满洲的普通货物的征税办法报告。"

奉总税务司命令，兹告知：贵署所汇报的瑷珲关邮寄包裹征税操作规程需与现行税则相一致。但根据哈尔滨关惯例，凡运至大连的包裹或由大连发寄的包裹情况除外，不应对其征收土货复进口半税，其原因详见哈尔滨税务司至瑷珲关令第 32/820 号。

　　同时，此令副本已抄送给哈尔滨关税务司。

　　　　　　　　　　　　　　　　　　　您忠诚的仆人

　　　　　　　　　　　　　　　　　　威厚澜（R. H. R. Wade）

　　　　　　　　　　　　　　　　　　代理总务科税务司

4. 为参照哈尔滨关处理运往南部地区邮递包裹征税办法事

SECTION No. 39

32.　Service.

CUSTOM HOUSE,

gun.　No. 820.

Harbin ,15th January, 1923.

Sir,

1.　　　I have to acknowledge receipt of your

Despatch No. 27 of the 5th instant:

> Postal Parcels: moved within North
> Manchuria.　Copy of correspondence
> to I. G., forwarded.　Information
> as to duty treatment by the Harbin
> Customs of Native cargo moved South
> of Harbin, soliciting.

2.　　　Cargo exported from Harbin by rail to

a southern destination is not controlled by

this office and, consequently, no duty is levied.

Native cargo, entrained at Manchouli or Suifenho

for transport inward by rail to a point on the

Chinese Eastern Railway or to any point South

of Harbin, is passed free of duty at the

Frontier Station.　　But as the _bona_ _fide_ Native

origin is difficult of establishment, practically

all

To

The Commissioner of Customs,

　　AIGUN.

all goods entrained at Manchouli or Suifenho are treated as foreign.

3.   Dairen is a free port and no duty is collected on goods entering its territory. As Coast Trade duty is payable at port of destination, it naturally is not paid on cargo shipped to Dairen, hence this Office exempts Native goods in postal parcel for Dairen from Coast Trade duty.

4.   As regards Practice Order No. 119, page <u>d</u>:- Parcels, posted at a Chinese Eastern Railway Station, at which there is no Custom House and <u>coming under the cognizance of Harbin Customs</u>, cannot reach a Trade Mart at which there is a Custom House, not on the Chinese Eastern Railway, without passing a Treaty Port, namely Harbin. From such an inland place to Aigun would be a different matter as parcels might not pass another Treaty Port <u>en route</u>. Such movement would, however, not come under the cognizance of a Custom House in Harbin District, for the guidance

of

of which Practice Order No. 119 was issued.

5.   A copy of this despatch, together with

a copy of your despatch under reply, is being

forwarded to the Inspector General.

I am,

Sir,

Your obedient Servant,

Commissioner.

致瑷珲关第 <u>32/820</u> 号函　　　　　　　　哈尔滨关 1923 年 1 月 15 日

尊敬的瑷珲关税务司：

1. 根据 1 月 5 日瑷珲关致哈尔滨关第 27 号函：

"邮政包裹：关于北满洲境内运输之邮政包裹，发送瑷珲关致海关总税务司署呈文抄件；请提供哈尔滨关对哈尔滨南部地区往来土货的征税办法相关信息。"

2. 凡货物经由铁路自哈尔滨运往南部地区者，均不在哈尔滨关管辖及征税之列；凡土货经由铁路自满洲里或绥芬河运往中东铁路沿线某地或哈尔滨南部地区者，皆于该两处边境分关免税放行；然因于满洲里分关或绥芬河分关而言，货物原产地难以确定，故几乎所有通过火车运输之货物皆视为洋货。

3. 大连为免税口岸，凡货物进入该地区者，皆免征税。因土货复进口半税均由目的口岸征收，故凡货物运往大连者，皆无须纳税；由此，凡土货以邮政包裹运往大连者，在哈尔滨关皆免征复进口半税。

4. 哈尔滨关第 119 号办法（d 页）所述之自中东铁路沿线未设税关之地寄发之邮政包裹，只要进入哈尔滨关管辖范围以内，在通过哈尔滨关之前，绝无机会抵达任何设有税关的贸易市场（不在中东铁路沿线）。然自中东铁路沿线未设税关之地寄发之邮政包裹若运往瑷珲关，途中或许不会经过另一通商口岸，但亦不会进入哈尔滨关的管辖范围。征税办法可参照哈尔滨关第 119 号办法。

5. 此函抄件及瑷珲关第 27 号函抄件已发送至总税务司。

您忠诚的仆人

（签字）覃书（R. C. L. d' Anjou）

哈尔滨关税务司

5. 为参照珲春关处理自中国寄入或寄出经由境外运至中国其他口岸、贸易市场等地之邮政包裹的征税办法事

SERVICE No. 47

No. 1.	Service.
AIGUN	No. 508.

CUSTOM HOUSE,

HUNCHUN, 11th April, 19 23

Sir,

As instructed by the Inspector General, I beg to append hereto copies of the correspondence exchanged between this office, the Inspectorate and the Harbin Postal Commissioner, with regard to the duty treatment of postal parcels, forwarded from or to China, across foreign territory, to other Chinese Ports, Marts, etc.

Should the question raised by the Hunchun office call for comments from yourself, I would be much obliged to you for sending me a copy of such comments.

I am,

Sir,

Your obedient Servant,

Commissioner.

APPEND.

To

The Commissioner of Customs,

AIGUN.

COPY.

A P P E N D.

THE HUNCHUN COMMISSIONER TO THE INSPECTOR GENERAL.

HUNCHUN DESPATCH NO. 1,189

OF 26th FEBRUARY,

1 9 2 3.

POSTAL PARCELS : forwarded from or to China across
foreign territory to other Chinese
ports, marts, etc. : duty treatment
of, queries concerning. Instructions
solicited.

Sir,

1.   The Harbin Postal Commissioner, Mr W. W. Ritchie,
informs me that he intends to establish a quick
delivery service for postal parcels forwarded to and
from the Hunchun and Lungchingtsun districts, whether
such parcels come from abroad, Treaty Ports or Inland
Places, or are intended for such places. Mr Ritchie is
of opinion - and I entirely agree with him - that
certain classes of parcels, whatever their provenance
might be, would reach our far-away districts much
quicker if they came or were forwarded through Korea,
a country where communications and rapid means of
transport are an example well worth imitating by China.

2.   The Hunchun and Lungchingtsun parcel post
procedure (examination, assessment of duty and general
control of the parcel post traffic) is entirely
governed by the instructions contained in your Despatches
Nos. 886/86,520 and 895/87,309. The rules laid down in
both these Despatches have, so far, worked very
smoothly and can easily be applied to any case coming
forward for the present.

3.   However, goods, foreign or native, contained in
parcels, whether for importation or exportation, are, I
take it, cargo and, therefore, subject to exactly the
same duty treatment as ordinary cargo reaching our

ports

ports by cart or pack animal, or leaving our
districts in the same manner.

4.   The question of native goods exported by parcel
post from either Hunchun, Lungchingtsun or Inland
Places and Marts, after being passed through our
Custom Houses, we can afford to leave as it is. It
is up to us, in Hunchun and Lungchingtsun, to ensure
prpper examination and assessment of duty. Such goods
are invariably covered by a postal declaration and
accompanied by a postal way bill. Both these
documents can be checked at any Treaty Port and it
is not all Treaty Ports, I make bold to say, that
will differentiate between parcels which have not left
Chinese territory on their way to destination and
parcels from China, passing through a foreign country
(Korea), on their way to a Chinese Treaty port or Inland
Place. The Provisional Regulations for the ports of
Hunchun and Lungchingtsun, approved by I.G. Despatch
No. 434/59,806 (1916) do not, so we think here,
apply to any ports but Hunchun and Lungchingtsun.
I beg, therefore, to suggest that we keep to the
existing practice as regards native goods exported by
postal parcels and intended for any place in China,
Treaty Port or Inland Places and that we ignore the
fact that such parcels are actually passing through
a foreign country (Korea or Russia).

5.   As regards import cargo - and goods imported by
means of postal parcels cannot very well be treated
differently under existing rules - we, the receiving
offices, if I may so put it, are confronted with a
technical difficulty. The Hunchun and Lungchingtsun
Provisional Regulations clearly state that :

           " Import

" Import duty according to the Revised
" Import Tariff of <u>1922</u> is leviable on all
"" goods (foreign or native) imported int
" China across the Russian and Korean
" frontiers, with the exception of the
" articles entitled to duty free treatment,
" etc. "

This means that, in the case of parcels coming from
Treaty Ports or Inland Places, forwarded through Korea
(or Russia), we have, in actual practice, to
ignore <u>totally</u> the actual <u>provenance</u> of import parcels
duty paid or not, and charge import duty once more.
The goods, whether foreign or native, lose their
status. We ignore postal and Customs declarations, Way
Bills, etc. and simply charge a full import duty.
The present procedure, which really applies to ordinary
cargo unaccompanied by documents, would not be quite
fair as regards duty-paid parcels coming from Treaty
Ports and Inland Places and I beg to suggest that,
in the case of parcels originating from China, whether
they are forwarded to destination <u>via</u> Korea (or
Russia ?) or not, we be guided by the original
Treaty Port declarations, Way Bills, etc. and assess
duty accordingly.

6.   Another complication is this : the duty
treatment of parcels originating from an Inland Place
and destined for Hunchun or Lungchingtsun and
forwarded through Korea, say, a parcel of native
goods from Changchun to Hunchun, <u>via</u> Korea over the
railroad and land routes. The goods (<u>cargo</u>)
contained in such a parcel will lose their native
status (according to our Provisional Regulations)
on reaching foreign territory. In Hunchun and
Lungchingtsun they ought to be simply treated as
foreign goods (coming from Korea direct) and

and charged duty accordingly, in addition to other duties leviable on native goods carried from an Inland Place to a Treaty Port. In other words, such parcels will have to pay : Transit Dues, Export Duty and full Import Duty. This, it will be admitted, is hardly fair on either the sender or the addressee. I am, therefore, again of opinion that we could waive all claims to our existing cargo practice in favour of the parcel post traffice

7.   My reasons for recommending the above are simple. Native cargo intended for Hunchun or Lungchingtsun comes mostly via Kirin. It is merely brought to us for examination. According to port practice of long standing such cargo is not even declared, i. e., no application is handed in. Foreign cargo from Treaty Ports or abroad reaches Hunchun and Lungchingtsun without any documents whatsoever and is invariably treated as imports direct. However, parcels, from any part of China, have either passed through responsible Custom Houses or Post Offices who send them forward with reliable documents which we always check. The case of ordinary cargo and goods carried by parcel post cannot be said to be quite on all fours, so to speak. The duty assessment on parcels originating from China, but forwarded through a foreign country, Korea (or Russia ?) is a question well worth considering, more especially as the real and earnest aim of the Manchurian Postal Authorities is - it is visible and palpable - to improve postal conditions in our remote districts. This means much real labour on the part of the Chinese Post Office and such labour is not always a pleasant nor an inexpensive one.

8.

8.　　　　　To conclude, I have the honour to ask for your authority to be allowed to assess duty on any parcel containing foreign or native goods, originating from any place (Treaty Ports, Inland Places or Marts) and destined for any place within Chinese territory, according to reliable proofs (Postal declarations, Way Bills, etc.) produced on each occasion, as to the origin or destination of such parcels, whether they are actually forwarded through a foreign country (Korea, Russia ?) or not. In other words, to assess duty, after due checking of postal declarations, way bills, etc., according to the real provenance of the goods concerned and irrespective of the fact that they have passed through a foreign country or not. I may add that Mr Ritchie's scheme for quick delivery of parcels forwarded via the Korean route is not only much appreciated locally but that it is bound to meet with success and that merchants, ordinary residents, etc. are very much interested in an enterprise which is bound to prove one of the steps forward in the development of our interesting districts.

　　　　　I have, etc.

　　(Signed :)　P. Bouinais,
　　　　　　　　Commissioner.

THE INSPECTOR GENERAL TO THE HUNCHUN COMMISSIONER.

I. G. Despatch No. 984/93,539
of 16th March, 1923.

Sir,

　　　　　I am directed by the Inspector General to acknowledge receipt of your despatch No. 1,189 :

reporting

reporting that the Harbin Postal Commissioner
intends to establish a quick delivery servic
for postal parcels forwarded to and from
the Hunchun and Lungchingtsun districts,
whether such parcels come from abroad,
Treaty Ports or Inland Places, or are
intended for such places, as he is of
opinion, with which you agree, that certain
classes of parcels, whatever their provenance
might be, would reach your districts much
quicker if they came or were forwarded
through Korea; stating that the Hunchun and
Lungchingtsun parcels post procedure is
entirely governed by the instructions
contained in I.G. Despatches Nos. 886/86,520
and 895/87,309, the rules laid down in
which have worked smoothly and can be
easily applied to any case coming forward
for the present; suggesting that the
existing practice be maintained as regards
native goods imported by postal parcels and
intended for any place in China, Treaty
Port or Inland Places, and that the fact
that such parcels pass through a foreign
territory (Korea or Russia) be ignored;
and requesting authority for permission to
assess duty on any parcel containing foreign
or native goods, originating from any place
(Treaty Ports, Inland Places or Marts)
and destined for any place within Chinese
territory, according to reliable proofs

(postal

(postal declarations, way-bills, etc.)
produced on each occasion, as to the origin
or destination of such parcels, whether they
are actually forwarded through a foreign
country or not - in other words, to assess
duty, after due checking of postal
declarations, way-bills, etc., according to
the real provenance of the goods concerned
and irrespective of the fact whether they
have passed through a foreign country or not:
and, in reply, to say that you should request the Harbin
Postal Commissioner to inform you officially of the
arrangements he intends to make for the transportation
of the parcels across Korea (or Russian territory),
i. e. :

1. Will the parcels be in closed mails ?
2. Will they be handed to the Korean Post
   Office on entering Korea and handed back
   to the Chinese Post Office on leaving
   Korea ?
3. Or will some freight arrangement only he
   made ?

I am also to request you to forward copy of your
despatch under reply, and of your reply to this despatch
to the Commissioners of the various Manchurian Ports for
their comments if any.

I am, etc.

(Signed :) Cecil A.V. B o w r a,

Chief Secretary.

THE HUNCHUN COMMISSIONER TO THE INSPECTOR GENERAL.

HUNCHUN DESPATCH NO. 1203 of 11th March,

1 9 2 3.

Sir,

1.   I have the honour to acknowledge the receipt of your Despatch No. 984/93,539 :

> Postal Parcels : forwarded from or to China across foreign territory to other Chinese Ports, Marts, etc. : Duty treatment of; I.G.'s further inquiries <u>re</u> and instructions :

and, in reply, to append hereto copy of the Harbin Postal Commissioner's despatch No. 454, which contains the information called for with regard to the transportation of postal parcels originating from China and forwarded <u>via</u> Korea (or Russia).

2.   I have nothing to add to the Harbin Postal Commissioner's very clear statements. I would merely call your kind attention to the precedents quoted by Mr W.W. Ritchie, with regard to postal parcels originating from China and forwarded across British or French territory. In my humble opinion, the Hunchun and Lungchingtsun Customs ought, in fairness to the Postal Administration and senders of parcels or addressees, to be guided by these long established precedents and levy duty on postal parcels forwarded from or to China across Korea (or Russia) to other Chinese Ports, Marts, tec. accordingly.

3.   As instructed, a copy of Hunchun despatch No. 1,189, of I.G. Despatch No. 984/93,539 and of the present despatch, dealing with the above question, is being sent to the Aigun, Harbin, Moukden, Antung,

Dairen

Dairen and Newchwang Commissioners.

I have, etc.,

(Signed :) P. Bouïnais

Commissioner.

THE HARBIN POSTAL COMMISSIONER TO THE COMMISSIONER
OF CUSTOMS AT HUNCHUN : HARBIN DESPATCH NO. 454
Of 4th APRIL,
1 9 2 3.

Sir,

I have the honour to acknowledge receipt of
your despatch No. 1 of 26th March, 1923 :

Requesting particulars of transit procedure for
postal parcels from Chinese Post Offices to
Chientao, via Korea :

and to reply to your queries as follows :

1. - Parcels will in all cases be in closed
        mails.

2. - These sealed bags will be handed over to
        the Korean Post Office on entering Korea,
        and delivered to the custody of the Chines
        Post Office at the Chientao frontier.

3. - In no case will parcels be forwarded
        through Korea as freight.

Shanghai and other Chinese Post Offices forward
through French territory, closed parcel mails for
Yunnan, and this transit is not considered by the
Customs as assuming foreign provenance. In a simila
way, carriage over British soil - Hongkong - of
Hoihow and Pakhoi closed parcel bags for Canton in
no way obscures the fact that China is the origin
of the parcels, and your attitude is therefore in
accordance

accordance with precedents of long standing. As all Parcels Way Bills, on which postal packets are entered one by one, bear series numbers, and as I have already requested that these documents be inspected and initialled by Customs officers at Hunchun and Lungchingtsun - the only two places of entry for Chinese mails to Chientao, <u>via</u> Korea - Custom revenue would appear to be fully safeguarded.

Your interest in postal developments in the Hunchun and Lungchingtsun areas, and the courteous assistance you continue to give freely, are much appreciated by the Co - Director General of Posts, to whom I am forwarding a copy of this correspondence.

I am, etc.,

(Signed :)   W. W. Ritchie

Postal Commissioner.

True copies :

Commissioner.

致瑷珲关第 1/508 号函　　　　　　　　　珲春关 1923 年 4 月 11 日

尊敬的瑷珲关税务司：

　　奉总税务司指令，兹附本关与总税务司及哈尔滨关邮务长往来信函抄件，事关自中国寄入或寄出经由境外运至中国其他口岸、贸易市场等地之邮政包裹的征税办法。

　　本关所遇问题如有需要贵署给予意见之处，还望将相关意见抄件发与本署，对此不胜感激。

您忠诚的仆人

（签字）濮义耐（A. P. A. Bouinais）

珲春关税务司

附件

珲春关税务司致总税务司信函抄件

呈海关总税务司署 <u>1189</u> 号文   珲春关 1923 年 2 月 26 日

尊敬的海关总税务司（北京）：

1. 哈尔滨关吉黑邮务长李齐（W. W. Ritchie）先生告知，其计划为珲春和龙井村地区寄入或寄出的邮政包裹建立一条快捷运输通道，无论包裹往来之地是外国，还是通商口岸或者内陆各地。其认为，某些类别的货物，无论源自何处，若经由朝鲜中转，可更快到达珲春关区，对此，本署完全同意。朝鲜的交通运输十分快捷，值得中国效仿。

2. 珲春和龙井村包裹邮寄手续（查验，估税及包裹邮寄运输监管）均照海关总税务司署致珲春关第 886/86520 号和 895/87309 号令之指示办理。截至目前，令文所载各项规定的执行十分顺利，且容易操作。

3. 然兹认为，包裹所载货物，无论为洋货或为土货，无论进口或是出口，均为货物，理应与通过车马往来海关口岸之普通货物享受同等征税待遇。

4. 关于土货通过邮政包裹自珲春、龙井村或内陆各地及贸易市场由海关查验放行后出口外国之事，暂时应不必做何更改。在珲春或龙井村，查验估税之事均由海关决定。此等土货包裹一直持有包裹报税清单和包裹运搬凭单，任何通商口岸均可予以查验。但恕本署冒昧，并非所有通商口岸皆会对在运输途中未曾离开中国境内之包裹和经由外国（朝鲜）转运至中国通商口岸或内陆各地之包裹进行区分。珲春和龙井村两处口岸的临时章程乃由海关总税务司署第 434/59806 号令（1916 年）批准，兹认为，该项章程并不适用于其他口岸。鉴于此，兹建议，对于通过邮政包裹出口外国或运往中国各地及通商口岸的土货，本关继续按照现行办法办理，至于包裹是否经由外国（朝鲜或俄国）转运，暂不予理会。

5. 对于进口货物及通过邮政包裹进口之货物，按照现行规定，很难区分对待。珲春关及龙井村关的临时章程已有明确规定：

> 根据 1922 年修订的进口税则，凡经由俄国或朝鲜进口之货物（无论洋土），概征进口正税，唯享受免税待遇之货物不在此列。

如此则意味着，对于自通商口岸或内陆各地经由朝鲜（或俄国）运来之包裹，无论实际源自何地，是否已税，本关均无法理会，只能再次征收进口正税。此等货物，无论洋土，均无法享受原有之待遇。于本关而言，包裹报税清单和运搬凭单均不在考虑之列，直接征收一次进口正税即可。然现行办事手续，实际上针对的是无相关凭证之普通货物，若对自通商口岸或内陆各地而来之已税包裹施行，颇有不公。鉴于此，兹建议，对于自中国寄出之包裹，无论是否经由朝鲜（或俄国）转运，本关均根据其原始口岸的报税清单和运搬凭单等凭证办理，并据此估税。

6. 此外，根据自内陆地区经由朝鲜转运至珲春或龙井村之包裹的征税办法，如果装有土货之包裹自长春经由朝鲜通过铁路及陆路运至珲春，那么在其进入外国境内之时，便已失去土货的性质（根据《珲春关临时章程》），珲春和龙井村两处口岸只能将之视为洋货（自朝鲜直接进口），并征收相应关税；而实际上，此等包裹此前已完纳自内陆地区运至通商口岸之税项，换言之，此等包裹须缴纳子口半税、出口税和进口正税。须承认，如此征税，无论对寄件人或是收件人，均非公允。因此兹认为不应再照现行征税办法处理邮政包裹的运输事。

7. 本署上述提议之理由十分简单。凡土货运至珲春或龙井村者，大多经由吉林，本关通常仅负责查验，而且按照口岸长期以来的惯例，此等货物甚至不会申报（即不递交申请）。凡洋货自通商口岸或外国运至珲春或龙井村者，均无任何凭证，一直按照直接进口货物办理。而包裹，无论自中国何地寄出，均会由尽职尽责的海关或邮政局检查并发给可靠凭证，对于此等凭证，海关均会核查。

当然，普通货物和邮政包裹运输之货物的情况并不完全一致，但经由外国（朝鲜或俄国）转运之问题的确值得细细斟酌，尤其目前，满洲邮政局殷切希望偏远地区的邮政运输工作可以得到显著改善。此则意味着中国邮政局将为此投入大量人力物力，随之而来的费用支出亦将不菲。

8. 最后，呈请批准允许本关对往来中国境内任何地方（通商口岸、内陆地区或贸易市场）的邮政包裹（无论装有洋货或土货），均根据包裹所持可靠凭证（包裹报税清单和运搬凭单等）进行估税，无论包裹是否经由外国（朝鲜或俄国）转运。换言之，估税之前，首先根据相关包裹的实际寄出地核查包裹报税清单、运搬凭单等，至于是否经由外国转运，不在核查之列。此外，李齐先生建立邮政包裹快捷运输通道之计划在当地十分受欢迎，相信一定会成功，而且对于此等促进地区繁荣发展之事，商人和普通居民等更是喜闻乐见。

您忠诚的仆人

（签字）濮义耐（A. P. A. Bouinais）

珲春关税务司

总税务司致珲春关税务司信函抄件

致珲春关第 <u>984/93539</u> 号令　　　　　海关总税务司署（北京）1923 年 3 月 16 日

尊敬的珲春关税务司：

珲春关致海关总税务司署第 1189 号呈收悉：

"汇报哈尔滨关吉黑邮务管理局计划为珲春和龙井村地区寄入或寄出的邮政包裹建立一条快捷运输通道，无论包裹往来之地是外国，还是通商口岸或者内陆各地。其认为，某些类别的货物，无论源自何处，若经由朝鲜中转，可更快到达珲春关区，对此，本署完全同意；珲春和龙井村包裹邮寄手续均照海关总税务司署致珲春关第 886/86520 号和 895/87309 号令之指示办理，截至目前，令文所载各项规定的执行十分顺利，且容易操作；建议对于通过邮政包裹出口外国或运往中国各地及通商口岸的土货，珲春关继续按照现行办法办理，至于包裹是否经由外国（朝鲜或俄国）转运，暂不予理会；呈请批准允许珲春关对往来中国境内任何地方（通商口岸、内陆地区或贸易市场）的邮政包裹（无论装有洋货或土货），均根据包裹所持可靠凭证（包裹报税清单和运搬凭单等）进行估税，无论包裹是否经由外国转运，换言之，估税之前，首先根据相关包裹的实际寄出地核查包裹报税清单、运搬凭单等，至于是否经由外国转运，不在核查之列。"

奉总税务司命令，现批复如下：请让哈尔滨关邮务管理局将其关于经由朝鲜（或俄国）转运包裹之计划正式发与贵署，具体内容包括：

1. 此等包裹是否会以装成总包（closed mail）的方式邮寄？

2. 包裹进入朝鲜境内后，是否会交与朝鲜邮政局，在离开朝鲜境内时，是否会交还与中国邮政局？

3. 或者是否有其他运输安排？

另请将珲春关第 1189 号呈抄件及对于此令文之回复抄件发与满洲各口税务司征询意见。

您忠诚的仆人

（签字）包罗（C. A. V. Bowra）

总务科税务司

珲春关税务司致总税务司信函抄件

呈海关总税务司署 <u>1203</u> 号文　　　　　　　　珲春关 1923 年 3 月 11 日

尊敬的海关总税务司（北京）：

　　1. 根据海关总税务司署第 984/93539 号令：

　　　"邮政包裹：关于自中国寄入或寄出经由外国运至中国其他口岸、贸易市场等地之邮政包裹的征税办法，提出相关问题并附指示。"

　　兹附哈尔滨关吉黑邮务管理局第 454 号信函抄件，内开关于自中国寄出经由朝鲜（或俄国）转运之邮政包裹运输事的相关信息。

　　2. 哈尔滨关吉黑邮务管理局之信函内容已十分清楚详尽，本署并无补充，唯李齐（W. W. Ritchie）先生于函中所提邮政包裹自中国寄出经由英国或法国转运之先例一事，还请贵署注意。本署愚见，珲春关和龙井村关若要公正对待邮政局和包裹寄件或收件之人，则应根据此等由来已久之先例办事，对自中国寄入或寄出经由朝鲜（或俄国）转运至中国其他口岸、贸易市场等地之邮政包裹采取相应征税办法。

　　3. 另已根据指示将珲春关第 1189 号呈、海关总税务司署第 984/93539 号令及珲春关第 1203 号呈之抄件发与瑷珲关、哈尔滨关、奉天关、安东关、大连关和牛庄关税务司。

您忠诚的仆人

（签字）濮义耐（A. P. A. Bouinais）

珲春关税务司

哈尔滨吉黑邮务管理局致珲春关税务司信函抄件

致珲春关第 454 号函　　　　　　哈尔滨吉黑邮务管理局 1923 年 4 月 4 日

尊敬的珲春关税务司：

1923 年 3 月 26 日珲春关第 1 号函收悉：

"询问关于邮政包裹自中国邮政局经由朝鲜至图们江的具体转运办法。"

兹回复如下：

1. 此等包裹一律以装成总包（closed mail）邮寄。

2. 印有中国邮政局印章之邮袋进入朝鲜境内后，会交与朝鲜邮政局，再由之运至图们江边境处的中国邮政局。

3. 邮政包裹绝不会以其他运输方式通过朝鲜。

上海及其他地区的中国邮政局将装成总包经由法国转运至云南，海关并未将此等转运包裹视作洋货。无独有偶，装成总包自海口和北海经由英国、香港转运至广东，亦被视作土货。因此，贵署亦应根据此等由来已久之先例办理。此外，邮政包裹的运搬凭单皆是按件签发，且有连续编号，本署此前业已提出请珲春关和龙井村关的海关关员予以核查签字，而且珲春和龙井村乃为中国邮政包裹经由朝鲜转运至图们江的唯一必经之地，因此，海关税收应会得到充分保障。

本署已将此函呈送至邮政总办，其对于贵署对珲春及龙井村地区邮政运输发展之关注以及日后之友好协助，深表感谢。

您忠诚的仆人

（签字）李齐（W. W. Ritchie）

哈尔滨吉黑邮务管理局邮务长

抄件内容真实有效，特此证明：

录事：濮义耐（A. P. A. Bouinais）珲春关税务司

6. 为汇报"半两"邮寄包裹征税情况事

POSTAL PARCELS: collection of duty on "half-tael" parcels; report in re, submitting.

165.

I.G.

Aigun   22nd. April, 1924.

Sir,

I have the honour to acknowledge receipt of your Circular No. 3486:

> Postal Parcels: collection of duty on " half-tael " parcels; report in re, called for;

and to submit the following replies to your two questions -

(1) Domestic Parcels:

When two or more parcels are posted by one sender at the same time to the same address it is the practice at this port to collect duty if this amounts to $0.45 in the case of native goods and $0.75 in the case of foreign goods.

(2) International Parcels:

(a) When two or more parcels are despatched by one sender at the same time to the same address it is the practice at this port to collect duty if this amounts to $0.45 and the contents are of native origin. Duty is not levied on foreign goods exported.

(b)

Inspector General of Customs,

Peking.

Entered in Card-Index.

(b) When two or more parcels are
received by the same mail for the
same addressee it is the practice
at this port to collect duty if
this amounts to $0.75.

The contents of such parcels are
not taken into consideration.

Instructions concerning the duty treatment
of Postal Parcels were conveyed to this office
in I.G. Despatch No. 14/87,199 (in reply to
Aigun Despatch No. 9) and the procedure now
reported has been in force at this port since
February, 1922.

I have the honour to be,

Sir,

Your obedient Servant,

R. F. Chengelun

Commissioner.

REFERENCES.	
DESPATCHES.	
From I.G.	To I.G.
Commrs. No.	Port No.
14/87,199	9
(C.3486)	

呈海关总税务司署 <u>165</u> 号文　　　　　　瑷珲关 1924 年 4 月 22 日

尊敬的海关总税务司（北京）：

　　根据海关总税务司署第 3486 号通令：

　　　　"邮寄包裹：请汇报'半两（half-tael）'邮寄包裹征税情况。"

　　兹回复如下：

　　（1）国内包裹：

　　凡两件或两件以上包裹由同一寄件人同时寄往同一地址者，按照本口惯例，若为土货且总价值达 0.45 银圆，则予以征税；若为洋货且总价值达 0.75 银圆，则予以征税。

　　（2）国际包裹：

　　① 凡两件或两件以上包裹由同一寄件人同时寄往同一地址者，按照本口惯例，若为土货且总价值达 0.45 银圆者，则予以征税；若为洋货，则免税出口。

　　② 凡两件或两件以上包裹由同一邮递工具送至同一收件人者，按照本口惯例，若包裹总价值达 0.75 银圆，则予以征税。征税与包裹内为何物无关。

　　关于邮政包裹征税办法的指示乃由海关总税务司署致瑷珲关第 14/87199 号令（回复瑷珲关第 9 号呈）下达，此呈所述征税办法乃自 1922 年 2 月起开始实施。

您忠诚的仆人

贺智兰（R. F. C. Hedgeland）

瑷珲关税务司

7. 为黑龙江省政府委任税捐局征税通知及要求海关停止代征厘金的子口税事

POSTAL PARCELS: appointment of Local Tax Office by
Provincial Authorities to collect duty on, notifying.
Collection of Transit Dues in Lieu of Likin by Customs
to cease; action taken in re, approval of soliciting.

413

I. G. Registered. Aigun 18th October, 1929

Sir

   I have the honour to forward, as an appendix
to this despatch a copy of a letter received
from the Provisional Mayor, dated the 7th September,
1929, from which it will be observed that he is
in receipt of instructions from the Provincial
Authorities to the effect that, as there is no
Parcel Duty Collection Bureau at Aigun, the
responsibility for the collection of parcel duties
is to devolve on the Local Tax Office; that
after correspondence with the Taheiho Post Office
a modus vivendi has been arranged as to the
manner in which the Local Tax Office shall examine
parcels and collect the new duties, and that,
as from the 1st September, 1929, the Customs is
to cease collecting Transit Dues in Lieu of
Likin.

   Previous to the receipt of the above
instructions, I had received a letter from the
Provisional Mayor, dated 25th January, 1929, copy
of which was forwarded with the Non-Urgent
Correspondence for January, 1929, transmitting the
instructions of the Provincial Authorities that

          a Special

THE INSPECTOR GENERAL OF CUSTOMS,
   SHANGHAI.

a Special Bureau was being organized for the collection of duties on parcels, the Post Office to assume the collection of the duties concerned in this district, and that the Customs was no longer to collect Transit Dues in Lieu of Likin.

In accordance with the action taken by the Harbin Commissioner, as reported in his despatch No. 3,804 to I.G., (vide my comments thereon dated 15th January, 1929), I was prepared at that time to hand over to the Post Office the function of collecting Transit Dues in Lieu of Likin on parcels but the Postmaster informed me that he had received no instructions in the matter.

Now that I have been informed by the Provisional Mayor of the completion of arrangements for the collection of the new parcel duties by the Local Tax Office and have been instructed by him, as noted in the first paragraph above, to turn over to that office the collecting of Transit Dues in Lieu of Likin, I have issued instructions to cease the collection of such dues. I trust that this action will meet with your approval. I should add that it has been the practice of this office to hand over quarterly to the Local Tax Office the dues collected under this heading after deducting 10%

for

for the cost of collection.

I have the honour to be,

Sir,

Your obedient Servant,

Acting Commissioner.

Appendix

呈海关总税务司署 <u>448</u> 号文　　　　　　瑷珲关 1929 年 10 月 18 日

尊敬的海关总税务司（上海）：

　　兹转呈暂代黑河市政筹备处处长来信抄件，意为其已收到黑龙江省政府之指示，鉴于瑷珲没有邮政包裹征税局，权宜之计为将大黑河邮局征税的职责移交给税捐局，由税捐局负责检验包裹，征收新税种，自 1929 年 9 月 1 日起瑷珲关停用对邮政包裹代征厘金的子口税。

　　此前，本署收到一封暂代黑河市政筹备处处长的来信，（信函抄件呈交于 1929 年 1 月的非紧急信件中）该信已说明省政府的意图，拟设立一个机构专门征收包裹税，由该邮局承担该地区的税收，海关无须再征收包裹子口税。

　　参照滨江关税务司所采取的行动（参阅哈尔滨关致海关总税务司署第 3084 号呈；1923 年 1 月 15 日瑷珲关对哈尔滨关致海关总税务司署第 3084 号呈的意见），当时本署正准备向邮局移交代征包裹厘捐的子口税的职责，但邮务管理局告知本署其并未收到相关指令。

　　现今，暂代黑河市政筹备处处长已做好各项安排，已通知税捐局承担包裹征税职责，接管代征包裹厘捐的子口税工作。本署也因此下令终止这些税款的征收，不知此举妥否。另外，再补充几句，本署历来遵循扣除 10% 海关征税佣金后，按季度向税捐局上缴税款的惯例。

您忠诚的仆人

铎博赉（R. M. Talbot）

瑷珲关署理税务司

附件

此抄件发送至滨江关税务司

录事：王德懋　二等一级税务员

8. 为批准移交邮递包裹子口半税征收权至黑河税捐局事

Reg^d

[4.—28]

497
I.G.

COMMRS. No. 124,779

Aigun No. 497

No.

SHANGHAI OFFICE OF THE

INSPECTORATE GENERAL OF CUSTOMS, 7th November, 1929.

Sir,

I am directed by the Inspector General to acknowledge receipt of your despatch No. 448:

reporting that you have received instructions from the Provincial Authorities to hand over the collection of Transit Dues in lieu of Likin on Postal Parcels to the Local Tax Office, that you have issued orders accordingly, and asking for approval of your action;

and, in reply, to say that your action, as reported, is approved.

I am,

Sir,

Your obedient Servant,

Chief Secretary.

The Commissioner of Customs,

AIGUN.

致瑷珲关第 <u>497/124779</u> 号令　　　　海关总税务司署（上海）1929 年 11 月 7 日

尊敬的瑷珲关税务司：

　　第 448 号呈收悉：

　　　"瑷珲关已收到省政府关于移交邮递包裹子口半税征收（代替厘金）权至黑河税捐局的指示，瑷珲关已发布相应命令，呈请批准瑷珲关安排。"

　　奉总税务司命令，现批复如下：对汇报中采取的行动予以批准。

　　　　　　　　　　　　　　　　　　　　　您忠诚的仆人

　　　　　　　　　　　　　　　　　　　　华善（P. R. Walsham）

　　　　　　　　　　　　　　　　　　　　总务科税务司

专题四

验估

1. 为构建口岸群由中心口岸提供货物估价和税目分类事

[A.—29]

COLLRS. No. 129,801

Aigun No. 549

No.

SHANGHAI OFFICE OF THE

INSPECTORATE GENERAL OF CUSTOMS, 29th August, 1950.

SIR,

1.   I am directed by the Inspector General to append for your information and guidance copy of I.G. despatch No. 2,692/129,017 to Dairen, embodying a description of the system of group ports now being introduced gradually throughout the Service.

2.   As outlined in the appended despatch, the procedure concerns only the ports of Antung and Newchwang as group ports under the group centre Dairen. Since the writing of that despatch, however, Harbin and Lungchingtsun have been added to the number, while your office has also been included, though not actually as a group port communicating direct with the group centre - Dairen. In view of the peculiar geographical situation of your port it has been decided that better results can be obtained by your collaboration with Harbin which, having an Appraising Desk and being in your more immediate neighbourhood, will be in a more favourable position to propose values for the ad valorem goods dealt with by you. Furthermore, as Harbin will be in closer touch with Dairen, it will obtain and transmit to you correct classifications and useful information for guidance in ascertaining duty-paying values.

3.   The procedure for your office will be as follows:

Commissioner of Customs.   from

A I G U N.

from the date of receipt of these instructions your
office is to commence to record, in rough form,
from the latest records kept and the applications
passed during the following six months, details of
all the ad valorem and specific duty-paying imports
from abroad and of ad valorem native exports actually
passing through your port. Exports paying specific
duties are, of course, not required.

4.   The description of the commodities should be a
full and accurate one, showing what each article
actually is and using, where possible, Tariff
nomenclature for purposes of easy identification by the
Harbin Appraiser. For ad valorem goods the duty-
paying values are to be given, calculated either on
reliable documentary evidence, or, if such is not
obtainable, derived from the market value ruling at
your port.

5.   At the end of the first quarter of 1931, the
items thus recorded are to be summarised and copied
alphabetically on forms A, B and C in duplicate -
specimens appended - with the information called for
by the various columns. The tables are then to be
forwarded to Harbin for the checking of classifications
and entering of values. Thereafter, that is from and
including June Quarter 1931, these quarterly lists,
supplemented by ad valorem imports and exports, and
specific duty-paying imports not appearing in the
previous quarters' lists, but passed during the quarter
under

under review, are to be sent to Harbin in original
only. Form "B" - classification of specific duty-
paying imports - need be sent on one occasion only
as, unlike values, the Tariff classification of goods
is not variable.

6.　　These value and classification lists, when
returned from Harbin, are to be kept properly filed
by a responsible Assistant in your General Office, and
the values and classifications thus supplied are to
be used for duty assessment purposes by the same
Assistant and not by the Examiners. The work of the
latter will thus be restricted to the verification of
the precise quantity, weight, nature and Tariff
description of the commodity to be passed. A copy of
these lists should, however, be supplied to your
Examination Shed for the purpose of instruction and
reference.

7.　　Throughout the year these forms should be kept
up to date in an easily accessible loose leaf file
until the end of December, when the particulars
transcribed into fresh forms for the coming year
have been checked by Harbin. They can then be bound
and filed away.

8.　　With reference to the description of commodities,
you are requested to note that in order to
facilitate their identification by the Harbin Appraising
Office, it is necessary to illustrate the items by a

full

full description of the " Brand," " Trade Mark,"
" Quality," "Measurement" and similar information, a
practice which will reduce to a minimum unnecessary
correspondence with the group centre.

9.   The forms A, B and C should not be lined
horizontally as the descriptions of different articles
require varying amounts of space. When the heading
for an article can be expanded by the addition of
sub-headings, space should be left for entries by
the group centre.

10.   Any fluctuations of importance occurring in the
values of goods entered in your lists by the Harbin
Office will be communicated to you by the Harbin
Commissioner by means of Value Memos. - specimen
appended. On receipt of such Value Memos., the
necessary alterations on the Value Lists are to be
made and initialled by the responsible Assistant
concerned.

11.   Similarly, should any new and/or doubtful cases
of classification or valuation arise at your port
during the quarter, they are to be referred
immediately to Harbin for decision, the cargo being
released on deposit, if necessary. Details of the
goods in question should be included in the lists
to be forwarded at the end of the current quarter.

12.   All correspondence with Harbin, in connection
with values and classifications is to be signed by
you and not by the Assistant or the Examiners. You
are

are also requested to satisfy yourself that such
correspondence is properly filed and indexed in the
General Office so as to be readily available for
reference. Any changes of values should also be
recorded and initialled in the Examiners' copies of
value Lists by yourself.

13.　　A supply of the forms A, B and C and the
value memos. will be sent to you by the Harbin
Commissioner as soon as he obtains them from Dairen.

14.　　In conclusion, I am directed by the Inspector
General to request that you and your staff will do
your utmost to make this scheme effective. To be a
success it requires close coöperation between General
Office and Examination Sheds and the whole-hearted
support of the Staff generally. When in full working
order it is hoped that it will ensure the correct
application of the Tariff and the uniform assessment
of values at all the ports where the Customs Service
is responsible for the collection of revenue.

　　　　　　I am,

　　　　　　　　Sir,

　　　　　Your obedient Servant,

　　　　　　　　　　　Chief Secretary.

Copy of I.G. despatch No. 2,692/129,017 to Dairen

10th July, 1930.

Sir,

The question of proper valuation of goods at the ports is one that has been raised many times in the history of the Customs Service. The last serious efforts to arrive at a solution of the problem were made in March 1914 and February 1915 when two conferences of examiners were held in Dairen and Newchwang to discuss the question of uniformity of valuation at these ports and at Antung, and to stop the loss of revenue due to lack of co-operation between the various Custom Houses (Circular No. 2357).

This system of meetings, although a new and interesting departure in Customs practice gradually fell into abeyance, as it could not be extended to other ports owing to the considerable dislocation of work it would have caused, and the heavy expenditure involved which the Service was not then prepared to meet

One practical idea, however, emerged from these discussions between the Examiners, and was made a standing practice throughout China in 1916. The ports were arranged into six group ports with Newchwang, Tientsin, Hankow, Shanghai, Amoy and Canton as the central points which began to send out quarterly value lists of imports and exports to the ports grouped with them (I.G. Circular No. 2487). The ports forming the groups around all central points were likewise to send

their

their quarterly value lists to their group centres and it was hoped that this correspondence and exchange of values would produce a mass of valuable information for ready reference. But this system, which was meant to awaken an intelligent interport interest in examination affairs, has failed to produce the desired result.

As regards the Newchwang group of ports, to which your office was attached, the principal cause of this failure lay in the impossibility of obtaining reliable market values. This was due, to a great extent, to the distance Custom Houses were situated from the local commercial centres, and the indifference to Customs interests and requirements displayed by Brokers Guilds and applicants generally, which precluded any but the most experienced and resourceful examiners obtaining anything approaching reliable values.

Furthermore, the fact that many Commissioners and Assistants in the past, have taken little or no interest in the most important work of examination, valuation and classification of cargoes and left the correspondence in connection with the exchange of values entirely in the hands of examiners, has contributed in no small measure towards the failure of this effort towards efficiency.

The new Tariff with its increased and varying ad valorem rates and more elaborate classifications, imposes on us the task of placing the verification, valuation and classification of goods on an entirely new basis and the carrying out of this task necessitates the making of the General Office responsible not only for the correct calculation of duties, but also for the proper. tariff classification and assessment of duty-paying values.

values. This has already been accomplished in your office where the Appraisers' work in the General Office is in close touch with the Assistants, and where co-operation between the wharves and the offices is as effective as it can be made for the present.

For obvious reasons this machinery cannot, however, be instituted at all the ports, and the Inspector General has decided, therefore, as an initial step in a scheme of reforms, to re arrange the ports into groups with the main Custom Houses as group centres, and gradually to provide these group centres with trained Appraisers, thus enabling them to prescribe for all minor ports grouped round them reliable duty-paying values as a guide to these offices in the assessment of duties.

A central Valuation Bureau will also be created at the Inspectorate which will check all the values from the group centres and generally keep the Inspector General posted on the work done at the ports in connection with the administration of the Tariff.

As a beginning, your port has been made a group centre for ports Antung and Newchwang.

In broad outline, the scheme is for the group ports to send to the group centre on forms A, B, and C - specimen of which are appended - quarterly lists of ad valorem and specific duty-paying imports from abroad and ad valorem Native exports passing through their Custom Houses with their present duty-paying values for the ad valorem commodities. The group centre, after checking the classifications and entering its duty-paying values, will return the lists to the group

group ports where they will serve as a guide in cases
where the correct classification and proper valuation
could not otherwise be ascertained, and will thus create
uniformity in the duty treatment of goods

In this connection, you will see from the despatches
to your group ports - a copy of which is appended -
the method those offices are to employ in compiling
their lists and the manner in which they are to be
forwarded to your office. There are several points of
which you are requested to take particular note. At the
end of the current (September) quarter these lists are
to be forwarded by group ports in duplicate; thereafter,
from and including December quarter, they are to be sent
in original only, in order to conform to the procedure
generally in force at the other groups where this scheme
is being operated.

As soon as your Appraising office has checked the
classifications and entered its duty-paying values for
the _ad valorem_ commodities, the originals of the lists
are to be returned and the duplicates sent to the
Inspectorate (Tariff Secretary) without covering despatch
together with lists - made out on the same forms - of
the commodities not included in the lists from group
ports, but passed by your office during the quarter
under review. When returned from the Inspectorate, these
duplicates with Shanghai values are to be retained by
your office as a guide until the proper scheme is
enforced at the end of the following quarter.

This somewhat irregular procedure is considered
advisable in view of the necessity for supplying your

office

office with Shanghai values as soon as possible, so that your Appraising Office, which is only in the initial stages of its development, and without the services of a trained recording typist, will not be called on suddenly to carry out the great deal of recording work entailed by the enforcement of the scheme in full.

Beginning with the December quarter, the procedure will be as follows: those lists of ad valorem Imports and Native Exports (Forms A and C) already sent by the group ports at the end of the September quarter, supplemented by all additional ad valorem Imports and Exports and additional specific duty-paying Imports, passed during the quarter under review, are to be forwarded - in original only - to your office for the usual check of classifications and entry of your port values. The specific duty-paying commodities (Form B) can be returned to the ports of origin immediately after checking - as no record of these is required at your office. Forms A and C, however, are to be returned only when your office has entered its quarterly values in the appropriate columns and transcribed each group port values to Forms D and E - specimen appended. These forms are to be retained by your office as a comprehensive record of the values sent by the group ports. And in order that they may be accessible and easily filed, they are to be printed on a light cardboard of the same texture and size as the value record cards used at present for archiving values in the steel cabinets in use at your office.

Having thus established contact with and obtained a check over the values at your group ports you will,

in

in turn, be required to keep in touch with the Inspectorate. As this has been assured for the current (September) quarter through the duplicates called for by the present instructions, values will not be required until later, probably at the end of the first quarter of next year, when the lists are being transferred to new forms at the group ports

Since, however, those values will be current for a quarter only, a further control is necessary. You will, therefore, have to forward to the Inspectorate at the end of each subsequent quarter the lists of values as recorded on forms D and E, which after being checked will be returned to your office in time for entry of the alterations and additions for the succeeding quarter. These instructions do not apply to the classification of specific duty-paying imports which, when once forwarded to and checked by you, remain in force unless changed by a T.Q.S. decision.

Apart from this quarterly supervision, you are to communicate alterations of importance either in the value or classification of goods on the lists to your group ports by means of Value Memos., specimen of which is appended, a copy being forwarded to the Inspectorate.

As regards the group ports, in cases of doubt or when a new commodity appears the value of which is not known, if the amount involved is of sufficient importance, the goods are to be released on deposit and the case referred to your Appraising Office for settlement.

All correspondence with your group ports in connection with values and classifications, as well as

the

the quarterly lists of commodities are to be signed by your Deputy Commissioner, never by the Examiners or Appraisers, and you are requested to satisfy yourself that such correspondence is properly filed and indexed so as to be readily available for reference.

It must be clearly understood that the above scheme does not in any way affect or alter the existing practice of submitting doubtful questions on (B.-30) to the Inspector General through the Shanghai Commissioner. But later on it may become advisable or necessary for group ports to submit their Tariff Questions on Form B.-30 through their group centre.

Owing to the pressure of work at the Statistical Department and the necessity for avoiding delay in putting this scheme into effect, you are requested to have the appended forms printed locally and those which concern group ports distributed. In due course they will be made Service forms and issued by the Statistical Secretary.

In conclusion, I am directed to say that it is hoped that this scheme will be successfully introduced into your group of ports. It is not expected, however, that it can become operative without certain initial difficulties arising, in which case any constructive recommendations and suggestions you can make to ensure its smooth working will be given full consideration.

I am,

Sir,

Your obedient Servant,

(Signed) P.R. Walsham

Chief Secretary.

True copy,

Assistant Secretary.

致瑗珲关第 <u>549/129801</u> 号令　　　　海关总税务司署（上海）1930 年 8 月 29 日

尊敬的瑗珲关税务司：

　　1. 奉总税务司命令，兹附海关总税务司署致大连关第 2692/129017 号令副本，以供参考。该令详述了目前正在整个海关推行的口岸分组估价体系。

　　2. 如所附令文所述，该办法仅涉及大连、安东和牛庄口岸，其中大连为中心口岸，安东和牛庄为周围口岸。自该令签发起，该口岸群新增哈尔滨和龙井村口岸，虽然贵关与中心口岸大连关不是直接联系，但也算该口岸群的成员。鉴于瑗珲口岸地理环境特殊，现决定，为达到更佳效果，贵关应同滨江关协作，滨江关既设有验估台，又是离贵关最近的口岸，能够更准确地给出贵关经办从价计征货物的价值。此外，滨江关将与大连关展开紧密合作，将获得的准确货物分类信息和有用的完税价值确定指导信息传达给贵关。

　　3. 贵关可遵照以下办法执行：自接受指示之日起，贵关可根据保存的最近记录以及未来六个月放行的报单，在草表中记录所有实际通过贵口岸的从价和从量计征国外进口货物与从价计征出口土货的详情。无须记录从量计征的出口货物详情。

　　4. 货物说明应全面准确，指明究竟是什么货物，尽可能使用税目名称，便于滨江关验估员辨认。对于从价计征货物，应给出完税价值，该价值一般通过可靠的记录文件计算得出，如果无法获得类似文件，则采用贵口岸现行市价。

　　5. 在 1931 年第一季度末，应将记录的项目分类汇总，按字母顺序抄写到表单 A、B 和 C（式样已随附）上，按要求填好每栏信息，每张表单一式两份。之后将表单寄送至滨江关，再由滨江关核查货物分类并登记估价。此后从 1931 年第二季度（包括第二季度）开始，新一季度由贵关放行，但没有登记在上一季度货物价值清单上的从价和从量计征进口货物都应添加在上一季度货物价值清单上，填好后，只需将原件寄送至滨江关。"表单 B 从量计征进口货物分类"只需寄送一次，因为不像货物价值经常变化，从量计征货物的税目分类一直保持不变。

　　6. 这些货物价值与分类清单由滨江关寄回贵关后，应从贵关总务课派一名负责任的帮办进行妥善保管和归档，由该名帮办使用且仅能用于征税估计目的，验货员无权使用。因此，验货员的工作仅限于核查放行货物的确切数量、重量、种类及征税说明。但可将这些清单副本提供给贵关验货厂，以供指示和参考。

　　7. 在每一年，这些表单都应装订为便捷的活页文件，一直更新到十二月末，届时滨江关将对其核查后誊写到新表单中，以供来年使用。那时就可以将原有表单装订成册并归档。

8.关于货物说明,贵口岸需注意：为方便滨江关验估课辨识,需详细说明货物"品牌"、"商标"、"质量"、"尺寸"及相关信息,这样可以最大限度地减少与中心口岸之间不必要的联系。

9.表单 A、表单 B 和表单 C 不应打印行线,因为不同货物的说明占用的空间各不相同。若一件货物的名目下面可进一步分出子名目,应当留出空间,以供中心口岸登记。

10.滨江关对于贵关清单中货物估价做出的所有重要变动,将会由滨江关税务司通过估价通函(式样已随附)传达至贵关。贵关收到估价通函后,由责任帮办对估价清单进行必要的修改并用姓名的首字母签字确认。

11.同样,如果贵关当季出现任何新增或有争议的分类/估价案例,请立即提交至滨江关进行决议,必要时可收取押金后放行货物。应将相关货物的详情填写在清单中,于当季季末呈交。

12.与滨江关往来的所有关于货物价值和分类的信函,须由您亲自签字,帮办或验货员均无权签字。请贵关确保上述文件已在总务课正确归档和索引,便于快速参考。您还应当在验货员估值清单副本上记录所有价值变动,并用姓名的首字母签字确认。

13.滨江关税务司一接收到大连关发来的表单 A、表单 B 和表单 C 以及估价通函,就会寄至贵关。

14.总之,奉总税务司命令,兹要求您与您的下属竭尽全力执行本方案。想要成功执行,需要总务课与验货厂之间的密切合作以及全体职员全心全意的配合。工作全面正常展开后,以期能保证在各海关征税口岸应用正确的关税率,实施统一的估价。

您忠诚的仆人

华善(P. R. Walsham)

总务科税务司

海关总税务司署致大连关第 2692/129017 号令副本

1930 年 7 月 10 日

尊敬的大连关税务司：

海关历史上已屡次提出过各口岸合理估价的问题。最近一次努力发生在 1914 年 3 月和 1915 年 2 月，在大连关和牛庄关分别举行了一次验估员会议，商讨大连、牛庄和安东口岸的统一估价事宜，以避免因各海关缺乏合作而导致的税收损失（第 2357 号通令）。

这种会议方式，虽然是一个有意义的新开端，但在海关实践过程中遭到搁置，因为可能引起征收工作陷入极大混乱，难以将其推行至其他口岸，再者巨大的开销也让海关始料未及。

但验货员们在讨论中想出一个可行的解决办法，并于 1916 年推行至全国。办法是将口岸分为六个群组，分别以牛庄、天津、汉口、上海、厦门和广州为中心点，将其季度进出口货物估值清单寄送至围绕中心口岸的各口岸（海关总税务司署第 2457 号通令）。围绕中心口岸的各口岸同样应将其季度估值清单寄送至中心口岸，希望往来信函中关于货物估价的交流可提供大量有用信息，以供参考。该办法企图使各口岸在验估方面建立整齐划一的估价制度，但最终并没有达到理想的效果。

贵关隶属于以牛庄为中心口岸群，其失败的主要原因在于无法获得可靠的市价。这很大程度上是因为海关距当地商业中心较远，经纪人协会及申请人漠视海关利益与需求，即便是经验最丰富的验货员也无法获取任何可靠的估价信息。

此外，过去许多税务司及帮办都极少关心甚至毫不关心最为重要的货物验估与分类工作，将估价交流这一工作全权交给验货员，对估价效率低下负有绝大部分责任。

新订税则的从价税率升高且不断变化，货物分类更为细化，这就要求我们按照全新的基准进行货物查验、估价及分类，总务课不仅要负责正确计算关税，还要负责合理分类税目，评估完税价值。贵关已成功实现这一点，总务课的验估员正同帮办密切合作，当前各码头与各课之间也处于高效的合作进程之中。

显然，这一机制无法适用于所有口岸，故总税务司决定，改革方案的第一步是重新将口岸分为几个群组，以最主要的海关作为中心口岸，逐步为这些中心口岸分配受过培训的验估员，以便为围绕中心的其他口岸提供可靠的完税价值，指导这些口岸的海关征税估计工作。

另外还会在海关总税务司署设立估价股,负责核查各中心口岸的所有估价,通常还向海关总税务司汇报各口岸关税管理的工作进度。

贵口岸已成为安东和牛庄口岸的中心,这是一个良好的开端。

大体上来讲,方案要求各口岸群将表单A、B和C(式样已随附)寄送给中心口岸。表单上显示了各海关发行的季度从价和从量计征国外进口货物和从价计征出口土货清单,以及从价货物的现完税价值。中心口岸核查货物分类并登记货物完税价值之后,将此清单寄回周围的口岸,作为案例指导征收,在分类或估价出现不确定时保持货物征税办法的统一。

鉴于此,从致贵口岸周围口岸的令文(副本已随附)中,贵关可以看出周围口岸海关的清单编制方法以及给贵关的发寄方式。贵署需特别注意以下几点:在本季度(第三季度)季末,周围口岸的清单应以一式两份的形式寄送。此后,为与实施该方案的其他口岸群保持一致的执行办法,从第四季度开始(包括第四季度)只发原件。

一旦贵关验估课结束分类核查并在清单上登记从价商品的完税价值之后,应将清单原件寄回各口岸,将复本寄至海关总税务司署(审榷科税务司),与呈文分开递送。在本季度,由贵关发行但没有登记在周围口岸的清单上的商品也应填写在清单上。在估价单从海关总税务司署寄回后,贵关应保留写有江海关完税价值的复本,可在下一季度末推行适当方案前提供参考。

考虑到贵关需要尽快按照江海关完税价值办理,这一看似不太常规的办法却是最得当的方法。贵关验估课正处于起步阶段,尚未配备经过培训的记录打字员,倘若要全面实施改革方案,记录工作量势必艰巨,而按照这种渐进的方案执行,贵关则不必冷不防地陷入忙乱之中。

从第四季度开始,按以下办法执行:周围口岸需在先前第三季度末寄送的"表单A从价计征进口货物价值清单"和"表单C从价计征出口土货价值清单"的基础上,添加本季度发行的所有新增从价计征进出口货物和从量计征进口货物。表单填好后,只需将原件寄送至贵关。贵关照例执行分类核查,登记贵关货物价值。对于表单B(从量计征商品统计表),检查完毕后即可寄回原口岸,因为这些统计无须在贵关再做记录。对于表单A和表单C,贵关则需先在其相应栏目填写好贵关的季度货物价值,并将周围各口岸的货物价值誊抄到表单D和表单E(式样已随附)之后,方可将表单A和表单C寄回原口岸。贵关应保存好表单D和表单E,它们是周围口岸的综合货物价值登记表。为了便于表单查询和存档,请将表单打印在薄纸板上,材质和尺寸与贵关钢制文件柜里储存的货物价值归档记录卡保持相同。

贵关已与周围口岸互通货物价值信息并进行核查工作，反之，贵关也需同海关总税务司署互通信息。鉴于本季度（第三季度）的货物价值已通过本指示要求提供的复本进行查明，可能直到明年第一季度末将这些统计数据誊写到周围口岸新表格之前，都不必呈报货物价值。

由于这些估价将仅在一个季度有效，因此接下来的管控措施十分必要。贵关将在此后的每一季度末都向海关总税务司署呈交表单 D 和表单 E，上报货物价值清单，海关总税务司署核查完毕后将及时寄回贵关，便于贵关在下一季度添加更正和新增记录。但这一指示不适用于从量计征进口货物分类，该表单寄至贵关并由贵关完成检查即可，除非《税则疑问核解》有更改，否则分类一直有效。

除了季度审查，贵署还需通过估价通函（式样已随附）告知周围口岸清单上货物价值或分类做出的重要更改，并将估价通函副本呈交至海关总税务司署。

在周围口岸，可能会出现估价争议或新货物估价不确定的情况，若数额巨大，货物缴纳押金后予以放行，该案件则移交至贵关验估课处理。

凡与周围口岸关于货物价值和分类的通信以及季度货物价值清单，一律应由贵关副税务司签字确认，验货员和验估员均无权签字。您需亲自确保上述文件正确归档和索引，便于快速参考。

必须指出的是，上述方案不会影响或者改变目前的问题提交办法，将问题登记在表B.30 表中，寄由江海关税务司转呈海关总税务司。但此后，周围口岸有必要将其各自口岸的关税问题登记到表 B.30 中，寄由中心口岸转呈。

由于造册处工作压力大，为了及时推行该方案，请贵关自己打印随附表单，给周围口岸分发与其相关的表单。日后这些表单将会制成海关通用表单，由造册处发行。

总之，奉总税务司命令，兹告知：希望本方案能够在贵关所在口岸群成功实施。但我们可以预见，万事开头难，初始阶段必定会出现一定困难，如果遇到，可给出确保顺利实施的建设性建议意见，我们会给予充分考虑。

您忠诚的仆人

华善（P. R. Walsham）

总务科税务司

2. 为呈报查验用秤相关信息事

EXAMINATION SCALES:report on, called for by Chief
Secretary's Circular Memorandum No.54,submitting.

511   <u>511</u>
                                                                              I.G

I.G.   A I G U N   3rd October 1930.

Sir,

    With reference to Chief Secretary's Circular
Memorandum No. 54 of 29th July 1930 :

    Calling for report on examination scales :
I have the honour to append, attached hereto, in
duplicate, a report on the examination scales and
steelyards of this office :

    3 Portable square platform scales,

    1 Counter scales, and

    4 Steelyards.

    I would recommend that the two missing bearing
balls (No.1164 in Howe's list of spare parts) of the
platform scale No.708874, now kept in the godown, be
supplied. This scale, when thus put into proper
working condition, will be used in the Tung-pei Shipping
Company's offices where most of the examination work of
this port is conducted. At present the Examiner has
to content himself with a Customs-owned steelyard which
he takes with him to the Tung-pei Company, a procedure
which, of course, causes a great deal of inconvenience.

    That there are no standard weights available
renders the testing of the scales, which is carried out
regularly at the beginning of every month, very difficult.
I would also recommend that two standard weights, say
of 50 pounds each, one for Taheiho Head Office and one
for Aigun Sub-station, be supplied, possibly by the
Harbin office, in order to save expense.

    I have the honour to be, Sir,

    Your obedient Servant,

The Inspector General of Customs,

              (H. G. Fletcher)

S H A N G H A I.

             Acting Commissioner   Append

A P P E N D.

Kind	(a) Maker's Name	(b) Type & description	(c) Capacity	(d) With or without fulcrum lever	(e) Platform	(f) Dimensions of Platform of Weight	(g) Standard of Weight	Condition	Location
Platform Scale No.1006470	Howe Co.	Portable, square	1225 catties	No	Metal and wood	44" x 35"	pounds and catties	good	Examiner's Office (Taheiho)
Platform Scale No.708974	"	"	1125	"	"	44½" x 30½"	"	Fairly good Not in use*	In godown
Platform Scale No.#### †	"	"	800	"	"	36" x 36"	"	good	Aigun Sub-station
Counter Scale No.1095589	"	Counter Scale	16 pounds				pounds	good	Examiner's Office (Taheiho)
Steelyard No.1	"	Single balance steelyard	510 catties				catties	good	"
Steelyard No.2	"	"	500				"	"	"
Steelyard No.3	"	"	210				"	"	"
Steelyard No.4	"	"	200				"	"	"

† Vide Aigun Dep. No.585/12.

The dates on and the authorities under which the above scales and steelyards were supplied, as well as their costs, are unascertainable. Probably they were supplied when this office was a sub-port of Harbin.
*Two bearing balls(No.1164 in Howe's list of spare parts)missing, rendering scale useless at present, and it is recommended that the two missing bearing balls be supplied to complete the apparatus.
No other repairs or replacement considered necessary.
Tests regularly carried out at the beginning of every month, and it is recommended that standard weights(two, say 50 pounds each)be supplied.

呈海关总税务司署 511 号文　　　　　　　瑷珲关 1930 年 10 月 3 日

尊敬的海关总税务司（上海）：

根据 1930 年 7 月 29 日总务科税务司第 54 号通函：

"请汇报查验用秤情况。"

兹附瑷珲关查验所用磅秤及杆秤报告表，一式两份，包括：

3 台便携式方形台秤，

1 台案秤，

4 个杆秤。

其中，序列号为 708874 的台秤现置于仓库，因遗失轴承滚珠（豪氏磅秤公司 ① 备件清单上的序列号为 1164），无法使用，建议提供滚珠。该秤修复后将置于主要验货地东北航务局货栈。目前，验货员需携带海关杆秤前往此货栈，十分不便。

验货用秤的检测工作定期于每月月初进行，然因无标准砝码，检测工作十分困难。为节约起见，建议由滨江关提供两个标准砝码（每个 50 磅），以供大黑河和瑷珲两口岸使用。

您忠诚的仆人

富乐嘉（H.G. Fletcher）

瑷珲关署理税务司

---

① 公司全称为 Howe Scale Co., Rutland, Vermont, USA（参见瑷珲关第 585 号呈），未查到确切中文译名，谨于此将之译为美国佛蒙特州拉特兰市豪氏磅秤公司，附表中简称豪氏。

附件

类别	（1）生产商	（2）说明	（3）承重量	（4）有无秤杆	（5）秤台	（6）秤台尺寸	（7）重量标准	（8）状况	（9）放置地点
台秤 序列号：1006470	蒙氏	*	1225斤	无	金属及木质	43.5"×35"	磅和斤	良好	验查课（大黑河）
台秤 序列号：708874	蒙氏	*	1125斤	无	金属及木质	43.5"×30.5"	磅和斤	非常好 未使用＋	关栈
台秤 序列号：2953*	蒙氏	*	800斤	无	金属及木质	35"×43"	磅和斤	良好	瑷珲分关
案秤 序列号：1093529	蒙氏	天平秤	16磅				磅	良好	验查课（大黑河）
杆秤 序列号：1		单杆秤	510斤				斤	良好	验查课（大黑河）
杆秤 序列号：2		单杆秤	500斤				斤	良好	验查课（大黑河）
杆秤 序列号：3		单杆秤	210斤				斤	良好	验查课（大黑河）
杆秤 序列号：4		单杆秤	200斤				斤	良好	验查课（大黑河）

注：

* 参阅瑷珲关致海关总税务司署第 585 号呈。

上述磅秤及杆秤的提供日期和依据，以及费用，均无法确定；或为于瑷珲关尚为滃江关分关时所提供。

⊕因两个轴承滚珠（蒙氏磅秤公司备件清单上的序列号为 1164）遗失，该台秤暂无法使用，建议配齐轴承滚珠。暂无其他维修替换之必要。

验货用秤检测工作定期于每月月初进行，建议提供标准砝码（2 个，每个 50 磅）。

3. 为瑷珲关 1931 年第一季度验货工作、货物估价与归类事

EXAMINATION WORK, VALUATION & CLASSIFICATION OF
CARGO: report on, for the March Qr., 1931,
submitted.

551

551
I.G.

I.G.   A I G U N   11th April 1931.

Sir,

In accordance with the instructions of your
Circular No. 4153 :

calling for a quarterly report on the
examination, valuation and classification of
cargo :

I have the honour to forward, appended hereto, my
report for the March Quarter, 1931.

I have the honour to be,

Sir,

Your obedient Servant,

(Signed) C. B. Joly

(C. H. B. Joly)

Acting Commissioner.

Appendix

The Inspector General of Customs,

S H A N G H A I.

Report on Examination Work, Valuation and Classification of Cargo at Aigun, March Quarter 1931.

GENERAL: As this is the first report of this kind to be prepared by this port, it is necessary to preface it with a brief outline of the abnormal conditions which have prevailed for the past eight years, and to describe the manner in which examination work is performed at Taheiho and Aigun.   To facilitate reference, two rough sketch plans - one of the Taheiho, and the other of the Aigun, harbour and river frontage - are appended hereto.

In 1923, the Soviet closed its frontier to individual trading and to Chinese shipping and the Heilungkiang authorities retaliated by adopting similar measures for Russian shipping and by prohibiting all imports and exports not covered by special permission. The result was an almost complete stoppage of all trans-frontier trade and the Aigun Customs had, in consequence, no cargo to deal with during the winter months.   During the navigation season, work was confined to goods moved along the Chinese bank of the Amur and to imports from and exports to Harbin and other Sungari ports.   All cargo moved along the Chinese side of the Amur is by local regulations passed free.   Conditions as above continued without change until the autumn of 1930, when the Soviet Far Eastern Trading Bureau, the Dalgostorg, was authorised by the Heilungkiang authorities to open an agency at Taheiho to import and export restricted quantities of goods under special permission issued through the Taheiho Mayor.   This change has led to the importation of small quantities of cargo, and to the exportation of beans, but the work entailed and the examination and appraising knowledge required have been negligible.   All goods conveyed across the ice at

Taheiho

Taheiho are controlled by the Winter Road Office, and are all examined on the Bund in front of the Custom House. At Aigun, only a small quantity of beans has been declared for export across the ice and examination will take place on the bund in front of the Custom House.

During the navigation season, steamers maintain a regular service between Harbin and other Sungari ports and Taheiho and Aigun. These vessels all belong to the Tung-pei Company, now changed to Harbin Shipping Syndicate (東北帆拖局今改為 哈尔滨官商航業包辦公局), a semi-Government organisation, which has its own wharf and godowns at Taheiho, as shown on the appended plan. One of the godowns, situated on the wharf, is recognised as a Customs-controlled import godown. It is locked by the Customs and examination work is performed by one officer. No special examination fees are charged for his services as the recognition of this godown as a registered import godown greatly facilitates control and examination work. Exports by vessel should, in theory, all be examined at the Customs Shed next door to the General Office, but, in practice, examination of nearly all exports takes place in another godown belonging to the Syndicate, vide plan, and a special examination fee of Hk. Tls. 5.00 per day per applicant is levied for this privilege. As the Shipping Syndicate applies for all cargo to be carried by its ships, the fees charged are not large. A few odd lots of export cargo are examined at the Customs Shed and are then escorted to the exporting vessel or to the godown, which is controlled and locked by the Customs until the cargo is loaded on to the vessel under Customs' supervision. Import cargo carried by non-Syndicate vessels is examined on board or on the foreshore, and no special examination fee is charged. The reason for this is that the Customs

Shed

Shed is only suitable for an office, being too small for the storage of cargo, and, if we did insist on this cargo being brought to the Custom House, it would still be necessary to examine it on the Bund or fore-shore in front of the Custom House. Export cargo for such vessels is examined on the Bund in front of the Custom House and escorted to the exporting vessel. If examined on the Bund or foreshore at some distance from the Custom House, special examination fees are levied. Cargo carried by junks is examined on board or on the foreshore of the Junk Anchorage and, all such cargo being duty free, no special examination fee is levied. Rafts are examined in the Raft Anchorage and, being free, no special examination fee is demanded. At Aigun the Customs have no examination Shed, and all cargo is examined on the foreshore in front of the Custom House. The quantities of goods dealt with by the Aigun Sub-station are very small.

I. STAFF:

Rank	Name	Where Stationed	Date of Appointment to Port.
(a) DESKS			
1st Clerk **A**	Wang Tê-mao	There is only one Desk in the General Office at which these two Clerks attend to all General Office work and to appraising work as instructed in I.G.desp.No. 549/129,801. They also do all Returns work. Mr.Wang also attends to all Russian correspondence and translations.	1.10.21 to 30.11.29(a transfer to Tientsin). Re-appointed on 1.2.30
3rd " **A**	Leung Wing Tat		1.5.30
(b) EXAMINATION SHEDS:			
Asst.Exmr.**A**	J. A. Crossland	At Custom House. Senior Outdoor Officer whose duties are those of a Tidesurveyor. Attends himself to as much examination work as possible. Acts also as Harbour Master during summer months.	6.4.30
" " **B**	N.Dikmann	Examination Shed, Custom House, Taheiho.	1.5.30

Rank

R a n k	N a m e	Where Stationed	Date of Appointment to Port
Supy.3rd Cl. Tidewaiter	Sun Hung Tsao	At Taheiho to 28.2.31. At Aigun in charge of Sub-station from 1.3.31	1.5.30
4th Class Tidewaiter	Wong Wen Tso	At Aigun in charge of Sub-station to 28.2.31. From 1.3.31 Examination Shed, Custom House, Taheiho. The two officers in the Examination Shed, Taheiho, attend to whatever work the Senior Out-door Officer details them to do. During the winter months, examination work forms a very small part of their duties. The Officer at Aigun has very little to do, especially during the winter.	1.5.30
(c) POSTAL PARCELS OFFICE:		One Officer attends three times a week, Mondays, Wednesdays, and Fridays, from 2 to 4 p.m. to deal with Parcels. An Officer attends all incoming letter mails. The same remarks apply to Aigun.	

II. WORK:

(a) APPRAISING DESKS:

No remarks, trade negligible.

(b) EXAMINATION SHEDS:

No remarks. Trade during winter almost nil.

(c) POSTAL PARCELS OFFICE:

No remarks. Parcels traffic very small.

III. EXAMINERS' CLASSES:

No classes. The Harbin Chief Appraiser has been requested to supply copies of his lectures for the information of the Aigun Staff.

IV. MISCELLANEOUS:

Replies to a Questionnaire supplied by the Tariff Secretary are given hereunder :- *Vide Tariff Sec. 8/... 7/6/0/31*

I. EXAMINATION SHEDS & OFFICES:

1. Nature of building?

   (a) Harbin Shipping Syndicate's Import Godown: wooden building on Wharf.

   (b) Harbin Shipping Syndicate's Export Godown: brick, in compound behind Wharf.

(c)

(c) <u>Customs Shed</u>: brick, adjoining General Office and
forming part of main building of Custom House.

2. Light, ventilation, tidiness?

Good.

3. Floor space adequate?

(a) and (b), yes. (c) is called an examination shed,
but is in fact the Examiners' Office; it is far too
small for an examination shed, its measurements being
24'6" x 12' and cargo has, in consequence, to be
examined on the Bund in front of the Custom House.

4. Suitable for Examination work?

(a) and (b), yes. (c) No (<u>vide</u> reply to 3).

5. Staff: number of officers and ranks?

One Assistant Examiner attends to all examination work.

6. Office hours?

9 a.m. to 4 p.m.

7. When does port close for winter and when does it
re-open?

Closed from 20th October to middle of May.

8. Which is busy time of day?

During navigation season, from 10 a.m. to 1 p.m.

9. Who provides shed-carrying coolies?

Shipping Syndicate in (a) and (b), ~~as above~~,& applicants at (c).

10. Files of Commissioner's Orders?

Yes, in Examination Shed at Custom House which is
Examiner's headquarters. When I took over charge of
this district in October 1930, I found that no Orders
were issued on subjects covered by I. G. Circulars.
The Circulars were circulated and each member of the
In-door Staff was required to initial it. The result
was that the Examination Shed and the Aigun Sub-station
had no record of Circular instructions. This practice
was changed and copies of all Orders are now provided
to the General, Tidesurveyor's and Examiner's Offices,
also to the Aigun Sub-station.

11.

11. Files of T. Q. S. Circulars?

Yes, in Examination Shed at Custom House. These copies were removed from Secretary's Office and given to Examiners.

12. Files of Instructions by Senior Examiners?

Harbin Chief Appraiser's Memos. on file.

13. List of Contraband and Prohibited Drugs?

Yes, in Examination Shed at Custom House. Copies also posted in public space of General Office and at Aigun.

14. I. G. Circulars re Drugs analysed by Shanghai Customs Analyst?

Yes, Secretary's copies handed to Examiners.

15. Value Records?

Yes, also in General Office as instructed in I. G. despatch No. 549/129,801.

16. List of Examiners' Library books ever referred to?

Yes.

17. Is there a Desk Memo.?

Yes.

18. Does Import Tariff contain "Definition of term 'Whole-sale Market Value'"?

Yes, bound in new Tariffs supplied by Statistical Department.

19. Rough sketch plan of port showing position of offices and sheds.

Plans of Aigun and Taheiho appended hereto, also plan of Custom House showing Customs Shed.

II. SAMPLES:

1. How kept, arranged?

Owing to absence of trade, collection small. What samples there are, are kept in bottles and glass-doored cupboards, and piecegoods in books.

2. Torresani's Textile Sample Book, how kept?

Satisfactory. Official copy, no samples available. Private copy (Senior Out-door Officer's) samples collected privately from other ports.

3.

3. Are samples renewed when spoiled?

    Yes, but very little scope for this here.

4. Are samples catalogued?

    Yes.

  III. SCALES:

    Please see Aigun despatch No. 511/I.G.

IV. APPLIANCES:

1. Microscope?

    No.

2. Appliances for testing goods?

    None.

V. SUPERVISION OF CARGO:

  Imports

1. How does cargo arrive at Shed?

    From steamer direct to godown on Wharf, under Customs' supervision.

2. How is cargo supervised in Shed until released?

    Godown locked at 6 p.m. and key kept by Customs.

3. Are Sheds opened and locked at night?

    Godown locked from 6 p.m. to 8 a.m.

4. Is substitution possible from ship to shed?

    No.

  Exports

1. How does cargo arrive at Shed?

    By carts.

2. How is cargo supervised while in Shed?

    Godown controlled and locked by Customs.

3. How does cargo leave Shed for steamer?

    Under supervision of Tidewaiter.

4. Is substitution of cargo possible from Shed to Ship?

    No.

VI. EXAMINATION OF CARGOES:

  Imports

1. Who receives applications? At what time of day usually presented?

                                        Clerk

Clerk in Charge of General Office.   10 a.m.

2. How sent to Shed?

By Customs T'ingch'ai.

3. Who distributes them to Examiners?

No remarks.

4. How are Examiner's calculations shown on applications?

In pencil on back of applications.

5. Is Examiner's work checked?   By whom?

Checked by Clerk in Charge of General Office.

6. What percentage of a lot is examined?

Large consignments from 10% to 40%.   Small consignments, all.

7. Who chooses packages for examination?

Examiner.

8. Can and is whole consignment seen by Examiner?

Yes.

9. What particulars of examination are given?

Number of packages weighed, opened, probed, tared; marks and numbers checked.

10 Shanghai Particular Stamp used?

No.

11. What happens if discrepancy is found in value or description?

Application corrected.   Cargo detained pending Commissioner's decision.

12. How are corrections made on applications?

In red ink.

13. Are packages opened and/or examined chopped?

Yes.

14. How is cargo to be examined, identified as the lot applied for?

By number of shipping order painted on each package.

15. Is cargo chopped with importing steamer's name and trip number?

No.

16

16. Is substitution of cargo possible under present practice?
Hardly.

17. Are ships' manifests supplied to Examiners and the items checked off after examination?
No, not necessary. There is only one steamer a week, on an average, and manifest is cleared almost immediately.

18. Is cargo passed without examination?
No.

19)
20) Who decides what cargo is to be p. w. e.? Is application marked P. W. E.?
No remarks.

21. Have Examiners access to invoices, contracts, weight bills?
Yes, but most of the cargo imported has paid duty at Harbin. For exports, very few documents available.

22. Are imports ever released before payment of duties?
No.

23. What happens in General Office when applications return from Sheds?
Checked and duty assessed.

24 Who is in charge of Import Desk?
Clerk in charge of General Office.

25 Who checks Examiners figures, values, classifications?
Clerk in charge of General Office.

26. What happens if Import Desk finds discrepancy?
Referred to Commissioner.

27. What happens if applicant finds valuation or classification too high?
Protest to Commissioner.

28)
29) Who discusses questions with Chinese and foreign applicants?
Clerk in charge of General Office.

30)
31) Are there any Assistants conversant with work of examination, valuation and classification of goods, and

with

with invoices and contracts?

No.

32. Any Assistants likely to become efficient in this work?

Not at present, trade too limited.

33. Office hours in General Office?

9 a.m. to 1 p.m., and 2 p.m. to 4 p.m., <u>vide</u> Aigun despatch No. 513/I. G.

34. Are these hours suitable?

Yes.

35. What is busy season in year?

No remarks.

36 Which are busy hours in day?

10 a.m. to 3 p.m.

37. What cargo examined and what not examined?

All examined.

VII. <u>EXAMINATION OF CARGOES, EXPORTS, RE-EXPORTS, TRANSHIPMENTS:</u>

1. Who receives Export Applications?

Clerk in charge of General Office.

2. At what time of day are Export Applications usually presented?

10 a.m. and 2 p.m.

3. Any fixed time for examining export cargo?

No.

4. Can all the consignment be seen before examination?

Yes.

5. What control of cargo while in Shed?

Shed locked and key kept by Customs.

6. Are exports ever released before payment of duty?

No.

7. Can substitution take place from Shed to ship?

Hardly.

8. Is Examiners' work ever checked? By whom?

By Clerk in charge of General Office.

9. What happens if discrepancy is found?

Referred to Commissioner, after application corrected and cargo detained.

10.

10. Are exports ever passed without examination?

No.

11) Who decides what cargo is to be p. w. e.? Is
12) application marked P. W. E.?

No remarks.

13. What cargo examined and what not examined?

All examined.

VIII. RE-EXPORTS:

  Nil.

IX. REPACKING:

Nil.

X. TRANSHIPMENTS:

Nil.

XI. SHUT-OUT:

1. State practice.

Shut-out Memo. made out by Clearance Officer and
Manifest endorsed.

2. Shut-out ever examined?

Yes.

XII. SUPERVISION OF EXAMINERS:

No remarks.

XIII. RELATIONS BETWEEN TIDESURVEYOR AND EXAMINERS:

No remarks.

XIV. CLEARING OF MANIFESTS:

1. Shipping Company's guarantee?

None in force at present. The practice has never
been to require annual guarantees from Shipping Companies.
This will be changed this summer. Registration of
firms having business with the Customs is being enforced
now.

2. Time limit for paying import duty.

In pro forma guarantee supplied to Shipping Companies,
a time limit of 6 days has been mentioned. In
practice, time limit unnecessary as duties paid promptly.

3. Is duty always paid within time limit?

Duty

Duty paid after examination, which takes place soon
after arrival of vessel.

4. How many accounts outstanding at present?

None.

5. Do you send notices of expiry of time limit?

Not necessary.

XV. VALUATION AND CLASSIFICATION:

Imports

1. How do you ascertain import values?

As instructed in Import Tariff. Harbin values adhered
to as far as possible.

2. Who assesses values on imports paying ad valorem rates?

Examiner, but procedure laid down in I. G. despatch No.
549/129,801 will be followed as soon as it has time
to adjust itself.

3. How is duty-paying value arrived at when there is no
invoice or contract?

Harbin values followed as far as possible. Tariff
rules would be applied in absence of such values and,
in case of doubt, cargo would be released on deposit
and Harbin written to.

4. Are contract values ever accepted as dutiable values?

No contracts ever produced and, with present trade
conditions, none likely to be available.

5. How is duty-paying value of contract arrived at in the
following cases: (a) c. i. f.; (b) c. i. f. duty paid;
and (c) c. i.f. ex-godown.

Scott Harding Schedule would be followed.

6. Are invoice values ever accepted as dutiable values?

If no local market value, yes, but, in case of doubt,
values obtained from Harbin.

7. What exchange rate is used for converting foreign
currencies to Haikuan Taels?

Harbin rates.

8. Is any record kept of values on which different
articles pay duty?

Yes,

Yes, I. G. despatch No. 549/129,801.

9. Who classifies the different articles?

Examiner.

10. Are there any records of your classifications?

Yes, I. G. despatch No. 549/129,801.

11. Who does the work of recording values and classifications?

Clerk in charge of General Office, I. G. despatch No. 549/129,801.

12. What method is followed in advising Examiners of changes in values?

Procedure laid down in I. G. despatch No. 549/129,801.

13. Table showing average daily number of applications passed in 1930 : -

Month in 1930	Import	Export	Re-export	Transhipment
1st January - 30th May: Nil, port closed.				
June	16	7	...	...
July	40	6	...	...
August	23	9	...	...
September	23	10	...	...
October	30	9	...	...
November	...	...	...	...
December	1 in 3 days	...	...	...

Note: 90% of Import Applications are duty paid at Harbin.

10% Duty free from Amur River Ports.

Applications for imports from, and exports to, abroad too few to be considered.

75% of Export Applications are duty free for Amur River Ports.

14. How is the Group system working?

So far satisfactory, but there is little opportunity for really testing it. The necessary forms have so far not been received from Harbin, and provisional

forms

forms have had to be typewritten here.

15. Are T. Q. S. and Tariff Decisions posted for information of public (Circular No. 3978) ?

Yes, in English and Chinese.

Exports

1. How do you obtain export values?

From wholesale market prices or from Harbin.

2. Are contracts ever produced?

No, and none likely with present trade conditions.

3. On what values do you assess duties on exports?

On local wholesale f. o. b. prices or on Harbin values.

4. How is the duty-paying value arrived at?

By enquiry from local dealers, but Harbin values followed as much as possible.

5. Are bills of sale from place of origin ever produced?

Yes, if required.

6. Is any record kept of your export values?

Yes, I. G. despatch No. 549/129,801.

7. Are export values up-to-date?

Yes, as far as possible. Export trade during winter months almost at a standstill.

XVI. BROKERS:

One, who is held responsible for all cargo passed by him. Special regulations not necessary as no cargo is released until duty has been paid.

XVII. INTERPORT EXCHANGE OF VALUE LISTS:

Procedure laid down in I. G. despatch No. 549/129,801 being followed.

XVIII. WEIGHERS:

None.

XIX. PROHIBITED DRUGS:

1. Are all drugs and chemicals examined?

Yes.

2. What is the procedure in cases of medicines suspected of containing drugs?

No such cases. Cargo would be detained and sample

sent

sent to Shanghai Customs.

XX. SKETCH PLAN OF GENERAL OFFICE SHOWING POSITION AND NAMES OF DESKS:

Only one Desk in General Office as shown in Sketch plan of Custom House appended, as mentioned in I. Examination Sheds and Offices, No. 19.

(Signed) C. B. Joly

(C. H. B. Joly)

Acting Commissioner.

[A.—27c]

C.OMMRS. No. 135,429
Aigun No. 606
No.

INDEXED

SHANGHAI OFFICE OF THE
INSPECTORATE GENERAL OF CUSTOMS, 18th June, 1931

SIR,

I am directed by the Inspector General to acknowledge receipt of your despatch No. 551:

forwarding your report on examination work, valuation and classification of cargo for the March Quarter, 1931;

and, in reply, to say that since this report is the first of its kind from your office, the introductory references to local trade conditions during the last few years were both appropriate and interesting. But they are not necessary for future reports which are each to begin with a list of the staff engaged in the work of examination, valuation and classification under heading I. Staff: (I.G. Circular No. 4153).

With regard to the remainder of your report, I am directed to say that its general composition in the form of questions and answers concerning every unimportant detail of your examination work is unnecessarily complicated, and apt to obscure the major issues. The Inspector General assumes that your office understands and is carrying out the ordinary routine of examination work, valuation and classification of cargo. All that he requires to be kept informed of are the important questions that arise in this connection and are being dealt with during the quarter under review.

You

The Commissioner of Customs,

A I G U N.

You are therefore requested in future to confine the substance of your reports to summaries of the salient points under heading II. Work: sub-headings (a), (b) and (c). The remaining sub-headings are not to be repeated in the report, as they were only meant to indicate in a general way the kind of information required. They need not be dealt with seriatim, nor is their sequence necessarily to be followed.

I am,

Sir,

Your obedient Servant,

Chief Secretary.

呈海关总税务司署 551 号文　　　　　　瑷珲关 1931 年 4 月 11 日

尊敬的海关总税务司（上海）：

根据海关总税务司署第 4153 号通令：

"为呈送验货工作及货物估价与归类季报事。"

兹附瑷珲关 1931 年第一季度验货工作、货物估价与归类报告。

您忠诚的仆人

周骊（C. H. B. Joly）

瑷珲关署理税务司

附录

瑷珲关 1931 年第一季度验货工作、货物估价与归类报告

综述：鉴于此乃瑷珲关首份验货工作、货物估价与归类报告，因此在正式汇报之前，有必要先简述本关区过去八年间之情况，以及大黑河与瑷珲两口岸的验货办法。另附大黑河与瑷珲两口岸之港口及江岸草图两份，以供参考。

1923 年，苏俄施行封锁边境政策，私人贸易及中国船只之航行皆遭禁止；黑龙江省政府亦采取相同的对抗手段，禁止俄国船只于中国一侧航行，并下令非经许可不得与俄贸易。如此一来，跨境贸易几近停滞。瑷珲关于冬季数月间几乎无货物往来，航运季期间，亦仅与黑龙江华岸各地、滨江关及其他松花江口岸有货物往来。而根据瑷珲关章程，凡货物往来黑龙江华岸者，均免税放行。

1930 年秋季，苏俄远东贸易公司经黑龙江省政府批准于大黑河设立分公司，但在进出口货物之前，须通过黑河市政筹备处获得省政府之特别许可，且货物之量亦有限制。至此，贸易停滞之情形方有所回转，逐渐有小宗货物自俄国运入，亦有大豆出口运至俄国，但海关所涉工作及所需验货估价知识，仍甚是微末。

大黑河口岸冬季跨江运输之货物皆由海关冬令过江检查处管理，验货工作则于海关办公楼前面的堤岸上进行；瑷珲口岸申报跨江出口之货物仅有少量的大豆，验货工作亦于海关办公楼前面的堤岸上进行。

航运季期间，大黑河及瑷珲口岸与滨江关及松花江其他口岸间有轮船定期往来，此等船只皆为东北航务局（现改为哈尔滨官商航业总联合局）所有。东北航务局属于准政府机构，于大黑河建有自己的码头和货栈（如随附草图所示）。其中一个货栈位于码头，现已由海关管理，成为公认的海关在册进口货栈，十分便于货物的管理和查验工作，仅一名海关关员便可应付，因此并未收取特别查验费。至于经由水运出口之货物的验货工作，于理而论，皆应于总务课旁的验货厂进行，但实际上，几乎皆于东北航务局的另一处货栈进行（参见随附草图）。凡于该货栈接受查验之报关人，每人每天收取 5 海关两的特别查验费，然因东北航务局为其船只将载的所有货物递交报关申请，故所收数额并不很多。

另有一些出口货物于海关验货厂接受查验，再由关员护送登船，或暂运至海关仓库，之后再于海关的监督下装船。非东北航务局船只运输之进口货物通常由关员登船验货，

或于前滩上接受查验,对此不征收特别查验费。

如此安排皆因海关验货厂面积过小,只宜办公,不宜存储货物,即使坚持要求货物运至海关办公楼,亦须于办公楼前面的堤岸或前滩上进行验货工作。因此,出口货物若由非东北航务局船只运输,可于海关办公楼前面的堤岸上接受查验,再由关员护送装船出口,然若验货之堤岸或前滩不在海关办公楼附近,则收取特别查验费。

民船所载货物由关员登船查验,或于民船停泊处接受查验,此等货物皆为免税,且不收取特别查验费。木筏所载货物于木筏停泊处接受查验,亦为免税,且不收取特别查验费。

瑷珲口岸尚无验货厂,验货工作皆于海关办公楼前面的前滩上进行,但所需处理之货物量非常小。

Ⅰ.人员配备:

级别	姓名	所在部门	本口委任日期
（a）验估台			
一等一级税务员	王德懋	总务课仅设一验估台;该两名税务员负责总务课一应事务并照海关总税务司署第549/129801号令指示完成货物估价工作,另负责统计工作;王德懋先生还负责所有俄文信件及相关翻译工作	1921年10月1日至1929年11月20日（调任至津海关）1930年2月1日再次任职
三等一级税务员	梁永达		1930年5月1日
（b）验货厂			
一等副验货员	克思澜（J.A.Crossland）	于海关办公楼办公;虽为超等外班关员,但职同监察长,并尽可能参与验货工作;夏季期间,职同港务长	1930年4月6日
二等副验货员	迪克满（N.Dickmann）	于大黑河海关办公楼内的验货厂办公	1930年5月1日
额外三等稽查员	孙鸿藻	于大黑河任职至1931年2月28日;自1931年3月1日起至瑷珲口岸负责分关事务	1930年5月1日

级别	姓名	所在部门	本口委任日期
四等稽查员	汪文卓	于瑷珲口岸负责分关事务至1931年2月28日；自1931年3月1日起至大黑河海关办公楼内的验货厂办公 大黑河验货厂的两名关员负责超等外班关员分派的一应工作。 冬季验货工作只占其日常工作的一小部分 瑷珲口岸关员工作较少，冬季更是如此	1930年5月1日

（c）邮政局包裹税征收处

		1名关员负责处理包裹（每周周一、周三、周五下午2点至4点）； 1名关员负责处理信件； 瑷珲口岸亦是如此	

Ⅱ.工作：

（a）验估台：

无建议；贸易可以忽略不计。

（b）验货厂：

无建议；冬季贸易基本停滞。

（c）邮政局包裹税征收处：

无建议；包裹运输量极小。

Ⅲ.验货员训练班：

无训练班。已请滨江关超等验估员提供其讲义抄件，以供瑷珲关关员参考学习。

Ⅳ. 其他事项：

对审榷科税务司调查表之回复如下：

（一）验货厂及办公室

1.建筑类型

（1）哈尔滨官商航业总联合局进口货栈：位于码头上的木制建筑。

（2）哈尔滨官商航业总联合局出口货栈：位于码头后方大院中的砖制建筑。

（3）海关验货厂：砖制建筑，毗邻总务课，为海关办公楼的一部分。

2. 照明、通风、清洁？

良好。

3. 地面空间是否足够使用？

哈尔滨官商航业总联合局的（1）进口货栈和（2）出口货栈的地面空间足够使用；（3）名为海关验货厂，实为监察课，因空间过小（24′6″×12′），验货工作只能于海关办公楼前面的堤岸上进行。

4. 是否适合进行验货工作？

哈尔滨官商航业总联合局的（1）进口货栈和（2）出口货栈适合进行验货工作；（3）海关验货厂不适合（参见3项之回复）。

5. 关员：人数及级别？

所有验货工作均由一名副验货员负责。

6. 工作时间？

上午9∶00至下午4∶00。

7. 口岸冬季关闭时间及重新开放时间？

自10月20日开始关闭，至次年5月中旬重新开放。

8. 每日最忙时段？

航运季期间上午10时至下午1时。

9. 将货物运至货栈的苦力雇用方？

哈尔滨官商航业总联合局的（1）进口货栈和（2）出口货栈由其自行雇用苦力，（3）海关验货厂由报关人雇用苦力。

10. 存有税务司令文？

是的，税务司令文存放于海关办公楼的验货厂（即验货员总部）内。但本署于1930年10月到任时发现已签发的令文中并无传达海关总税务司署通令所涉内容者。通令皆由关员相互传阅，内班关员传阅后会按照要求于通令上签字（姓名的首字母）。因此验货厂和瑷珲口岸此前并无通令指示的相关记录。而今此惯例业已更改，所有令文抄件均会发送至总务课、监察长办公室、监察课以及瑷珲口岸。

11. 存有税则疑问核解通令？

是的，税则疑问核解通令存放于海关办公楼的验货厂内。此等通令抄件此前存放于文案房。

12. 存有超等验货指示文件？

存有滨江关超等验估员备忘录。

13. 存有违禁药品清单？

是的，违禁药品清单存放于海关办公楼的验货厂内。清单抄件亦张贴于总务课公共空间及瑷珲口岸。

14. 存有海关总税务司署有关江海关化验员所化验之药物的相关通令？

是的，抄件均发与验货员。

15. 存有估值簿？

是的，此外亦照海关总税务司署第 549/129801 号令指示存放于总务课。

16. 是否参阅验货员参考书籍清单？

是的。

17. 是否有验估台备忘录？

是的。

18. 进口税则中是否有"'批发市价'定义"一节？

是的。含于造册处提供的新税则中。

19. 口岸草图中是否显示了办公室和验货厂的位置？

兹附瑷珲及大黑河两口岸的平面图，及标注海关验货厂的海关办公楼平面图。

（二）货物样品：

1. 如何存放，处理？

因贸易停滞，货样收集较少；现有货样皆用样品瓶、玻璃门橱柜存放，按件货样已编制成册。

2. 托雷萨尼（Torresani）纺织品货式册簿的存放情况？

十分妥善。官方抄本中无可用货样；（超等外班关员）私人抄本中有自其他口岸私下搜集之货样。

3. 货样损坏后是否修复？

是的。但瑷珲关几无货样损坏之事。

4. 货样是否列入目录？

是的。

（三）验货范围：

请参阅瑷珲关致海关总税务司署第 511 号呈。

（四）仪器：

1. 有无显微镜？

无。

2. 有无检测货物的仪器？

无。

（五）货物监管：

进口货物

1. 货物如何运至验货厂？

在海关的监督下，货物自轮船直接运至码头货栈。

2. 货物放行前于验货厂内如何监管？

关栈每日下午 6 时关闭，钥匙由海关保管。

3. 验货厂夜间是否开放？

关栈每日下午 6 时至次日 8 时关闭。

4. 自轮船至验货厂，货物有无替换之可能？

无。

出口货物

1. 货物如何运至验货厂？

由货车运送。

2. 货物于验货场内如何监管？

关栈由海关负责管理和关闭。

3. 货物如何自验货厂运至轮船？

在稽查员的监督下。

4. 自验货厂至轮船，货物有无替换之可能？

无。

（六）货物查验

进口货物

1. 何人受理报单？送交报单的时间通常为？

由负责总务课事务的税务员受理报单，时间为上午 10 时。

2. 报单如何送至验货厂？

由海关听差运送。

3. 何人负责将报单分发与验货员？

无。

4. 验货员如何将估价填入报单？

使用铅笔于报单背面填写。

5. 是否有人核查验货员之工作？由谁核查？

是的，由负责总务课事务的税务员核查。

6. 货物查验比例？

大宗货物：10% 至 40%；小宗货物：全部。

7. 何人选取接受查验之货物？

验货员。

8. 验货员能否看到所有货物？

能。

9. 验货清单上载有？

货物中被称重、开封、探查及称净重之数量；标记和号数的核查情况。

10. 是否使用江海关特殊邮票？

否。

11. 若货价或货色存有差异，如何处理？

更正报单，暂扣货物，以待税务司裁夺。

12. 如何于报单上做出更正？

使用红色墨水笔填写。

13. 开箱查验后是否加盖戳记？

是。

14. 验货依据为何？

根据包装上的装货单号。

15. 货物上是否印有运输轮船名称和航行次数？

否。

16. 按照现行惯例，货物有无替换之可能？

几无可能。

17. 船只舱单是否交与验货员？舱单上已查验完之项是否会划掉？

每周平均仅有一艘轮船到港，舱单几乎皆可当即完成结关手续，故无须如此。

18. 货物未经查验可否通关？

不可。

19/20. 何人决定货物可享免验放行？报单上是否标明免验放行？

无此类情况。

21. 验货员是否有权使用发票、合同及重量清单？

是的，但进口货物大多已于滨江关完纳税款。而于出口货物而言，可用凭据甚少。

22. 进口货物有无未完税即放行之情况？

无。

23. 若验货厂将报单退回，总务课如何操作？

核查并计税。

24. 何人负责进口台？

负责总务课事务的税务员。

25. 何人核查验货员的数据、估价及归类？

负责总务课事务的税务员。

26. 进口台发现误差时如何处理？

上报税务司。

27. 报关人认为估价或归类过高时如何处理？

向税务司提出异议。

28/29. 何人与华洋报关人交涉？

负责总务课事务的税务员。

30/31. 帮办中有无熟悉验货、估价和归类工作，以及发票和合同者？

无。

32. 帮办有无胜任验货工作之可能？

目前贸易有限，暂无可能。

33. 总务课的工作时间？

上午9时至下午1时，下午2时至下午4时（参阅瑷珲关致海关总税务司署第513号呈）。

34. 工作时间是否适宜？

是的。

35. 一年当中最繁忙的季节？

暂无。

36. 每日最忙的时段？

上午 10 时至下午 3 时。

37. 货物接受查验及免验者为？

全部接受查验。

（七）出口、复出口及转运货物之查验：

1. 何人受理出口报单？

由负责总务课事务的税务员受理出口报单。

2. 每日送交出口报单的时间为？

上午 10 时至下午 2 时。

3. 出口货物有无固定的验货时间？

无。

4. 验货员于检查之前能否看到所有货物？

能。

5. 货物于验货场内如何监管？

关栈关闭，钥匙由海关保管。

6. 出口货物有无未完税即放行之情况？

无。

7. 自验货厂至轮船，货物有无替换之可能？

几无可能。

8. 验货员的工作由谁核查？

负责总务课事务的税务员。

9. 发现误差时，如何处理？

更正报单，暂扣货物，以待税务司裁夺。

10. 货物未经查验可否通关？

不可。

11/12. 何人决定货物可享免验放行？报单上是否标明免验放行？

无此类情况。

13. 货物接受查验及免验者为？

全部接受查验。

（八）复出口货物：

无。

（九）重新包装货物：

无。

（十）转运货物：

无。

（十一）短装货物：

1. 请说明口岸惯例。

由办理结关的关员填写短装货物记录，并于舱单上签注。

2. 是否查验短装货物？

是的。

（十二）监督验货员：

无。

（十三）监察长与验货员之关联：

无。

（十四）舱单结关：

1. 是否要求航业公司填具保税单？

迄今尚无要求航业公司填具年度保税单之惯例，但今年夏季将会调整；现已开始要求与海关有业务往来之航业公司于海关登记注册。

2. 进口税收缴纳时限？

发与航业公司的形式保税单上注明的时限为 6 天。但实际上，关税皆为即时缴纳，时限要求无甚必要。

3. 关税是否一直于要求时限内缴纳？

船只抵港后即接受查验，查验后即行缴纳关税。

4. 目前尾数未清者多少？

无。

5. 是否发送时限到期通知？

并无必要。

（十五）估价与归类：

进口货物

1. 如何对进口货物进行估价？

主要依照进口税则，同时尽量与滨江关保持一致。

2. 应从价纳税之进口货物由谁计价？

由验货员计价；若时间允许，将照海关总税务司署第 549/129801 号令所规定之手续重新调整。

3. 若无发票或合同，如何确定完税价格？

尽量与滨江关保持一致；若滨江关无相关价格，则依照税则办理，若仍有疑虑，则于收取押款后放行货物，同时致函滨江关。

4. 合同价格可否作为应税价格？

迄今尚无签署合同之情况，鉴于目前的贸易环境，亦无合同可用。

5. 如何确定（1）到岸价格，（2）完税到岸价格，及（3）关栈外到岸价格三种情况下的合同完税价格？

遵循斯科特哈丁价目表。

6. 发票价格可否作为应税价格？

若无当地市价可循，发票价格则可作为应税价格；如有疑问，则向滨江关询问价格。

7. 外币兑换海关两所用汇率？

滨江关汇率。

8. 有无各类货物缴税记录？

有（参阅海关总税务司署第 549/129801 号令）。

9. 何人负责为不同货物归类？

验货员。

10. 有无货物归类记录？

有（参阅海关总税务司署第 549/129801 号令）。

11. 何人负责记录估价与归类？

负责总务课事务的税务员（参阅海关总税务司署第 549/129801 号令）。

12. 验货员改价参照办法？

参照海关总税务司署第 549/129801 号令所规定之办事手续。

13. 1930 年平均每日放行报单数量表：

1930 年	进口	出口	复出口	转运
1 月 1 日–5 月 30 日：无，口岸关闭				
6 月	16	7	……	……
7 月	40	6	……	……
8 月	23	9	……	……
9 月	23	10	……	……
10 月	30	9	……	……
11 月	……	……	……	……
12 月	3 天通过 1 份	……	……	……

注：进口报单中有 90% 已于滨江关完税。

另有 10% 为黑龙江华岸各地免税进口。

外国进出口报单数量甚少，可忽略不计。

出口报单中有 75% 为免税前往黑龙江华岸各地。

14. 现行机制如何？

迄今尚可，但实际检测机会甚少；另目前尚未自滨江关收到所需表单，只得自行打印临时表单。

15. 税则疑问核解及税则决定是否已向公众发布？（参阅海关总税务司署第 3978 号通令）

已发布（汉文及英文）。

出口货物

1. 如何对出口货物进行估价？

依照批发市价或滨江关价格。

2. 有无签署合同之情况？

暂无，鉴于目前的贸易环境，亦无合同可用。

3. 出口货物计价依据？

根据批发离岸价格或滨江关价格。

4. 如何确定完税价格？

通过询问当地经销商，但尽量与滨江关保持一致。

5. 有无开具原产地销售单据之情况？

如有要求，会开具原产地销售单据。

6. 有无出口估价记录？

有（参阅海关总税务司署第 549/129801 号令）。

7. 出口价格是否已更新？

是的,已尽量更新。但冬季出口贸易几乎停滞。

（十六）报关行：

现有一家报关行,负责所有其经手之货物。但因货物皆于完税后放行,故无须制定专章。

（十七）转口价格换算：

遵照海关总税务司署第 549/129801 号令所规定之手续办理。

（十八）司秤：

无

（十九）违禁药品：

1. 是否检查所有药品和化学品?

是的。

2. 若药品中疑有违禁药品,如何操作?

暂无此等情况。如有,则扣留货物,并将样品送至江海关。

（二十）总务课平面草图（显示验估台位置）：

如随附海关办公楼平面草图所示,总务课仅设一验估台（参阅上述（一）验货厂及办公室第 19 项）。

您忠诚的仆人

周骊（C. H. B. Joly）

瑷珲关署理税务司

致瑷珲关第 <u>606/135429</u> 号令　　　　海关总税务司署（上海）1931 年 6 月 18 日

尊敬的瑷珲关税务司：

　　根据瑷珲关第 551 号呈：

　　"呈交瑷珲关 1931 年第一季度验货工作、货物估价与归类报告。"

　　奉总税务司命令，现批复如下：鉴于此为瑷珲关首份验货工作、货物估价与归类季报，因此对瑷珲关区过去数年间之贸易情况加以概述甚为妥当，内容亦颇有价值。但今后报告中不必如此，唯以"Ⅰ.人员配备（与验货工作、货物估价与归类有关之人员列表）"开篇即可（参阅海关总税务司署第 4153 号通令）。

　　至于报告其他部分，总税务司表示，以问答形式呈现验货工作有关内容，太过面面俱到，反而容易模糊重点。其相信瑷珲关已知悉验货工作、货物估价与归类办法，且一直遵照办理，唯须知晓当季所涉重要问题及解决办法。

　　于此，贵署日后呈交报告时仅对要点进行总结并将之列于标题"Ⅱ.工作：副标题（a）（b）（c）"下即可。其余无关紧要之副标题，无须于报告内重复列明，亦无须遵循其顺序连续排列。

您忠诚的仆人

岸本广吉（H. Kishimoto）

总务科税务司

4. 为申请按照大黑河批发市价为当地出口货物估价事

VALUATION OF CARGO: authority to apply local wholesale market values in case of local exports, requested.

573
573
I.G.

I.G.
                                    A I G U N   21st July 1931.

Sir,

1.   With reference to your despatch No. 549/129,801:

        notifying the formation of group ports, each
        group having a centre to supply values and
        Tariff classifications; directing that, owing
        to its peculiar geographical position, Aigun
        was to collaborate with Harbin instead of
        Dairen, the group centre; and instructing
        that value and classification lists, when
        returned from Harbin, are to be used for
        duty assessment purposes:

    and to your despatch No. 4,505/135,406 to Harbin (copy
    of which was supplied to this office):

        establishing Harbin as a separate group
        centre controlling and supervising the
        valuation and classification work of its
        sub-stations and of the port of Aigun:

    I have the honour to enquire whether the instructions
    of §6 of despatch No. 549/129,801 are intended to
    deprive the Aigun Commissioner of authority to use his
    discretion in the matter of values for local exports
    liable to an _ad valorem_ duty.

2.   The port of Aigun is the outlet for the
    products of the Upper Amur regions - virgin country,
    thinly populated, with a low standard of life -, where
    timber, skins and furs and a few other articles are
    produced at very low cost and are transported to
                                                    Taheiho

The Inspector General of Customs,

    S H A N G H A I.

Taheiho for sale and distribution. To attempt to apply to such articles values ruling at a group centre from 1,000 to 1,500 miles from the source of production and 1,000 miles from the place of distribution would, I venture to submit, be manifestly unfair and would lead to serious complaints and opposition. Amur trade is already handicapped by local taxation and by heavy freight rates and I do not think we should add to the burdens of the trading community, thus helping to retard the development of this almost untapped region.

3.   The principal articles affected by the above ruling are timber and skins and furs. In the case of the former, the Taheiho wholesale market value is Hk. Tls. 0.12 per cubic foot (and this value will probably have to be reduced owing to the lack of demand from Harbin for local timber) as compared with Hk. Tls. 0.24 at Harbin.

4.   After careful consideration, I have instructed the staff to follow local wholesale market values for local exports liable to an ad valorem duty and I now beg to request your approval of my action and to seek a ruling for future guidance. No difficulty should be experienced by this office in applying Harbin values to foreign imports.

I have the honour to be,

Sir,

Your obedient Servant,

(Signed) C. B. Joly

(C. H. B. Joly)

Acting Commissioner.

[A.—27 c]

COLLRS. No. 136,538
Aigun No. 621
No.

SHANGHAI OFFICE OF THE
INSPECTORATE GENERAL OF CUSTOMS, 11th August, 1931.

SIR,

I am directed by the Inspector General to acknowledge receipt of your despatch No. 573:

enquiring, with reference to I.G. despatch No. 549/129,801 and I.G. despatch No. 4,505/135,406/ Harbin, a copy of which was sent to you, whether the instructions of § 6 of the former were intended to deprive the Aigun Commissioner of authority to use his discretion in the matter of values for local exports liable to an _ad valorem_ duty; submitting, in this connection, that to attempt to apply to such articles values ruling at a group centre 1000 or 1500 miles away would be unjust; reporting that you have instructed the staff to follow local wholesale market values for local exports liable to an _ad valorem_ duty; and requesting approval of your action;

and, in reply, to approve your action as reported.

It is not intended that group centre values shall be imposed arbitrarily, but only that they shall serve as a guide to group ports in the appraisement of duty paying values. The instructions referred to apply more particularly to foreign imports into group ports, the

values

The Commissioner of Customs,

A I G U N.

1000 / 4.31.

values for which are usually either not ascertainable
locally or, if obtained, may not be supported by
reliable documentary evidence. As regards exports, it
is of course the value of the goods at the port of
origin that is to be applied.

  I am,

   Sir,

  Your obedient Servant,

         Chief Secretary.

呈海关总税务司署 <u>573</u> 号文　　　　　　　瑷珲关 1931 年 7 月 21 日

尊敬的海关总税务司（上海）：

　　1. 根据海关总税务司署第 549/129801 号令：

　　　　"通知构建口岸群事，各群组均由中心口岸提供货物估价与归类办法；瑷珲关因地理位置特殊归入滨江关一组，而非大连关一组，故须以滨江关所提供之估价与归类表为估税参照。"

及海关总税务司署致滨江关第 4505/135406 号令（抄件已发送至瑷珲关）：

　　　　"将以滨江关为中心口岸划分一组，监督管理下属分关及瑷珲关的估价与归类工作。"

　　特此询问，根据海关总税务司署第 549/129801 号令第 6 项指示，瑷珲关税务司是否无权自行决定应从价纳税之当地出口货物的估价办法。

　　2. 黑龙江上游地区尚未开发，人烟稀少，生活标准相对较低，但盛产木料、皮货等，价格十分低廉，主要运至大黑河销售或分销。滨江关与此等货物的原产地相距 1000 至 1500 英里，距大黑河亦有 1000 英里，瑷珲关若依照滨江关标准对此等货物进行估价，实有不公，难免会迎来抱怨反对之声。黑龙江沿岸贸易已因当地苛捐杂税及高昂的运费严重受阻，兹认为，海关不应再增加其负担，影响地区发展。

　　3. 若照滨江关标准估价，主要受影响的是木料和皮货。木料方面，大黑的批发市价为 0.12 海关两每立方英尺（由于滨江关对本地木料并无需求，此价或会更低），而滨江关批发市价为 0.24 海关两每立方英尺。

　　4. 经审慎考虑后，本署已向关员下达指示，对于应从价纳税之当地出口货物，均照大黑河批发市价估价。对此，还望署予以批准，另请对日后估价办法予以指示。不过，对于进口洋货，若照滨江关标准估价，应不会有何问题。

　　　　　　　　　　　　　　　　　　　　　　　　您忠诚的仆人

　　　　　　　　　　　　　　　　　　　　　　　周骊（C. H. B. Joly）

　　　　　　　　　　　　　　　　　　　　　　　瑷珲关署理税务司

该抄件发送至审榷科税务司及滨江关税务司。

录事：陈培因　　四等一级帮办

致瑷珲关第 <u>621/136538</u> 号令　　　　海关总税务司署（上海）1931 年 8 月 11 日

尊敬的瑷珲关税务司：

瑷珲关第 573 号呈收悉：

"根据海关总税务司署致瑷珲关第 549/129801 号令及致滨江关第 4505/135406 号令（抄件已发送至瑷珲关），询问若照第 549/129801 号令第 6 项指示，瑷珲关税务司是否无权自行决定应从价纳税之当地出口货物的估价办法；滨江关与货物原产地相距 1000 至 1500 英里，与大黑河相距 1000 英里，瑷珲关若依照滨江关标准对当地货物进行估价，实有不公，故已命关员按照大黑河批发市价对应从价纳税的当地出口货物进行估价，请求予以批准。"

奉总税务司命令，现批复如下：批准报告所述估价办法。

中心口岸所供价格并非必须遵照办理，而仅为同组各口岸估价计税之参照。进口洋货之价，地方常难确定，即使可确定，亦常无可靠凭证，总税务司相关指示乃主要针对此等货物而定，至于出口货物，自应依照原产口岸之价而估。

您忠诚的仆人

岸本广吉（H. Kishimoto）

总务科税务司

此抄件发送至滨江关税务司。

5. 为呈交瑷珲关 1931 年第二季度验货工作、货物估价与归类报告事

EXAMINATION, VALUATION AND CLASSIFICATION OF CARGO:
report on, for June Quarter, 1931, submitted.

572
I.G.

572

I.G.

A I G U N   10th July 1931.

INDEXED

Sir,

In accordance with the instructions of your Circular No. 4153 :

calling for a quarterly report on the examination, valuation and classification of cargo :

I have the honour to forward, appended hereto, my report for the June Quarter, 1931.

I have the honour to be,

Sir,

Your obedient Servant,

(Signed) C. B. Joly

(C. H. B. Joly)

Acting Commissioner.

Appendix

The Inspector General of Customs,

S H A N G H A I.

APPENDIX.

REPORT ON EXAMINATION WORK, VALUATION & CLASSIFICATION OF CARGO

AT AIGUN, JUNE QUARTER, 1931.

I. STAFF:

Rank	Name	Where stationed	Date of appointment to port
(a) DESKS:			
1st Clerk B	Wang Te-mao	There is only one Desk in the General Office at which these two Clerks attend to all General Office work and to appraising work as instructed in I.G.desp.No.549/129,801. They also do all Returns work. Mr.Wang also attends to all Russian correspondence and translations.	1.10.21 to 30.11.29(on transfer to Tientsin). Re-appointed on 1.2.30
3rd " A	Leung Wing Tat		1.5.30
(b) EXAMINATION SHEDS:			
Asst.Exmr.A	J. A. Crossland	At Custom House. Senior Out-door Staff Officer whose duties are those of a Tdyr. Attends himself to as much examination work as possible. Acts also as Harbour Master during summer months.	6.4.30
1st Class Tidewaiter	Fan Chin Tsao	Examination Shed, Custom House, Taheiho.	10.4.31
4th Class Tidewaiter	Wong Wen Tso	- do - Note: The two Officers in the Examination Shed,Taheiho, attend to whatever work the Senior Out-door Staff Officer details them to do. Most of the examination work is done during the navigation season in the godowns of the Harbin Shipping Syndicate, but the Officers attending to this work are based on the Custom House as there is not enough work to call for the constant services of an Officer.	1.5.30
Supy.3rd Cl. Tidewaiter	Sun Hung Tsao	At Aigun from 1st March 1931, in charge of Sub-station.	1.5.30
(c) POSTAL PARCELS OFFICE:		One Officer attends 3 times a week, Mondays,Wednesdays, & Fridays,from 2 to 4 p.m. to deal with Parcels. An Officer attends all incoming letter mails. The same remarks apply to Aigun.	

II. WORK:

During the Quarter there were only 16 applications for direct exports abroad and 19 applications for Interport Exports.

Exports. All imports from the Sungari arrived under duty-paid documents from the Harbin Customs. Goods moved along the Chinese bank of the Amur are duty-free and entail little work. With reference to I. G. despatch No. 606/135,429, I beg to state that this office understands the ordinary routine of examination work, valuation and classification of cargo, but that owing to the almost complete absence of trade there is little scope for its application.

(Signed) C. B. Joly
(C. H. B. Joly)
Acting Commissioner.

Custom House,
A I G U N, 10th July 1931.

呈海关总税务司署 <u>572</u> 号文　　　　　　　瑷珲关 1931 年 7 月 10 日

尊敬的海关总税务司（上海）：

根据海关总税务司署第 4153 号通令：

"为呈送验货工作及货物估价与归类季报事。"

兹附瑷珲关 1931 年第二季度验货工作、货物估价与归类报告。

您忠诚的仆人

周骊（C. H. B. Joly）

瑷珲关署理税务司

附录

瑷珲关 1931 年第二季度验货工作、货物估价与归类报告

1. 人员配备：

级别	姓名	所在部门	本口委任日期
（1）验估台			
一等一级税务员	王德懋	总务课仅设一验估台；该两名税务员负责总务课一应事务，并照海关总税务司署第549/129801 号令指示完成货物估价工作，另负责统计工作；王德懋先生还需负责俄文信件及相关翻译工作。	1921 年 10 月 1 日至1929 年 11 月 20 日（调任至津海关）1930 年 2 月 1 日再次任职
三等一级税务员	梁永达		1930 年 5 月 1 日
（2）验货厂			
一等副验货员	克思澜（J. A. Crossland）	于海关办公楼办公；虽为超等外班关员，但职同监察长，并尽可能参与验货工作；夏季期间，职同港务长。	1930 年 4 月 6 日
一等稽查员	樊金藻	于大黑河海关办公楼内的验货厂办公。	1931 年 4 月 10 日
四等稽查员	汪文卓	于大黑河海关办公楼内的验货厂办公。注：大黑河验货厂的两名关员负责超等外班关员分派的一应工作。航运季期间，验货工作主要于哈尔滨官商航业总联合局的关栈内进行，但因工作不多，负责此项工作的关员仍主要于海关办公楼办公。	1930 年 5 月 1 日
额外三等稽查员	孙鸿藻	自 1931 年 3 月 1 日起至瑷珲口岸负责处理分关事务。	1930 年 5 月 1 日

级别	姓名	所在部门	本口委任日期
（3）邮政局包裹税征收处			
		1名关员负责处理包裹，（每周周一、周三、周五下午2点-4点）； 1名关员负责处理信件； 瑷珲口岸亦是如此。	

2. 工作：

1931年第二季度仅有16份直接出口报单和19份转口出口报单。凡自松花江运来之货物，皆持有滨江关签发的完税凭证；而往来黑龙江华岸货物皆享免税待遇，因此所涉工作很少。根据海关总税务司署第606/135429号令，特此说明，本关知悉验货工作、货物估价与归类之常规流程，然因贸易基本停滞，可用之处寥寥。

您忠诚的仆人

周骊（C. H. B. Joly）

瑷珲关署理税务司

6. 为瑷珲关 1931 年第三季度验货工作、货物估价与归类事

EXAMINATION, VALUATION & CLASSIFICATION OF CARGO:
report on, for September Quarter, 1931, submitted.

582
I.G

582

I.G.   A I G U N   8th October 1931.

Sir,

In accordance with the instructions of your
Circular No. 4153 :

calling for a quarterly report on the
examination, valuation and classification of
cargo :

I have the honour to forward, appended hereto, my
report for the September Quarter, 1931.

I have the honour to be,

Sir,

Your obedient Servant,

(Signed) C. H. B. Joly

(C. H. B. Joly)

Acting Commissioner.

Appendix.

The Inspector General of Customs,

S H A N G H A I.

APPENDIX

REPORT ON EXAMINATION WORK, VALUATION & CLASSIFICATION OF CARGO

AT AIGUN, SEPTEMBER QUARTER, 1931

I. STAFF:

Rank	Name	Where stationed	Date of appointment to port
(a) DESKS:			
1st Clerk B	Wang Te-mao	There is only one Desk in the General Office at which these two Clerks attend to all General Office work and to appraising work as instructed in I.G.desp.No.549/129,801. They also do all Returns work. Mr.Wang also attends to all Russian correspondence and translations.	1.10.21 to 30.11.29(on transfer to Tientsin). Reappointed on 1.2.30.
3rd " A	Leung Wing Tat		1.5.30 Transferred to Lappa & relieved from duty on 17.9.31.
3rd " A	Ch'ang Fu Yuan	In General Office from 18.9.31 to replace Mr.Leung Wing Tat.	1.5.30
(b) EXAMINATION SHEDS:			
Asst.Exmr.A	J.A.Cross-land	At Custom House.Senior Out-door Staff Officer whose duties are those of a Tdyr.. Attends himself to as much examination work as possible. Acts also as Harbour Master during summer months.	6.4.30
1st Class Tidewaiter	Fan Chin Tsao	Examination Shed,Custom House, Taheiho	10.4.31
4th Class Tidewaiter	Wong Wen Tso	- do -	1.5.30
		Note: The two Officers in the Examination Shed Taheiho, attend to whatever work the Senior Out-door Staff Officer details them to do. Most of the examination work is done during the navigation season in the godowns of the Harbin Shipping Syndicate, but the Officers attending to this work are based on the Custom House as there is not enough work to call for the constant services of an officer.	
3rd Class Tidewaiter	Sun Hung Tsao	At Aigun from 1st March 1931, in charge of Sub-station.	1.5.30
(c) POSTAL PARCELS OFFICE:			
		One Officer attends 3 times a week, Mondays, Wednesdays, & Fridays,from 2 to 4 p.m.to deal with Parcels. An Officer attends all incoming letter mails. The same remarks apply to Aigun.	

II.

II. WORK:

Trans-frontier trade was conspicuous by its absence throughout the quarter. For local exports to Harbin it was impossible to establish wholesale market values as this trade has been exceptionally dull this year. The few consignments of _ad_ _valorem_ goods dealt with were given values obtained from documents produced by applicants. The Harbin Shipping Syndicate (哈爾濱官商航業總聯合局) was, owing to internal dissensions, dissolved on the 15th August and all vessels concerned were placed under the management of their respective owners. This necessitated the recognition by the Customs of another registered godown, situated on the bund not far from the Custom House.

(Signed) C. B. Joly

(C. H. B. Joly)

Acting Commissioner.

Custom House,

A i g u n, 8th October, 1931.

[A.—27d]

COMMRS. No. 137,906

Aigun No. 633

No.

SHANGHAI OFFICE OF THE

INSPECTORATE GENERAL OF CUSTOMS, 3rd November, 1931.

SIR,

I am directed by the Inspector General to acknowledge receipt of your despatch No. 582:

submitting your report on examination, valuation and classification of cargo for the September quarter;

and, in reply, to say that the list of staff employed in connection with the examination, valuation and classification of cargo, which you were instructed by I.G. Circular No. 4153 to forward with each report is, in future, required only in the June and December quarters' reports after the periodical staff movements have taken place, and that, furthermore, this table is to show the situation of the staff at the end of these two quarters without any reference to transfers or local moves.

I am also directed to request you to confine these staff tables solely to the information called for by the headings of the various columns, without reference to the work performed by each member. Such matters, if considered of sufficient interest, should be embodied in the report itself.

I am,

Sir,

Your obedient Servant,

Chief Secretary.

The Commissioner of Customs,

A I G U N.

呈海关总税务司署 <u>582</u> 号文　　　　　　　　　瑷珲关 1931 年 10 月 8 日

尊敬的海关总税务司（上海）：

根据海关总税务司署第 4153 号通令：

"为呈送验货工作及货物估价与归类季报事。"

兹附瑷珲关 1931 年第三季度验货工作、货物估价与归类报告。

您忠诚的仆人

周骊（C. H. B. Joly）

瑷珲关署理税务司

附录

瑷珲关 1931 年第三季度验货工作、货物估价与归类报告

1. 人员配备：

级别	姓名	所在部门	本口委任日期
（1）验估台			
一等一级税务员	王德懋	总务课仅设一验估台；该两名税务员负责总务课一应事务，并照海关总税务司署第549/129801号令指示完成货物估价工作，另负责统计工作；王德懋先生还需负责俄文信件及相关翻译工作	1921年10月1日至1929年11月20日（调任至津海关）1930年2月1日再次任职
三等一级税务员	梁永达		1930年5月1日调任至此 1931年9月17日离职
三等一级税务员	常福元	自1931年9月18日起替代梁永达任职总务课	1930年5月1日
（2）验货厂			
一等副验货员	克思澜（J. A. Crossland）	于海关办公楼办公；虽为超等外班关员，但职同监察长，并尽可能参与验货工作；夏季期间，职同港务长	1930年4月6日
一等稽查员	樊金藻	于大黑河海关办公楼内的验货厂办公	1931年4月10日

级别	姓名	所在部门	本口委任日期
四等稽查员	汪文卓	于大黑河海关办公楼内的验货厂办公 注：大黑河验货厂的两名关员负责超等外班关员分派的一应工作。航运季期间，验货工作主要于哈尔滨官商航业总联合局的关栈内进行，但因工作不多，负责此项工作的关员仍主要于海关办公楼内办公	1930 年 5 月 1 日
额外三等稽查员	孙鸿藻	自 1931 年 3 月 1 日起至瑷珲口岸处理分关事务	1930 年 5 月 1 日

（3）邮政局包裹税征收处

		1 名关员负责处理包裹，（每周周一、周三、周五下午 2 点—4 点）； 1 名关员负责处理信件； 瑷珲口岸亦是如此	

2. 工作：

1931 年第三季度跨境贸易已然停滞。因贸易太过萧条，已无法为自本埠出口至滨江关的货物确定批发市价。从价纳税货物之运输量更是少之又少，此类货物皆照报关人提供之凭证估价。哈尔滨官商航业总联合局因内部纠纷已于 8 月 5 日解散，所有下属船只均由各自船主管理。如此一来，海关则须将距离海关办公楼不远处堤岸上的关栈收为己用。

您忠诚的仆人

周骊（C. H. B. Joly）

瑷珲关署理税务司

此抄件发送至审榷科税务司。

录事：陈培因　四等一级帮办

致瑷珲关第 633/137906 号令　　　　海关总税务司署（上海）1931 年 11 月 3 日

尊敬的瑷珲关税务司：

瑷珲关第 582 号呈收悉：

"呈交 1931 年第三季度验货工作、货物估价与归类类报告。"

奉总税务司命令，现批复如下：贵署照海关总税务司署第 4153 号通令指示于季报中所列之与验货工作、货物估价与归类相关人员配备列表，今后，仅需在人员定期变动后于第二、第四季度报告中列明，且此表仅示该两季度末的人员情况，无须载明人员调任或当地变动情况。

此外，表内信息应严格按照各栏标题要求填写，无须列明人员具体工作内容。如有值得汇报之事，可体现于报告正文。

您忠诚的仆人

岸本广吉（H. Kishimoto）

总务科税务司

7. 为呈送瑷珲关 1931 年第四季度验货工作、货物估价与归类报告事

EXAMINATION, VALUATION & CLASSIFICATION OF CARGO:
report on for December Quarter 1931, submitted

Aigun   597

5th   January   1932.

In   accordance   with   the   instructions   of   your
Circular   No. 4153 :

       calling   for   a   quarterly   report   on   the
       examination,   valuation   and   classification   of
       cargo :

I   have   the   honour   to   forward,   appended   hereto,   my
report   for   the   December   Quarter   1931.

       I   have   the   honour   to   be,

          Sir,

       Your   obedient   Servant,

       (signed) C. H. B. Joly

       (C. H. B. Joly)

       Acting   Commissioner.

Appendix.

The   Inspector   General   of   Customs,

S H A N G H A I.

A P P E N D I X.

REPORT ON EXAMINATION WORK, VALUATION & CLASSIFICATION OF CARGO

AT AIGUN, DECEMBER QUARTER 1931:

I. STAFF:

Rank	Name	Where stationed	Date of appointment to port
(a) DESKS:			
1st Clerk B	Wang Tê-mao	General Office	1.10.21 to 30.11.29 Reappointed on 1.2.30.
3rd Clerk A	Ch'ang Fu Yuan	- do -	1.5.30
(b) EXAMINATION SHEDS:			
Asst.Exmr.A	J.A.Crossland	Examination Shed, Custom House, Taheiho	6.4.30
1st Cl.Twtr.	Fan Chin Tsao	- do -	10.4.31
3rd Cl.Twtr.	Sun Hung Tsao	Sub-office, Aigun	1.5.30
(c) POSTAL PARCELS OFFICE:	An Officer attends 3 times a week from 2 to 4 p.m..		

II. WORK:

Apart from a few imports from Blagovestchensk, consisting mainly of kerosene oil and benzine, trade was almost at a standstill throughout the quarter. The Soviet Far Eastern Trading Bureau (the Dalgostorg) appears to have more or less monopolised the local kerosene oil market and this led to an increase in the import duty collected by this office.

(C. H. B. Joly)
Acting Commissioner.

Custom House,
A i g u n, 5th January 1932.

呈海关总税务司署 <u>597</u> 号文　　　　　　　　瑷珲关 1932 年 1 月 5 日

尊敬的海关总税务司（上海）：

根据海关总税务司署第 4153 号通令：

"为呈送验货工作及货物估价与归类季报事。"

兹附瑷珲关 1931 年第四季度验货工作、货物估价与归类报告。

您忠诚的仆人

周骊（C. H. B. Joly）

瑷珲关署理税务司

附录

瑷珲关 1931 年第四季度验货工作、货物估价与归类报告

1. 人员配备：

级别	姓名	所在部门	本口委任日期
（1）验估台			
一等一级税务员	王德懋	总务课	1921 年 10 月 1 日至 1929 年 11 月 30 日 1930 年 2 月 1 日再次任职
三等一级税务员	常福元	总务课	1930 年 5 月 1 日
（2）验货厂			
一等副验货员	克思澜（J. A. Crossland）	大黑河海关验货厂	1930 年 4 月 6 日
一等稽查员	樊金藻	大黑河海关验货厂	1931 年 4 月 10 日
三等稽查员	孙鸿藻	瑷珲分关	1930 年 5 月 1 日
（3）邮政局包裹税征收处			
		1 名关员负责处理包裹（每周周一、周三、周五,下午 2 点-4 点）; 1 名关员负责处理信件; 瑷珲口岸亦如此	

2. 工作：

　　1931 年第四季度的贸易几乎处于停滞状态,仅自布拉戈维申斯克（Blagovestchenk）有一些货物进口,主要为煤油和轻质汽油。苏俄远东贸易公司似乎已基本垄断当地煤油市场,瑷珲关进口税收因此有所增加。

您忠诚的仆人

周骊（C. H. B. Joly）

瑷珲关署理税务司

专题五

查缉

1. 为黑河金商运金过境携带枪弹者之验照办法事

No. 2557.   COMMRS.   INSPECTORATE GENERAL OF CUSTOMS.

Harbin   No.84,003.

Peking,   9th May, 1921.

      Sir,

        I append, for your information and guidance, copy of Shui-wu Ch'u despatch No. 616, from which you will see that arms and ammunition carried for defence purposes, when consignments of gold are transported to places on the frontier by Heiho merchants, are to be passed provisionally under Huchao issued by the Heiho Taoyin and countersigned by the Aigun Customs.

              I am,

                 Sir,

              Your obedient Servant,

                (signed) F. A. Aglen,

                  Inspector General.

The Commissioner of Customs,

    H A R B I N .

        True copy.

        Unclassed Assistant.

[K.1-21]

I.G. despatch No. 2557 to Harbin

Append No. 1.

税務處令第六一六號　中華民國十年五月四日

案查前准黑龍江省長來咨大致以據黑河道尹呈據黑河商會轉據商號慶升恒等帖

稱商等於沿邊解運金項全藉槍械以資護衛現奉轉知不准請發大槍護

照是直置商等於傅止營業之地務祈轉請稅務處或海關監督專為運金一事仍

准逕由道署發給大槍護照不限子彈數目並手槍子彈亦不限數等情據此

是查可行應咨請查核見復等因當經本處轉咨陸軍部核辦旋准陸軍部咨

復以黑河商號慶升恒等護衛槍械歷由黑河道尹發給護照由海關簽字

發行各節本部並無此項案牘等由又經本處按照咨內所查各節轉咨黑龍江

省長查復飼准黑龍江省長將飾由黑河道并查明情形咨復到處原咨內並稱

黑河與俄密邇係屬邊防要區該道發給該商護照准其攜帶槍彈雖為部處

定章所無然為商人自衛起見與無故攜帶醫購運者有別且此種辦法由愛琿關

簽字放行已歷年所尚屬有利無弊似難中途廢止應請咨部將前項發照辦法

[K₁—21]

特准該道仍行照舊辦理所有該商携帶大槍即由該道事前取具保結確係

運金自衛不作別用者即行發給護照子彈數目亦責令詳加審核以每次運金之

多寡量為酌定不得任意携帶漫無限制並於每月終將發出護數及領照商人姓各携

帶槍彈數目列表呈送轉洛備查一俟邊夹靖再行改章辦理以符慎重軍火

之意等語復經本處查核向來不准商民自由携帶槍枝子彈者原為重視地方治安

起見今黑龍江省長既以為黑河金商運金銷售有携帶槍彈自衛之必要請准仍行

照舊辦理其必無得地方治安無疑且金商所携帶之槍彈須經黑河道尹核發護照

由關查驗放行尚非漫無限制原洛所擬辦法似應照准以便商情爰以此意洛行

陸軍部請其查酌去後兹准洛復稱查黑河道尹查復各節雖接諸部處定章所

無然既係黑河與俄境密邇通道路不靖商人運金萬分危險不得不携帶大槍與彈

以為自衛之計且由道尹先取商人保結確係以運金若干酌令携帶槍與彈若干

始能發照並由海關簽字技行黑龍江省長亦聲明實行負責本部自應通融

[K.—21]

照准惟必須確照所稱各節詳慎妥切辦理一俟邊境稍平仍照定章核辦應咨復

貴處轉達黑龍江省長查照等因前來本處復查此案既准陸軍部咨復前因自可照辦

嗣後黑河金商運金自衞攜帶大小槍枝子彈應准仍舊請由黑河道尹核發護照送

由爰琿分關簽字後給予頒用其沿途經過關卡驗照放行仍作為黑省暫行特別辦法

除分行益咨復黑龍江省長轉飭黑河道并遵照外相應令行總稅務司查照迅即轉令

濱江等關稅務司遵辦又黑龍江省長咨復本處原文茲孟抄交備查可也此令附抄件

照錄黑龍江省長咨文 十年四月十六日

為咨復事案查前據黑河道尹呈稱黑河商會以商號慶升恒等運金困難懇請由

道發給大槍護照孟免限制子彈數目一案經本署咨行貴處查核見復嗣准復開以應

來黑河金商攜帶護衞槍械由道發給護照係憑何項章程以及爰琿海關所引中央

軍械章程究係何年所定本處與陸軍部查一均無案咨請轉飭分別查明復由本處轉咨

陸軍部核辦以照詳慎等因當經轉令該道查復去後茲據復稱查黑河地處極邊交通不

便兼以道路不靖商人運金萬分危險自非攜帶槍械不足以資自衛凡過運金商人如有

商會結保經本署核明確係正當者即行填發護照並由愛琿海關簽字放行此等辦法

已歷多年歷住皆係如此辦理非自今始至愛琿海關所引軍械章程何年所定一節本署

無案可稽即經洛請該關查明速復茲准哈爾濱海關洛稱業據愛琿分關呈請

將關巷商人攜帶自衛手槍及大槍章程所定年月查明飭知以便遵照轉復黑河道尹等情

到關巷查關於獵槍及子彈進口辦法曾於民國六年間由陸軍部規定辦法凡中國人必須

購買獵槍者須先取具在京薦住以上三人切實保結呈由本省長官洛轉陸軍部由部查

核明確填給護照洛行本省長官發交准購惟祇限於獵槍且槍不得逾一枝彈不得逾

五百粒以俟該槍運到後即將護照繳部註銷並一面由陸軍部洛行稅務處飭關驗放以

免阻碍經由稅務處令行總稅務司轉令到關歷經遵辦有案嗣後對於中國人須購獵

用之槍枝子彈者即遵照上開辦法辦理驗照徵稅放行此項規定僅限於中國人運進槍械

非許攜帶槍械

尚冒儱奉總稅務司第二四三六號通令內開有如得有關監督同意則外人購用槍械章

[K₁—21]

程亦適用於中國人惟須斟酌隨時更改等語以法理而言本不應承認貴道尹所發之

護照然黑河地方情形與他處不同又非關監督駐在地是以從權辦理而有上年通融

之辦法也本稅務司又為過止其他下級地方官更濫發護照並防範軍械貿易起見故

於上年曾經規定攜帶槍枝子彈辦法凡正當商人每人祇准攜帶手槍一枝子彈二

十五粒憑貴道尹所發護照放行令行愛琿分關遵照辦理在案此不過按照當地情

形所擬之當地變通辦法不能指為愛琿海關之關章亦非中央政府規定之章程以前

云云想係愛琿分關誤會所致至於中國人攜帶自衛大槍子彈一節亦係向無定章雖

上年曾經本稅務司飭令愛琿分關承認貴道尹發給庫瑪金礦總辦護金衛兵之

槍彈護照然此種辦法不能視為定例亦不能適用於私人或商人凡屬私人資格欲攜帶

大槍有衛者必須先得有陸軍部特准始准攜帶擾本稅務司之意以為對於商人攜帶

手槍大槍必須從嚴限制不宜輕於允准蓋商人攜帶軍械一旦途遇胡匪則所攜

軍械極易被其刦奪以商人一人或數人之力絕難與之抵抗故危險亦屬極大除指令愛

[K.—21]

琿分關遵照辦理外相應咨復貴道尹查照辦理可也等因前來商人運金究竟應否仍

由本署給照准其攜帶自衛大槍並免限制子彈數目之處理合具文呈請鑒核轉咨等

情據此查黑河與俄密邇係屬邊防要區本省各礦所產沙金均以此處為聚集銷售

之所值此羌帖低落錢法毛荒之際端賴該商等運銷金沙維持本省金融現在俄難未

平匪氛未息該道發給該商護照准其攜帶槍彈雖為處部定章所無然為商人

自衛起見與無故攜帶槍彈暨購運者有別且此種辦法由愛琿關簽字放行已歷年所尚

屬有利無弊似難中途廢止應請

貴處體念黑（河）地方情形特別轉咨陸軍部將前項發照辦法特准該道仍行照舊辦

理所有該商攜帶大槍即由該道節令事前取具保結確係連金自衛不作別用者

即行發給護照子彈數目亦責令詳加審核以每次運金之多寡量為酌定不得任

意攜帶漫無限制並於每月終將發出護照數及領照商人姓名攜帶槍彈數目

分別詳細列表呈送轉洛備查此係本省救濟金商困難暫行特別辦法一俟邊境

[K.₁—21]

安靖匪氛肅清再行改照定章辦理以符處部慎重軍火之意除指令外相應

咨請

貴處轉咨查照核准見復施行此咨

稅務處

致哈尔滨关第 <u>2557/84003</u> 号令　　　　海关总税务司署（北京）1921 年 5 月 9 日

尊敬的哈尔滨关税务司：

　　兹附税务处第 616 号令之抄件，以供参考。从中可知，今后凡黑河金商运金过边境为自卫而携带枪弹者，仍暂由黑河道尹核发大枪护照，并由瑷珲分关签字后给予领用，途经关卡验照放行。

您忠诚的仆人

（签字）安格联（F. A. Aglen）

总税务司

2. 为防止俄国赤塔及苏维埃政府发行的纸币进入中国之指令事

[A.—20]

No. 3   COMMRS.

Aigun   No. 86,088.

INSPECTORATE GENERAL OF CUSTOMS,

PEKING, 6th October, 1921.

Sir,

I append, for your information and guidance, copy of Shui-wu Ch'u despatch No.1531, from which you will see that General Chang Tso-lin wishes you to take all possible measures to prevent the introduction into China of paper money issued by the Chita and Soviet Governments in Russia.

I have to request you to act accordingly.

I am,

Sir,

Your obedient Servant,

Inspector General.

The Commissioner of Customs,

AIGUN.

APPENDIX.

APPENDIX .

税務處令第一五三一號　中華民國十年十月三日

准盛京張巡閱使電稱從前俄國羌帖灌輸我國旋因無處兌換幾等廢紙商民受損極鉅

正在調查核辦現聞赤塔及勞農政府又發行二種羌帖頗流入我國境內無知商民每多

收受應用流弊滋大亟應嚴禁免蹈覆轍希速飭吉江沿邊關卡嚴密查禁不准中外來往

之人攜帶羌帖入境以過來源并盼見復因前來查俄國羌帖流行中國市面前因俄亂

頻仍以致價格跌落幾等廢紙商民已大受損失此次赤塔暨勞農政府又發行二種羌帖

頗流入中國境內不特於幣制有礙且恐商民收用損害滋多自應令關嚴密查禁以杜來

源而防流弊除電復并分行外相應令行總稅務司轉令吉江沿邊各關稅務司遵照辦理

此令

柏　春　同　校
陳　書　龢

[A.—19]

No. **237** COMMRS.

Aigun No. 103,642

INSPECTORATE GENERAL OF CUSTOMS,

PEKING, **23rd June 1925.**

Entered in Card-Index.

Sir,

I append, for your information and guidance, copy of Shui-wu Ch'u despatch No. 732, from which you will see that the importation in bulk into China of the banknotes of Soviet Russia is to be strictly prohibited.

You are, therefore, requested to prevent the entry of these notes, whether blank of effective, but are to read these instructions as applying only to notes carried as freight.

I am,

Sir,

Your obedient Servant,

Officiating Inspector General,
ad interim.

The Commissioner of Customs,

A I G U N.

Appendix.

Appendix.

I. G. despatch No. 237/103,642 to Aigun

稅務處令第七三二號　中華民國十四年六月二十日

查蘇俄新紙幣派人中國邊境請飭東省沿邊稅關嚴禁一事前准吉林省長來咨當經本

處以此項新幣派入我國邊境行使若不嚴重取締實於圖法大有關礙應如何由東省沿

邊稅關嚴密查禁以杜來源之處令總稅務司遵振辦法呈復以遵核辦在案關據

總稅務司呈復將此項蘇俄發行之新紙幣如係大批運輸綸係寫空白抑為發行有效

者在海關若果奉有中國政府之命令禁止進口即可遵照實行惟以此項紙幣運進中國

時大約皆係旅客等星攜帶並非由火車裝運大批報運進口按此如由海關將旅客攜帶

之紙幣扣留充公即不能不以現款兌換交與旅客也竊以此事最妙辦法係由政府禁止

該幣在中國流通並通令中國各銀行對於該幣一律不准收受脂此辦理則該幣在中國

卽成廢紙矣趙台復請鑒核等情復經本處以此項蘇俄新幣運入中國邊境實於幣制有

礙若照總稅務司所擬辦法由政府通令禁止流通並令中國各銀行不准收受自屬根本

取締之法咨行財政部核擬辦法復並分咨外交部吉林省比查脂各在案茲准財政部咨復

稱宜蘇俄政府所發新紙幣流入我國不惟有礙主權且應慮為舊虜布票之續既准吉林省

比咨請查禁自應脂辦應請貴處通令沿邊各關卡並飭知各該關稅務司嚴密查禁大批

蘇俄新紙幣進口以重圖法面保主權除咨行奉天吉林黑龍江新疆各省地方行政長官

脂辦外咨行脂辦並見復等因前來除咨復並分行外相應令行代理總稅務司轉令

各該關稅務司遵脂辦理此令

[A.—29]

No. 248   COMMRS.   INSPECTORATE GENERAL OF CUSTOMS,

Aigun   No.104,653   PEKING, 11th September 1925.

Entered in Card-Index.

Sir,

    With reference to my despatch No. 237/

103,642 :

        instructing you to prevent all importations
        in bulk of Soviet Russian banknotes,
        whether blank or effective, when such
        notes are carried as freight:

I now append, for your information and guidance,

copy of Shui-wu Ch'u despatch No. 1110, from which

you will see that the above instructions have been

extended to all Russian banknotes whether new or

old.

        You are requested to act accordingly.

                    I am,

                        Sir,

                    Your obedient Servant,

The Commissioner of Customs,

    A I G U N.   Officiating Inspector General,
                                    ad interim.

                                        Appendix.

Appendix.

I. G. despatch No. 248/104,653 to Aigun

税務處令第一二一◯號　中華民國十四年九月九日

准財政部咨開查中俄接壤俄國紙幣流用於吾國境內者以東三省為最多尤以中東

鐵路沿線一帶及吉林黑龍江新疆沿邊等處一切貿易通行為最暢比年市價漲落無

定商民重受虧損現在中俄會議業已開幕照協定第十四條凡商民所受俄鈔損失應

提出要求賠償此案正在進行尚未解決前項俄鈔若欲其輸入日多恐商民受害亦日

甚應請貴督辦迅速行知應稅務司電飭與俄接壤邊弄之海關自奉文日起不准新舊

俄幣入境以斷來源而輕商累應咨請查照辦理等因前來相應令行代理總稅務司電

飭璦琿濱江垂所屬各關稅務司遵照部咨自奉文日起不准新舊俄幣入境可也此令

文桂
趙學謙
同校

致璦珲关第 <u>3/86088</u> 号令　　　　　海关总税务司署（北京）1921 年 10 月 6 日

尊敬的璦珲关税务司：

　　为了便于贵署顺利执行,兹附中方税务处令第 1531 号,以供参考。据该令所示,张作霖将军希望贵署尽可能采取一切措施,防止俄国赤塔及苏维埃政府发行的纸币进入中国。

　　敬请遵照此令执行。

您忠诚的仆人

安格联（Francis Arthur Aglen）

海关总税务司

致瑗珲关第 <u>237/103642</u> 号令　　　　海关总税务司署（北京）1925 年 6 月 23 日

尊敬的瑗珲关税务司：

　　兹附中方税务处第 732 号令副本，以供参考。据该令所示，严禁苏俄新纸币大量流入中国。

　　故，无论苏俄纸币是空白抑或发行有效，请贵署严禁该纸币流入，仔细阅读适用于禁止火车装运纸币进口的指令。

您忠诚的仆人

泽礼（J. W. Stephenson）

暂代总税务司

致瑷珲关第 <u>248/104653</u> 号令　　　　海关总税务司署（北京）1925 年 9 月 11 日

尊敬的瑷珲关税务司：

　　根据第 237/103642 号令：

　　　　"指示贵署禁止由火车装运的苏俄新纸币进入满洲，无论纸币是空白抑或发行
　　有效。"

兹附中方税务处第 1110 号令，以供参考。据该令所示，上述指令已将禁运范围增加到所
有俄国纸币，无论新旧。

　　敬请遵照此令执行。

您忠诚的仆人

泽礼（J. W. Stephenson）

暂代代理海关总税务司

3. 为禁止俄国军火进入满洲境内事

[1—29]

.89　COMMRS.

ligun　No. 91,843

INSPECTORATE GENERAL OF CUSTOMS,

PEKING, 2nd November 1922.

Sir,

I append, for your information and guidance, copy of Shui-wu Ch'u despatches Nos. 1519 and 1525, from which you will see that, in connection with the unauthorised importations into Manchuria, by General Chang Tso-lin, of arms, etc., from Vladivostock and other Russian territory alleged to be taking place, the Central Government, while instructing that the Custom Houses concerned are to prevent such importations as far as possible, wishes to be supplied with particulars of any consignments which, in the absence of I. G. authority, you endeavour to detain but which may be forcibly removed from your control by the Fengtien Military Authorities.

I have to request you to act accordingly and to report any cases of this nature that may

have

The Commissioner of Customs,

A I G U N.

have taken place at your port recently or that

may occur in future.   Your report is to be

accompanied by a Chinese version in duplicate.

I am,

Sir,

Your obedient Servant,

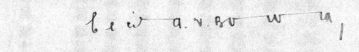

for Inspector General.

Appendix.

Appendix.

I. G. despatch No. 89 to Aigun.

税务处令第一五一九号 中华民国十一年十月三十日

關於由俄境運入中國之軍械一事接據總稅務司來字第三四六號來呈以按照東三省

現時情形而論所有緩關對於黑龍江司令由俄境所運來華之軍械似難施之之權理

合備文復請飭核施行等因前來本處查東三省將未經中央核准購運之軍械由俄運入

國現以現時情形而論在海關權力自屬難予施察應由陸軍部另行設法阻止惟此項軍

械究竟運入若干中央亦須知其催飭應由總稅務司轉行東三省各關稅務司詞後遇有

未奉處令擅放之軍械運入東三省者仍以扣留為正當辦法倘實有難以扣留之處亦須

將運入廠目隨時報告本處以憑轉報院部查核除咨復院部外相應令行總稅務司遵照

辦理可也此令

税务处令第一五二五号 中华民国十一年十月三十一日

准外交部函開據駐海參崴總領事報告赤軍已抵崴埠舊黨將所有鎗械裝載敵艦日內

運往營口等語希查照轉飭總稅務司迅電東省各關一體嚴查儻有軍火發現務即扣留

233

並將辦理情形隨時報告又開日軍代官僱人軍被關有私營奉天情事並有被海關查出

扣留麵稻之說究竟內關驗證疑竇查考干封識及稻件形狀何似其案經迅速到奉省軍機

以經何路由何人過付希飭總稅務司轉令哈爾濱綏芬安東營口各關迅將調查情形詳

概以貨考查等函飭來全數查做人軍被私營奉天被關扣留一案飭據總稅務司來字第

三四六號來呈全數兼將對於此舉之辦法於第一五一九批文令行總稅務司飭關迅辦

在案茲准關調函相應將令行總稅務司查照飭令飭關迅辦可也此令

趙桂山同校
趙學蘭

82.

I. G.   Aigun/Taheiho 25th November, 1922.

Sir,

I have the honour to acknowledge the receipt

of your despatch No. 89/91,845 :

calling for a report on the alleged importation into Manchuria from Russia of Arms and
Ammunition, in connection with the importation
of Arms by General Chang Tso-lin ;

and, in reply, to say that arms are continually being

imported over the border from Russia, and that, now

that the war against the "Whites" is over, there is

a chance of the Russians being more willing to

sell their arms into China.

Most often, the arms are imported in small

lots at places far from Aigun or Taheiho, beyond the

control of our Patrols, and are resold to Hunghutze.

Recently however I have been informed that a large

consignment was to be imported here, and that the

russian

The Inspector General of Customs,
        P E K I N G.

Russian Authorities stopped it; the local Military Authorities were implicated in this plot, which failed.

Since Customs patrols have been inaugurated, they make a certain amount of seizures, but they cannot operate too far from their basis; if an attempt to smuggle arms is detected, the arms are seized according to instructions. - No large consignment has been reported to me as having been actually imported or as being on the point of being smuggled, nor did so far the Military Authorities try and remove from Customs control any such consignment; but it is impossible to know the importance and circumstances of the traffic in arms which takes place along the whole frontier.

Any future case of importation, or attempt by the Military Authorities to move arms by force, will be reported.

A Chinese version of this despatch, in duplicate, is enclosed.

I have the honour to be, Sir,

Your obedient Servant,

J. Bohm

Acting Commissioner.

2593

Appendix.

wchwang   92,125   27th November, 1922.

Sir,

1.   I have to acknowledge the receipt of your

despatches Nos.5428 and 5429 :

reporting unauthorised importations of

articles governed by the Arms Regulations;

and, in reply, to approve of your action as reported.

2.   These cases have demonstrated the futility

of the so-called Foreign International Arms Embargo as

a means of preventing the introduction of arms and

ammunition into China, and, as political developments

in the Three Eastern Provinces have now reached a

stage when the Central Government is powerless to

enforce observance of its own enactments in that

region, I have to instruct you in future and until

further orders to pass all consignments of goods, which

under

R.L. Warren, Esquire,

Acting Commissioner of Customs,

NEWCHWANG.

under standing regulations require Lu-chün Pu
Authority to be conveyed through myself, if they
are properly covered by huchao issued by the
Tuchün.

3.   You will endeavour so far as possible
to secure compliance with instructions in regard
to the duty treatment of such articles coming
under the category of arms and ammunition and
military supplies as are imported under purely
provincial authority and you will be careful to
record all such importations in your Arms Return.

4.   Generally speaking, while using to the
fullest extent the discretion now accorded to you
to carry out the instructions of the de facto
provincial government, and to avoid any action
calculated to bring you and the Service into
collision with the Manchurian Provincial Authority,
you will be careful to note that this discretion
stops short at matters in respect to which the
Chinese Government has bound itself by Treaty or
by international agreement.   In this connection

you

you are requested to re-read my S/O Circular No.34.

A copy of this despatch is being sent

to the Commissioners at Harbin, Aigun, Hunchun,

Moukden, Antung and Dairen.

I am,

Sir,

Your obedient Servant,

(Signed) F. A. Aglen,

Inspector General.

True copy :

A. H. Forbes

ating Assistant Secretary.

致瑷珲关第 89/91843 号令　　　　　　海关总税务司署（北京）1922 年 11 月 2 日

尊敬的瑷珲关税务司：

　　为了便于贵署顺利执行，兹附税务处第 1519 号及第 1525 号令，以供参考。据该令所示，现有从俄国符拉迪沃斯托克（Vladivostok）及其他地区将张作霖将军禁运军火运入满洲境内，中央政府指示海关尽可能阻止这种进口，希望贵署呈报走私军火数目详情，并且（未经海关总税务司署授权）要求贵署竭力扣留禁运军火，但贵署对禁运军火的管控权可能被奉系当局强制接管。

　　请遵照此令执行。假如贵港口近期已发生类似案件或将来发生类似案件，请予以上报。贵署报告需一式两份，附中文版。

您忠诚的仆人

包罗（C. A. Bowra）

受海关总税务司委托签发此文

呈海关总税务司署 <u>82</u> 号文　　　　　瑷珲关／大黑河 1922 年 11 月 25 日

尊敬的海关总税务司（北京）：

　　根据海关总税务司署第 89/91843 号令：

　　　"关于张作霖将军运入军械一事，请汇报据称有军火自俄国运入满洲之详情。"

　　兹汇报，自俄国跨境输入之军火历来源源不绝，近期因新旧两党已停战，俄国人谋求向中国出售军械之机会较往日更甚。

　　军械多为自远离瑷珲或大黑河之处零散运入，躲避瑷珲关巡缉，后辗转售予土匪（红胡子）。然近来本署得知有一大批军火妄图运入此地，遭俄国政府阻止；当地军方亦曾牵连其中。

　　因瑷珲关巡缉正常履职，大量军械得以被查获，但职责之外则鞭长莫及；按照指令，若察觉涉嫌走私，则扣押军械。然本署尚未收到关于大宗输入或正在走私军火之报告，本地军人亦无胁迫海关放行此类军火之情况；但边境沿线运输军械之境况，本署尚无从知晓。

　　日后若存在大宗军火运入及军人强制运送等情况，本署将呈报情形。

　　兹附此呈中文译本，一式两份。

　　　　　　　　　　　　　　　　　　　　您忠诚的仆人

　　　　　　　　　　　　　　　　　　　　包安济（G. Boezi）

　　　　　　　　　　　　　　　　　　　　瑷珲关署理税务司

附件

致牛庄关第 2593/92125 号令　　　海关总税务司署（北京）1922 年 11 月 27 日

尊敬的牛庄关署理税务司霍李家（R.L.Warren）先生：

　　1. 第 5428 号及第 5429 号呈收悉：

　　"汇报现有军火章程禁运的武器进口。"

　　奉总税务司命令，现批复如下：对汇报中采取的行动予以批准。

　　2. 出现这些案件已表明，所谓的《国际军火禁运公约》在阻止军火进入中国方面几乎毫无作用。东三省（满洲）的政治发展，已经到了中央政府无力在当地施行法规的阶段。故指示贵署，根据现行法规，将来若托运货物已获得督军签发的护照许可，须由本署转交陆军部呈请批准后，才能根据本署指示放行托运货物。

　　3. 凡完全系由满洲省政府批准进口的军火类与军需类物品，贵署须竭尽全力确保进口与此类物品征税办法的指令相符，请贵署在"军火物品清单"中详细记录此类进口情况。

　　4. 为了方便贵署贯彻落实实际统治者满洲省政府的指示，避免任何海关可能与满洲省政府发生冲突的行为，曾授予贵署自由裁量权。一般而言，贵署须知，虽然贵署可以最大限度地使用该权力，但在处理中国政府受条约或国际协定约束的事宜时，不得使用该权力。关于这一点，贵署须重读本署第 34 号机要通令。

　　同时，此令副本已抄送给哈尔滨关税务司、瑷珲关税务司、珲春关税务司、奉天关税务司、安东关税务司及大连关税务司。

您忠诚的仆人

安格联（Francis Arthur Aglen）

海关总税务司

此副本内容真实有效，特此证明。

确认人签字：福贝士（A. H. Forbes）

代理总务科副税务司

4. 为瑷珲关护兵之武器军火应否归还事

SERVICE No. 36

No. 30.   Service No.

Aigun/Taheiho. 817.

CUSTOM HOUSE,

Harbin, 30th December 19|22

Sir,

I beg to append a copy of the Superintendent of Customs letter No. 288, asking whether the Arms and Ammunitions which had been supplied to the Aigun Customs Guards at the time when Aigun was still a sub-station, have been returned to this port or not ?

Will you please supply me with the necessary information.

I am ,

Sir,

Your obedient Servant,

Commissioner.

The Commissioner of Customs,
    AIGUN/ TAHEIHO.

APPENDIX.

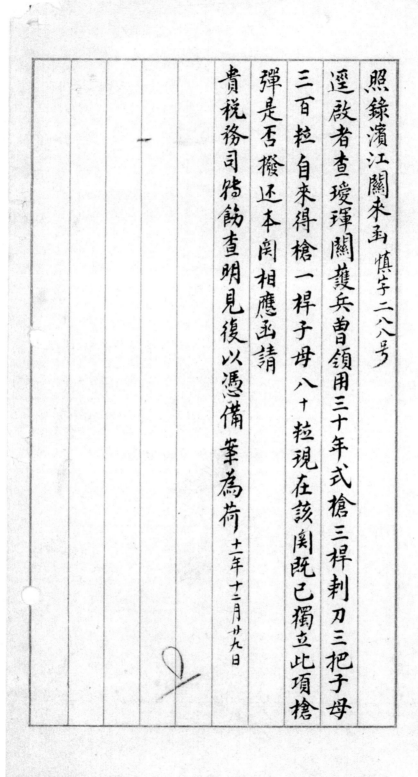

照錄濱江關來函　慎字二八八号

逕啟者查瑷琿關護兵曹領用三十年式槍三桿刺刀三把子母

三百粒自來得槍一桿子母八十粒現在該關既已獨立此項槍

彈是否撥还本關相應函請

貴稅務司飭餉查明見復以憑備筆爲荷　十一年十二月廿九日

致瑷珲关（瑷珲／大黑河）第 <u>30/817</u> 号函　　　　哈尔滨关 1922 年 12 月 30 日

尊敬的瑷珲关（瑷珲／大黑河）税务司：

　　兹附哈尔滨关海关监督第 288 号信函抄件，请告知在瑷珲关仍为分关时，哈尔滨关发给瑷珲关护兵的军火武器归还与否。

　　请提供必要信息。

您忠诚的仆人

（签字）覃书（R. C. L. d'Anjou）

哈尔滨关税务司

5. 为汇报查获印花税票请指示处理办法事

POSTAL PARCELS: collection of duty on "half-tael" parcels; report in re, submitting.

165.

I.G.

Aigun   22nd. April, 1924.

Sir,

I have the honour to acknowledge receipt of your Circular No. 3486:

> Postal Parcels: collection of duty on " half-tael " parcels; report in re, called for;

and to submit the following replies to your two questions -

(1) Domestic Parcels:

When two or more parcels are posted by one sender at the same time to the same address it is the practice at this port to collect duty if this amounts to $0.45 in the case of native goods and $0.75 in the case of foreign goods.

(2) International Parcels:

(a) When two or more parcels are despatched by one sender at the same time to the same address it is the practice at this port to collect duty if this amounts to $0.45 and the contents are of native origin. Duty is not levied on foreign goods exported.

(b)

Inspector General of Customs,

Peking.

Entered in Card-Index.

(b) When two or more parcels are
received by the same mail for the
same addressee it is the practice
at this port to collect duty if
this amounts to $0.75.

The contents of such parcels are
not taken into consideration.

Instructions concerning the duty treatment
of Postal Parcels were conveyed to this office
in I.G. Despatch No. 14/87,199 (in reply to
Aigun Despatch No. 9) and the procedure now
reported has been in force at this port since
February, 1922.

I have the honour to be,

Sir,

Your obedient Servant,

R. F. Chengelun

Commissioner.

REFERENCES.	
DESPATCHES.	
From I.G. Commrs. No.	To I.G. Port No.
14/87,199 (C.3486)	9

呈海关总税务司署 <u>165</u> 号文　　　　　　　瑷珲关 1924 年 4 月 22 日

尊敬的海关总税务司（北京）：

　　根据海关总税务司署第 3420 号通令：

　　　　"印花税票：凡未持有财政部所签发之护照者，印花税票均不予放行；相关指示。"

　　兹报告，瑷珲关查获两个装有印花税票之包裹。

　　包裹内含：

　　（1）寄自北京之包裹。

　　印花税票：10000 张面值为 10 分的印花税票；藏于腌菜罐坛底（可移动）中。发件人申报之物为"腌萝卜（Corned Raddish）"。

　　（2）寄自湖南之包裹。

　　印花税票：6000 张面值为 1 分的印花税票，2500 张面值为 2 分的印花税票；包裹内之物未申报，寄件人于申报单上添加汉字布包。

　　兹请求指示，此番查获之印花税票是否应移交海关监督，若移交，可否要求其发放奖励。另查获包裹事宜已呈报海关监督。

您忠诚的仆人

贺智兰（R. F. C. Hedgeland）

瑷珲关税务司

6. 为没收军火之处理办法事

Aigun Confiscation Report: certain outstanding unsettled cases: requesting I. G. 's instructions re settlement.

I.G.   Aigun.   11th December, 1925.

Replied to in No. 272.

Sir,   INDEXED

With reference to certain Unsettled Confiscation Cases in the Aigun Customs Accounts, some of them outstanding since 246th/March quarter, 1922, and to the Chinese Secretary's Memorandum of 9th April, 1925:

requesting that a report be given whether or not arrangements could be made to settle these cases:

to the Aigun Commissioner's reply by Memorandum of 18th September, 1925:

reporting the difficulties in bringing about a settlement:

and to the Chinese Secretary's Memorandum of 3rd October, 1925:

forwarding a request that the whole question be officialised by despatch:

I now have the honour to forward appended hereto copies of the above correspondence and a precis of subsequent Chinese correspondence with the Superintendent in re, from which it will be noted that difficulties in

The Officiating Inspector General of Customs,
                    Peking.

in settling the outstanding cases arose over a question of values of the seized munitions, the Heilungkiang Tuchun - the military authority to whom the seizures were referred by the Superintendent - eventually deciding that $210.848 was an equitable sum to be given as 2/10ths rewards, a cheque being forwarded for this amount, whereas the Customs, having placed a value on the seizures which established <u>Hk. Tls.</u> 210.848 as the reward money to be remitted, reported this fact to the Superintendent, at the same time informing him that the munitions could not be handed over on the Tuchun's basis for settlement without instructions from the Inspectorate.

All of these cases have been outstanding three years or more, the delay in settling the matter threatens to retard and complicate the discussions of other questions arising between the Customs, the Superintendent, and other Provincial Officials, the munitions in the meantime are deteriorating from dampness in a poor Seizure Room (the only available one under present building arrangements) in a very damp cellar, and a lengthy correspondence has developed

and

and taken a direction which seems to admit no other
means of settlement except an Inspectorate decision:
I have the honour to request your authority to
accept the Tuchun's offer, hand over the munitions
in question, and bring these cases to a close.
It may be added that the difficulty over values
arose prior to the issuance of I. G. Circular No.
3576 and that the instructions and the Lu Chun Pu
scale of values as outlined therein will be the basis
for settlement of future cases.

        I have the honour to be,

          Sir,

          Your obedient Servant,

          Assistant-in-Charge, temporarily.

        APPENDIX.

APPENDIX.

<u>Chinese Secretary's Memorandum of 9th April, 1925 to Aigun</u>:

 With reference to your Confiscation Report for the 257th Quarter, 1924, I am to call your attention to the following remarks:-

 Unsettled Cases: You are requested to report by Memo addressed to the Chinese Secretary whether arrangements cannot be made for the arms, ammunition, etc., detailed in these cases, to be handed over to the local military authorities in exchange for rewards due.

   (signed) A. C. E. Braud

    Chinese Secretary.

<u>Aigun Commissioner's Memorandum of 18th September, 1925 to the Chinese Secretary</u>:

 <u>Chinese Secretary's Memorandum of 9th April, 1925, with reference to Aigun Confiscation Report for the 257th Quarter, 1924.</u>

   <u>A.</u> Ordinary Cases.

 248th/September Quarter, 1922: Case No. 57. This has been settled.

   <u>B.</u> <u>Arms Cases already reported to Superintendent.</u>

 246th/March Quarter, 1922: Nos. 1, 2, and 10.

 247th/June Quarter, 1922: Nos. 34, 35, and 36.

 248th/September Quarter, 1922: Nos. 42, 45, 46, 49, 60, 79, 82, 91, and 95.

 249th/December Quarter, 1922: Nos. 110, 117, 122, and 123. These cases are still outstanding but you will see from the precis of correspondence attached that attempts have been made to settle them. The Tuchun

Tuchun complains that our values are far too high
and points out that the rifles are of an obsolete
type and practically useless owing to lack of
ammunition. He says that it is absurd to value
75 catties of gunpowder at Hk.Tls. 207 and insists
that the correct value is at the rate of $1 per
catty. In August 1923 he offered to issue rewards
on condition that the value of the arms was
reduced from Hk.Tls. 979.24 to $979.24 and that we
agreed to a sum of $75 as representing the value
of the gunpowder. If we come into line with the
Tuchun's wishes the total value of the arms will
amount to $1,054.24 and the rewards to $210.848.
Rewards calculated on the basis of the Tuchun's
valuation were applied for by the Superintendent
in December, 1923, but they have never been issued
and I have since made it clear on various occasions
that I have no authority to accept the offer.
The Taoyin has taken this matter up once again
and he tells me that if Customs Regulations
preclude acceptance of the $210.848 which the Tuchun
has offered he will write and tell him so.
He thinks, however, that we are asking for far
too big an amount and that we should be well
advised to accept the Tuchun's offer. Will the
Chinese Secretary authorise the undersigned to close
these cases on the basis suggested by the Taoyin/
Superintendent? The undersigned wishes to add
that the fire-fighting appliances in this town are
of a most crude and primitive nature and such as
may be said to offer no defence against dangerous
fire risks. A burst of flame from the crude
wooden shelters that stand in the closest proximity
to

to the Custom House would be likely to start a
conflagration which would rapidly invade the Custom
House and Staff Quarters and in case of disaster
the gunpowder which is at present stored in the
basement beneath the General Office would materially
help to wipe out everything and everybody. It is
hoped, therefore, that the Chinese Secretary will
allow the undersigned to hand over the gunpowder
to the local military authorities without further
delay.

C. Arms Cases not yet reported to Superintendent.

252nd/September Quarter, 1923:   No. 31.

254th/March Quarter, 1924:   No. 6.

255th/June Quarter, 1924:   No. 14.

258th/March Quarter, 1925:   No. 2.

The seizures as per above four cases have been
separately stored and it is not proposed to report
these cases to the Superintendent until the earlier
cases have been disposed of. The undersigned has
informed the Superintendent that values recently
fixed by the Lu-chun Pu (C. 3576) should apply to
all seizures made after the 1st. January, 1925, and
that it is on the basis of these values that
rewards will be calculated in the future by this
office.

(Signed) R. F. C. Hedgeland.
Commissioner.

Appendix.

Precis of correspondence in re Arms Seizures.

To Supt. No. 111 of 2nd. February, 1923. Applying for
rewards @ 2/10 of values.

From

From Supt. No. 343 of 4th. February, 1923. Requesting
   Commissioner to forward detailed list of contraband.

To Supt. No. 119 of 2nd. March, 1923. Enclosing detailed
   list and again applying for rewards @ 2/10.

From Supt. No. 422 of 21st. May, 1923. The Taoyin's
   idea was to sell the arms to the Magistrate,
   Superintendent of Police, etc., and to issue
   rewards from sale price, but he has been
   instructed by the Shui-wu Ch'u to dispose of the
   arms to the Tuchun.

From Supt. No. 442 of 29th. June, 1923. The list gives
   the number of rifles, cartridges, etc., but omits
   to record whether these are in a serviceable
   condition or not and the Tuchun is therefore
   unable to say whether the values given are
   correct. Seizures being of small amounts rewards
   should be @ 1/10. The arms will be inspected
   and a fresh list drawn up.

To Supt. No. 150 of 2nd. July, 1923. Explaining the
   Customs rule re issue of rewards.

From Supt. No. 456 of 9th. August, 1923. The Tuchun
   points out that the rifles are of the _____
   and _____ category and that they are practically
   useless because the ammunition required is now no
   longer manufactured. Moreover, the Customs values
   are considerably higher than they should be. E.G.
   it is absurd to value 75 catties of gunpowder at
   Tls. 207. It is suggested that the tael amount
   be changed into a dollar amount and rewards
   issued accordingly. The value of the rifles, etc.,
   should be altered from Taels 979.24 to Dollars 979.24
   and the gunpowder should be valued at $75, the
   proper value of this latter article being $1

                                             per

per catty.   The total value thus amounts to
$1,054.24 and the rewards to $210.848.

To Supt. No. 202 of 5th. December, 1923. Amongst the
seized arms there is a revolver (No. 7494) which
is being retained for Customs use and is
considered as the property of the Superintendent.
The value of the weapon is Hk.Tls. 10 and the
rewards due @ 2/10 = $3.13 (Tl. 2). Supt. is
requested to send the reward and to close the
other cases.

To Supt. No. 388 of 20th. August, 1925. The
Commissioner thinks that the gunpowder at any
rate should no longer be stored at the Custom
House. He has no authority to accept the Tuchun's
offer of a dollar for a tael. A further attempt
should be made to close these outstanding cases.

From Supt. No. 850 of 25th. August, 1925. Rewards were
long ago applied for but to date no money has
been received. The matter is being taken up
again.

(Signed) R. F. C. Hedgeland.
Commissioner.

Chinese Secretary's Memorandum of 3rd October, 1925 to
Aigun:

Cases of Arms, etc., seized at Aigun and still
reported as "Unsettled" in Confiscation Reports.
With reference to your memorandum of 18th September,
as there are points at issue which can only be
decided by the Inspector General you are requested
to officialise the whole question in a despatch
addressed to him.

(Signed) A. C. E. Braud.
Chinese Secretay. Precis

Precis of Additional Correspondence in re. (For Chinese
Texts, see Summary of Non-urgent Correspondence, Sept.,
1925.

From Superintendent No. 880 of 25th September, 1925.

Certain Outstanding Confiscation Cases:

(Vide Fines and Confiscations Report, 260th/September
Quarter, 1925) Enclosing a draft for $210.848 from
Tsitsihar Government as 2/10ths reward for certain
arms, etc., seized and requesting that seizures be
forwarded together with list.

To Superintendent No. 400 of 28th September, 1925.

Acknowledging receipt of draft and stating that case
was being reported to the Inspector General for
instructions re settlement on basis suggested.
(Vide Chinese Secretary's Memo of 9. 4. 25 and Aigun
reply of 18. 9. 25)

True Copy:

Assistant-in-Charge, temporarily.

呈海关总税务司署 <u>249</u> 号文　　　　　　　瑷珲关 1925 年 12 月 11 日

尊敬的海关总税务司：

根据瑷珲关账户中未了结之没收案件［其中含 1922 年第一季度（246 笔）未了结之案件］，及 1925 年 4 月 9 日汉文秘书科税务司通函：

"请汇报，关于此等案件有无解决办法。"

及 1925 年 9 月 18 日瑷珲关税务司通函：

"报告解决过程中所遇之困难。"

及 1925 年 10 月 3 日汉文秘书科税务司通函：

"请正式呈文汇报。"

兹附上述往来信件抄件，及本署与海关监督关于此事之中文通信摘录，从中文通信中可见，解决此等案件之难处在于判定没收军火之价值。海关监督将没收军火事提请黑龙江督军指示后，黑龙江督军将 20% 的海关缉私奖金最终定为 210.848 银圆，认为此为合理之数，并已开具支票。但在此之前，海关判定之缉私奖金为 210.848 海关两，本署已向海关监督汇报此事，并说明若无海关总税务司署指示，没收军火不得移交黑龙江督军处理。

此等没收案件已拖延三年有余，海关、海关监督及省级官员间的其他问题亦因此而变得更加复杂，受到阻碍；此外，军火因置于潮湿的地下室（当前唯一可供利用之扣押室）而日渐受损；瑷珲关已于另一封长文中表示此事唯有提请总税务司裁定方可解决。鉴于此，兹请批准接受黑龙江督军之提议，移交未决之军火，由此结案。本署另需补充说明此等没收军火价值之判定问题乃出现于海关总税务司署第 3576 号通令发布之前，因此，今后若再有此等案件发生，便可以此通令指示及陆军部制定之价值表作为判定参考。

您忠诚的仆人

裴德生（C. M. Petterson）

瑷珲关暂行代理税务司

附录

1925 年 4 月 9 日汉文秘书科税务司致瑷珲关通函：

关于瑷珲关 1924 年第四季度（第 257 笔）没收货物报单，意见如下：

未了结的案件：请以通函形式向汉文秘书科税务司汇报关于此等案件有无解决办法，能否将没收之军火等移交至当地军方，换得海关缉私奖金。

（签字）伯乐德（A. C. E. Braud）

汉文秘书科税务司

1925 年 9 月 18 日瑷珲关税务司致汉文秘书科税务司通函

根据汉文秘书科税务司 1925 年 4 月 9 日通函：

"关于瑷珲关 1924 年第四季度（第 257 笔）没收货物报单。"

甲、普通案件

1922 年第三季度第（248 笔）：第 57 号案件：已解决；

乙、军火案件（已汇报至海关监督）

1922 年第一季度（第 246 笔）：第 1、2 和 10 号案件：未解决；

1922 年第二季度（第 247 笔）：第 34、35 和 36 号案件：未解决；

1922 年第三季度（第 248 笔）：第 42、45、46、49、60、79、82、91 和 95 号案件：未解决；

1922 年第四季度（第 249 笔）：第 110、117、112 和 123 号案件：未解决。

此等军火案件虽尚未解决，但如随附信函摘录所示，本署确已尽力。黑龙江督军诉瑷珲关对没收军火估价过高，指出步枪款式皆为过时之类，又无弹药，实无用武之地；其认为 75 斤火药估价 207 海关两实为荒谬，坚称正确估价应为每斤火药 1 银圆。1923 年 8 月，黑龙江督军提出，若可将武器之估价由 979.24 海关两降至 979.24 银圆，并将火药之估价定为 75 银圆，其便同意发给海关缉私奖金。按照黑龙江督军所提之估价，军火总价值为 1054.24 银圆，海关缉私奖金为 210.848 银圆。海关监督于 1923 年 12 月提出按照黑龙江督军之估价计算海关缉私奖金，但迄今仍未发放。本署已多次明确表示无权接受此出价。道尹随后表示若根据海关规定，无法接受黑龙江督军所提之金额数 210.848 银圆，其将致信告知督军，但认为，海关估价过高，应接受督军之报价；然不知汉文秘书科税务司会否同意按照道尹兼海关监督之建议了结此等案件。

此外，本署另需补充说明，城内灭火设施皆为最简陋最原始一类，对防止火灾毫无作用。海关办公楼附近建有简陋木屋，此等木屋内一旦起火，便会迅速殃及海关办公楼和职员宿舍；若发生火灾，储存于征税汇办处下方地下室内之火药将会成为倾覆之源。故望汉文秘书科税务司可允许本署立即将火药移交至当地军方。

丙、尚未汇报至海关监督之军火案件

1923 年第三季度（第 252 笔）：第 31 号案件

1924 年第一季度（第 254 笔）：第 6 号案件

1924 年第二季度（第 255 笔）：第 14 号案件

1925 年第一季度（第 258 笔）：第 2 号案件

上述四起案件之没收物已单独存放，计划于此前案件了解后，再向海关监督汇报。本署已向海关监督说明，1925 年 1 月 1 日后没收之物应照陆军部（C.3576）最近制定之价值表估价，而海关缉私奖金则应由瑷珲关按此估价计算。

（签字）贺智兰（R.F.C.Hedgeland）

瑷珲关税务司

1925 年 10 月 3 日汉文秘书科税务司致瑷珲关通函

瑷珲关没收军火案件于没收货物报单中仍汇报为"未了结的案件"

关于瑷珲关 9 月 18 日通函，鉴于此事唯有提请总税务司裁定方可解决，故请瑷珲关将全部问题正式呈文汇报至总税务司。

（签字）伯乐德（A. C. E. Braud）

汉文秘书科税务司

附录

军火起获相关信函摘录

1923 年 2 月 2 日致海关监督第 111 号信函：申请按照没收军火价值之 20% 发放海关缉私奖金。

1923 年 2 月 4 日自海关监督第 343 号信函：请瑷珲关税务司呈送没收禁运军火清单。

1923 年 3 月 2 日致海关监督第 119 号信函：随附清单并再次申请按照没收军火价值之 20% 发放海关缉私奖金。

1923 年 5 月 21 日自海关监督第 422 号信函：道尹本欲将军火售于地方官、警察长等人，再从售卖金额中发放海关缉私奖金，但税务处命将军火移交黑龙江督军处置。

1923 年 6 月 29 日自海关监督第 442 号信函：瑷珲关所呈交清单虽列明步枪和弹药筒等数目，但未载明此等军火是否可用，黑龙江督军因此无法辨明海关估价正确与否；鉴于没收物数量较少，海关缉私奖金应按照没收军火价值之 10% 发放；重新检查军火后，再列清单。

1923 年 7 月 2 日致海关监督第 150 号信函：阐明海关对缉私奖金之规定。

1923 年 8 月 9 日自海关监督第 456 号信函：黑龙江督军指出，步枪因所需弹药现已停止生产，毫无用处；海关估价较军火本身之价值高出甚多，如 75 斤火药估价 207 海关两难合情理，建议以银圆计价，海关缉私奖金亦应据此发放。鉴于此，步枪等武器估价应降为 979.24 银圆，火药应照每斤 1 银圆之数估价，即为 75 银圆，故该批没收军火总价值应为 1054.24 银圆，海关缉私奖金应为 210.848 银圆。

1923 年 12 月 5 日致海关监督第 202 号信函：没收军火中有左轮手枪（型号 7494）一把，由海关留用，现已为海关监督所有。该左轮手枪值 10 海关两，应缴纳海关缉私奖金 3.13 银圆（2 海关两）；故请海关监督据此发给奖金，同时了结其他案件。

1925 年 8 月 20 日致海关监督第 388 号信函：瑷珲关税务司认为无论如何火药皆不应再储存于海关办公楼，但其无权接受督军一银圆换一两之提议。此等未了结案件之处理办法需再行商议。

1925 年 8 月 25 日自海关监督第 850 号信函：海关缉私奖金申请已久，但时至今日仍未收到分文，需继续商讨。

（签字）贺智兰（R. F. C. Hedgeland）

瑷珲关税务司

其他相关信函摘录（中文文本见于 1925 年 9 月非紧急信件摘要）

1925 年 9 月 25 日自海关监督第 880 号信函：未结没收案件：

（参阅 1925 年第三季度（第 260 笔）罚款和没收货物报单）随附齐齐哈尔政府发来之 210.848 银圆汇票作为海关缉私奖金（按照没收货物价值之 20%），请将没收军火随清单一并呈送。

1925 年 9 月 28 日致海关监督第 400 号信函

汇票收悉，已将案件汇报至总税务司，提请解决指示。（参阅 1925 年 9 月 4 日汉文秘书科税务司通函及瑷珲关 1925 年 9 月 18 日回函）

7. 为报告瑷珲关现有军备及相关详情事

ARMAMENT MAINTAINED BY THE AIGUN CUSTOMS: report on, as called for by I.G. Circular No.3921, forwarding.

437.

I. G.   Aigun   24th July, 1929.

Registered.

Sir,

With reference to I. G. Circular No.3921:
requiring a report on the
armaments maintained at the various
Custom Houses, hulks, light -
stations, etc.:

I have the honour to append a statement showing
the particulars of arms in possession of the
Aigun Customs and stored in the Custom House at
Taheiho. They were apparently seized as contraband
in 1922 and retained for Customs use without
being reported as seizures to the Inspectorate or
local authorities. The rifles are of an obsolete
Russian military type of no indicated calibre. A
very small stock of doubtful ammunition is on
hand and it would probably be impossible to obtain
a fresh supply. The Mauser pistol is in good
condition.

At the time these rifles were taken over
they were issued to the Boatmen/Guards on patrol
at Liangchiat'un Barrier. Upon the closing of
this Barrier they were sent to the Upper and

Lower

THE INSPECTOR GENERAL OF CUSTOMS,
SHANGHAI.

Lower Barrier established for the prevention of smuggling across the Amur. These Barriers ceased to function in 1927, owing to the closing of the frontier by the Soviet, since when the arms have rested in the Customs strong room. They are periodically overhauled and are in a fair condition.

As both Aigun and Taheiho are frontier garrison towns and adequate military forces are always maintained at the two places, I see no present need for any armament for the protection of the Customs and would not recommend that the present weapons be replaced. The time may come, however, with the reopening of the frontier, when armed patrols may have to be reestablished. If this eventuates they should be provided with new weapons.

I have the honour to be,

Sir,

Your obedient Servant,

Acting Commissioner.

Appendix

Appendix.

Statement of Armament maintained by the Aigun Customs,
with certain particulars regarding, as called for by
I. G. Circular No.3921.

(a) At Custom House, Taheiho:

4 old military rifles and 12 rounds.

2 " " carbines.

1 Mauser with case and 58 rounds.

2 revolvers with 31, and 36 rounds.

(b) Make and calibre of each weapon:

2 military rifles, Imperial Russian Arms Factory,
model 1917, calibre uncertain.

1 military rifle, apparently of Japanese make,
calibre uncertain.

1 military rifle, Remington, model 1918, calibre
uncertain.

1 carbine, Remington, model 1916, calibre uncertain.

1 carbine, Vos Suhl, model 1906, calibre uncertain.

1 Mauser, calibre 403.

1 Russian Army revolver, apparently 32 calibre.

1 Browning, 32 calibre.

(c) When were they purchased and how are fresh supplies
of ammunition obtained.

A note on a Seizure Report of 1922 states that the
4 rifles and 2 carbines were confiscated for Customs
use.   There is no record of how the Customs came into
possession of the Mauser and the two revolvers.   It
is believed that it would be practically impossible to
obtain fresh supplies of ammunition for any but the
Browning and Mauser.

(d)

(d) <u>Do you consider that these weapons are a real protection to the Staff?</u>

With the exception of the Mauser and the Browning, the protection afforded the Customs Staff would arise from the moral effect produced by the appearance of the weapons.

(e) <u>Do you recommend the replacement of all obsolete weapons?</u>

Not at present; if the frontier is reopened and armed patrols reestablished it may be necessary.

(f) <u>Do you consider it necessary to retain any of the existing armaments?</u>

No, with the possible exception of the Mauser and Browning.

Acting   Commissioner.

CUSTOM HOUSE,

Aigun, 24th July, 1929.

呈海关总税务司署 <u>437</u> 号文　　　　　　　　瑷珲关 1929 年 7 月 24 日

尊敬的海关总税务司（上海）：

根据海关总税务司署第 3921 号通令：

"要求瑷珲关报告海关各旧船及灯塔管理处等的军备状况。"

兹附一份报表，详细报告瑷珲关及大黑河境内海关的军械情况。这些都是 1922 年扣押的违禁军械，留作海关自用，未向海关总税务司署或地方政府报告。步枪为老式俄国军用类型，未标明口径。现存有少量军火规格不明，新弹药不能补给。毛瑟枪保存完好。

自瑷珲关接手这些步枪后，即派梁家屯巡缉的卫兵进行保管。梁家屯分卡关闭之际，这些枪被送至图西分卡和图东分卡，此两分卡为防备跨黑龙江走私而建。因苏维埃关闭边境，此两分卡于 1927 年停止运行，自此军械储存在海关保险库。这些军械定期进行检修，状况良好。

由于瑷珲及大黑河是边境要塞市镇，其军事力量相对强大，因此本署认为当前瑷珲关不需要任何军备，且无须替换现用武器。如果边境重新开放，届时可能需要重建武装巡缉队，如此则需给他们装配新武器。

您忠诚的仆人

铎博赉（R. M. Talbot）

瑷珲关署理税务司

附件

报告瑷珲关现有军备及相关详情

（1）在大黑河境内海关：

4把老式军用步枪及12发子弹。

2把老式军用卡宾枪。

1把带壳毛瑟枪及58发子弹。

2把左轮手枪，分别带31发及36发子弹。

（2）每件武器的构造及口径：

2把军用步枪，俄国高级军火厂（Imperial Russian Arms Factory）制造，1917年版，口径未知。

1把军用步枪，日本制造，口径未知。

1把军用步枪，雷明顿，1918年版，口径未知。

1把卡宾枪，雷明顿，1916年版，口径未知。

1把卡宾枪，苏尔（Vos Suhl），1906年版，口径未知。

1把毛瑟枪，403口径。

1把俄式军用左轮手枪，32口径。

1把勃朗宁，32口径。

（3）购买时间及新弹药补给方式：

据1922年海关查获货物类别清单中备注所示，缴获了4把步枪及2把卡宾枪，留作海关自用。至于海关如何获得毛瑟枪及2把左轮手枪，并无记录。本署认为除勃朗宁及毛瑟枪，其他武器几乎不可能获得新弹药补给。

（4）瑷珲关认为武器真的可以保护职员吗？

佩戴武器有一定震慑作用，因心理作用海关职员会觉得受到保护。

（5）瑷珲关是否建议更换所有旧武器？

目前不换；如果边境重新开放，重建武装巡缉队时可能需要更换。

（6）瑷珲关认为是否有必要留下现用武器？

没必要，可以留下毛瑟枪和勃朗宁。

铎博赛（R. M. Talbot）

瑷珲关署理税务司

瑷珲关，1929 年 7 月 24 日

8. 为通告东北各机关由外洋购运军火所持护照不必经驻外使领签字事

[A.—29]

COMMRS. No. 136,420

Aigun No. 620

No.

SHANGHAI OFFICE OF THE
INSPECTORATE GENERAL OF CUSTOMS, 4th August, 1931.

INDEXED

SIR,

 With reference to Circulars Nos. 4087 and 4100:
instructing, inter alia, that when arms are
imported from abroad, the covering Huchao must
bear the visé of the Chinese Legation, or if
there is no Legation, of the Chinese Consulate
in the country of shipment;

 I append, for your information and guidance, copy of
telegrams exchanged with the Kuan-wu Shu from which
you will see that, in reply to my enquiry, the Shu
state that the Government has authorised a special
procedure for Manchuria, and that in the case of arms
imported from abroad by the Manchurian authorities,
visé of the Huchao by the Chinese Legation or
Consulate is therefore to be dispensed with.

 You are requested to act accordingly.

  I am,

   Sir,

   Your obedient Servant,

    Inspector General.

The Commissioner of Customs,

 AIGUN.

2000 / 9.

總稅務司電　關務署第一九三號　中華民國二十年七月二十二日

9900南京張署長鈞鑒案查現行驗放各機關由外洋購運軍火辦法所有國府

所發護照必須經駐外使領簽字海關方能放行惟近來常有由秦皇島報運

進口之軍火雖已奉有鈞署令放之電而進口護照並未經駐外使領簽字此

後所有各關驗放軍火時是否應僅以鈞令爲憑並不論其護照是否已經駐

外使領簽字抑或除鈞署電令外其護照必須經駐外使領簽字方准放行之

處敬祈電示祗遵總稅務司梅樂和叩養

文　郁
周啓明　同校

關務署電第八七七號　中華民國二十年七月二十九日

梅總稅務司覽奫（二十二日電悉查各機關由外洋購運軍火進口按照定章

均應驗憑府照及駐外使館簽證方可放行惟東北方面情形特殊會經國府

核准該處購買外國軍火准予電由中央轉電駐外使館核明起運在案嗣後

各機關由外洋購運軍火進口除東北方面外均應按照定章辦理仰即遵照

署長張藝印

文郁同校
張哲生

致瑷珲关第 620/136420 号令　　　　　海关总税务司署（上海）1931 年 8 月 4 日

尊敬的瑷珲关税务司：

根据海关总税务司署第 4087 号及 4100 号通令：

"凡由外洋购运军火者，所持护照须经中国驻外公使签字，若当地无驻外公使，则由起运国家之中国领事签字。"

兹附本总税务司与关务署往来电报抄件，以供参考。从中可知，关务署已说明嗣后东北各机关由外洋购运军火，所持护照不必经驻外使领签字，照特殊办法办理即可。

请遵照办理。

您忠诚的仆人

梅乐和（F. W. Maze）

总税务司

9. 为汇报每月走私情况事

[A.—28]

COMMRS. No. 138,405

Aigun No. 637

No.

SHANGHAI OFFICE OF THE

INSPECTORATE GENERAL OF CUSTOMS, 1st December, 1931.

SIR,

In view of the importance that the prevention of smuggling is assuming in our administration, I have to request you to submit a monthly report setting forth the extent and trend of smuggling in your district, the methods adopted to defraud the revenue, including particulars of cases presenting peculiar features by reason of special ingenuity, etc., and the steps taken to endeavour to check illicit trade.

These reports are to be forwarded to me during the second week of each month and are to be numbered in the regular despatch series, a copy of the report itself being sent to the Preventive Secretary. One of the objects of calling for these reports is to enable the Inspectorate to serve as a sort of "clearing house" for the dissemination of information regarding the methods employed to defraud the revenue and the nature of our counter-action.

I am,

Sir,

Your obedient Servant,

Inspector General.

The Commissioner of Customs,

AIGUN.

590

590
I.G

I.G

Aigun   15th December 1931.

Sir,

     I have the honour to acknowledge receipt of your despatch No. 637/138,405 :

          calling for a monthly report, to be forwarded during the second week of each month, on the extent and trend of smuggling, the methods adopted to defraud the revenue, and the steps taken to endeavour to check illicit trade :

and to report that the abnormal conditions reported in Aigun despatch No. 542 continue unchanged and that smuggling along this frontier is, in consequence, almost completely absent. As far as can be ascertained, the Soviet Far Eastern Trading Bureau (Dalgostorg) has so far not taken advantage of the unprotected state of the Chinese frontier, but has on each occasion applied for special permission to import and export certain articles in accordance with the regulations of the Heilungkiang Government. Such permission is applied for through the local Mayor, who is concurrently Superintendent of the Aigun Customs, and full particulars of what goods may be moved inwards or outwards are transmitted to this Office to ensure collection of duty.

     I have the honour to be,

         Sir,

         Your obedient Servant,

         (Signed) C. H. B. Joly

          (C. H. B. Joly)

         Acting Commissioner.

The Inspector General of Customs,

    S H A N G H A I.

致瑷珲关第 <u>637/138405</u> 号令　　　　海关总税务司署（上海）1931 年 12 月 1 日

尊敬的瑷珲关税务司：

　　鉴于防范走私乃为海关职权范围以内之要事，遂请每月递交一份报告，内容包括瑷珲关区走私之范围和趋势，走私逃税之办法，可详细列举奇案特案，以及海关为查获非法贸易所采取之措施。

　　此等报告均须于每月第二周呈交至本署，与正常呈文采用相同编号办法，报告抄件须发送至缉私科税务司。要求呈交此类报告，亦为使海关总税务司署发挥信息"交流所"之作用，将各处走私逃税之办法以及海关所采取之应对措施通报各处知悉。

　　　　　　　　　　　　　　　　　　您忠诚的仆人

　　　　　　　　　　　　　　　　　　梅乐和（F. W. Maze）

　　　　　　　　　　　　　　　　　　总税务司

呈海关总税务司署 <u>590</u> 号文　　　　　　　瑷珲关 1931 年 12 月 15 日

尊敬的海关总税务司（上海）：

根据海关总税务司署致瑷珲关第 637/138405 号令：

"请于每月第二周汇报走私范围与趋势、逃税漏税之方法以及海关为制止违法贸易所采取之措施。"

兹汇报，瑷珲关致海关总税务司署第 542 号呈中所汇报之异常情况仍未有所改变，边境走私之事已几近消失。据调查，苏维埃远东贸易局（Dalgostorg）已不再利用中国边境无保护之状态谋取利益，而是每次按照黑龙江政府之规定，为特定物品申请特殊许可。此类特殊许可须向黑河市政筹备处处长兼瑷珲关海关监督申领，而进出口之物品明细皆送至瑷珲关以确保征税事宜。

您忠诚的仆人

（签字）周骊（C.H.B.Joly）

瑷珲关署理税务司

专题六

征税汇率

1. 为呈交 1924 年 7 月为完税所用之通货统计表事

104.

I.G.

Enclosure.
Report on Currencies actually used in the Payment
of Customs Dues and Duties for the month of July,
1924; enclosing.

Aigun   25th. August, 1924.

Entered in Card-Index.

Sir,

I have the honour to acknowledge receipt
of your Circular No. 3533 :

Revenue: return of currencies actually
used for payment of duties to be
forwarded in June and December;
instructions;

and to hand you herewith the report for the month
of July, 1924, prepared in the manner directed.

I have the honour to be,

Sir,

Your obedient Servant,

Commissioner.

The Inspector General of Customs,

Peking.

AIGUN NO. 184 OF 1924 (See I.G. Circular No. 3533, Second Series.)

[R—45]

A I G U N   *Customs.*

Report on Currencies actually used in the Payment of Customs Dues and Duties

For the Month of **July** 19 24

CURRENCY USED.	Rate of Equivalence to Hk.Tls. 1.	Approximate Percentage of Revenue paid during Month in this Currency.
Sycee: Name of Tael (English and Chinese):—	. . .	. . .
Large Silver Coins: *i.e.*, Dollars—Mexican, Dragon, Yuan Shih-k'ai, Hongkong (clean or chopped); Japanese Yen (gold or silver); Piastres; etc.:—		
Dragon (Pei-yang) Dollar	156.65	3
Yuan Shih-k'ai Dollar	156.65	7
Small Silver Coins: *i.e.*, 50, 20, and 10 cent pieces	. . .	. . .
Copper Cents …	. . .	. . .
Cash …	. . .	. . .
Bank-notes: Name of Issuing Bank:—		
Bank of China (中國銀行)	156.65	10
Bank of Communications (交通銀行)	156.65	15
Bank of Manchuria (東三省官銀號)	156.65	35
Kuang Hsin Kung Ssu (廣信公司)	156.65	30
		100.00

If Drafts on a large trading centre, such as Shanghai, Hankow, or Canton, are accepted in payment of duty, the following paragraph is to be filled in:—

Approximately . . . % of the Revenue is paid by Drafts on the . . . Bank,

. . . , at the rate of $\frac{\text{Dollars}}{\text{Taels}}$ . . . to Hk.Tls 1.

CUSTOM HOUSE,

R. F. Chengchi

/Taheiho, 25th. August, 19 24.

Commissioner.

呈海关总税务司署 <u>184</u> 号文　　　　　　　　　　　瑷珲关 1924 年 8 月 25 日

尊敬的海关总税务司（北京）：

根据海关总税务司署第 3533 号通令：

"税收：为完税所用之通货统计表应于 6 月及 12 月份报送事；附相关指示。"

兹报告，已照指示编制 1924 年 7 月统计表，特此呈交。

您忠诚的仆人

贺智兰（R. F. C. Hedgeland）

瑷珲关税务司

1924 年瑷珲关致海关总税务司署第 184 号呈附件

［根据海关总税务司署第 3533 号通令（第二辑）］

[B-45]

瑷珲海关

用以完纳海关税捐之通货报告

1924 年 7 月

所用之通货	对关平两兑换率	本月以此通货完税之比百分数
通货名称（英文及汉文）：	……	……
大银币（即银圆）：墨西哥银圆、龙纹银圆、袁世凯头像银圆、香港银圆（光银圆或被加戳记者），日元（金币或银币），比塞塔，等等		
龙纹银圆（北洋）	156.65	3
袁世凯头像银圆	156.65	7
小银币：50、20 及 10 分硬币	……	……
铜分币：	……	……
制钱：	……	……
钞票：发行银行名称：		
中国银行	156.65	10
交通银行	156.65	15
东三省官银号	156.65	35
广信公司	156.65	30
		100.00

如大贸易中心付款之汇票,诸如上海、汉口或广州等接受付税,则需填写以下部分税款约＿··%系以＿·····＿银行付款之汇票支付,＿·····＿汇率为 1 海关两（元）等于＿·····＿关平两。

您忠诚的仆人

贺智兰（R. F. C. Hedgeland）

瑷珲关税务司

1924 年 8 月 25 日,瑷珲关／大黑河

2. 为按照市场汇率调整税收汇率及薪资发放汇率事

DOCKET: <u>COLLECTION RATE</u>: to be approximately that of market rate of the day, and salary paying rate to be raised accordingly, recommending.

303.

I.G.

303

I.G.

Aigun   15th February, 1927.

Sir,

1.   Since my arrival at this port last October I have been acutely aware of the great disparity between the fixed collecting rate between Haikuan Taels and the local dollar, i. e. 156.65, and the actual market rate which now averages from 180 to 188. I have hesitated, however, about reporting the matter officially until I knew the outcome of the steps that were being taken by the Harbin Commissioner to raise the rate there to a point that would compensate for the loss to the revenue in accepting depreciated paper notes.

2.   The problem of the Harbin Office and its sub-offices at Lahasusu, Manchouli, etc., is exactly reproduced in Aigun. The same paper notes are used and the same economic conditions

that

Inspector General of Customs,

Peking.

that determine their value in the Harbin District obtain here. In short it is an anomaly that (say) Bank of China notes should be accepted in the payment of duty at Lahasusu at the Harbin rate of \$170 = 100 Hk.Tls. whereas at Aigun, a bit further up the river, the same notes should be accepted by the Customs at the fictitiously low rate of 156.65.

3.   As it is so well known in the Inspectorate that conditions affecting the collection rate in the Harbin and Aigun Districts are identical it seems to me only necessary to refer you to the correspondence that has passed between the Inspectorate and Harbin for the necessary support of, and reasons for, the recommendation I now have the honour to make, namely, that the Aigun Customs collection rate be more nearly that of the market rate of the day.

4.   At the time the Harbin District was opened the collection rate appears to have been

fixed

fixed (early records are not complete in this office) between Roubles and Haikwan Taels. This fixed rate apparently continued until after the Russian Revolution when it was made to conform with the market rate of the day. At the end of 1919 the rouble (Kerensky) reached such an absurdly low rate - Rbls.30,000 = 100 Hk.Tls. - that it was decided to accept the dollar, also, for the payment of duty. In an agreement with the Bank of China at the time, appointing them as Customs Bankers, the rate between dollars and Haikwan Taels was to be fixed on consultation between the Customs and the Bank; and was notified to the public as 154 on the 3rd January, 1920. On the 1st April, 1921, it was raised to 156.65 and at Aigun this is still the collection rate. It will be seen from the above that there is precedent for making the collection rate the market rate of the day.

5.   The local rates between dollars, Yen

and

and Shanghai taels for remittance are the same as those of Harbin and are notified daily by wire by the Harbin Banks to their branches here. The remittance rate for dollars from Aigun to Harbin is at par. For January the remittance rate on dollars to Shanghai (via Harbin) averaged 188 for 100 Hk.Tls. There is at present no occasion to remit revenue from Aigun as any surplus is absorbed as Office Allowance.

6.   In-as-much as the Harbin and Aigun exchange rates are the same it seems to me that the collection rate could be the same. As I understand it the Harbin rate for the coming month is notified the 23rd of each month and is based on the average of the preceding three months. If this rate could be wired monthly by the Harbin office, as soon as it is determined there, it could be notified as the collection rate here also.

7.   The principal item in the collection

of

of Aigun is River Dues and this will not be affected as the tariff is in dollars and not Haikwan Taels. The actual collection last year, excluding River Dues and Surtax, amounted only to some Hk.Tls.11,700. Of this amount it may be estimated that some Hk.Tls.5,700 was for duty on furs which was paid by foreign firms. It will thus be seen that the Chinese public will not be largely concerned in the proposed increase.

8.   With reference to salaries, the local practice since 1922 has been to issue part pay in Shanghai Taels to those foreign and Chinese employees who have Tael accounts in Shanghai. The amounts drawn in Shanghai, however, are only a small proportion of the total salaries issued. As a result of the great depreciation of the Manchurian paper dollar and the consequent considerably increased cost of living I venture to recommend this

phase

phase of the situation to your sympathtic

consideration and to suggest that if the

collection rate is raised that the salary paying

rate be brought into line with it.

9.   At present the rate at which

salaries are paid (156.65) appears as an anomaly

in our accounts. For example I am now

transferring Hk.Tls.6,000 from the Aigun Customs

Official Account at Shanghai which is fed from

the Inspectorate for the most part in the form

of grants as Office Allowance. The proceeds of

this transfer will amount to some $10,800 in

depreciated notes in Aigun, at the estimated

rate of 180. This sum will be used largely

in the payment of salaries at the rate of

156.65 resulting in a gain of some $1,400 to

the Service and a corresponding loss to the

Staff.

10.   I have been in correspondence with

the Harbin Commissioner and understand and

appreciate

appreciate fairly well all the difficulties with which he had to contend in instituting the present system of a variable collecting rate. Now that it has been accepted by the Harbin and Moukden authorities and by the Chambers of Commerce concerned I believe, with such precedents to quote, that the local Superintendent and Chamber of Commerce will accept the same system without undue protest. I have not sounded the local authorities as yet, however, as I prefer to have your views and instructions first.

I have the honour to be,

Sir,

Your obedient Servant,

Acting Commissioner.

Reference:

From I.G.   To I.G.
                298.

333
1.G.

No. 333   **COMMRS.**   INSPECTORATE GENERAL OF CUSTOMS,

Aigun   No. 111,451   PEKING, 1st March 1927.

Sir,

       I have to acknowledge receipt of your

despatch No. 303 :

> suggesting the fixing of the Customs
> duty-paying rate of exchange on the
> basis of the market value of the
> local dollar <u>vis-à-vis</u> the Haikwan
> Tael instead of the fixed rate of
> $156.65 as at present, in order to
> fall into line with the new procedure
> at Harbin;

and, in reply, to say that your proposal is

approved in principle but that you are first to

obtain in writing the agreement of the

Superintendent to the change.

       In your correspondence with the

Superintendent you should refrain as far as

possible from reference to the past history of

the collection rate, and content yourself with

pointing out the anomaly of different rates ruling

                                     under

The Commissioner of Customs,

     A I G U N.

under similar currency conditions at Harbin and Aigun, and stating that the rate which would be adopted would be the same as that ruling at Harbin and which would be notified you telegraphically by the Harbin Commissioner.

In the event of your proposal meeting with no opposition from the Superintendent, you are authorised to issue a Notification to the Public and to make the necessary change in procedure without further reference here. At least two weeks' notice should be given to the public, however.

You are requested to report in due course the result of your negotiations with the Superintendent, and further to note that, when revision of the collection rate has been effected, the amount of your office allowance drawn locally

as

as well as the amount of salaries paid locally
are to be calculated at the collection rate
ruling at the time.

      I am,

        Sir,

     Your obedient Servant,

     Officiating Inspector General.

呈海关总税务司署 <u>303</u> 号文　　　　　　　　　　　　　瑷珲关 1927 年 2 月 15 日

尊敬的海关总税务司（北京）：

1. 本人于去年十月到达瑷珲关后,便察觉到海关两与当地哈大洋的固定汇率与市场汇率之间相差较大,目前固定汇率为 100 海关两兑换 156.65 哈大洋,市场汇率为 100 海关两兑换 180 到 188 哈大洋。哈尔滨关税务司已将汇率提高,从而弥补因所收货币贬值而带来的损失。本署在得知该措施之成效后,方决定正式汇报此事。

2. 瑷珲关与哈尔滨关及拉哈苏苏、满洲里等分关所使用的纸币相同,影响各自纸币汇率的经济因素也相同。因此若瑷珲关与拉哈苏苏同样使用中国银行的纸币,但拉哈苏苏使用哈尔滨关汇率（100 海关两兑换 170 哈大洋）,而瑷珲关却使用固定汇率（100 海关两兑换 156.65 哈大洋）,则实在是一件反常的事情。

3. 鉴于海关总税务司署已知晓影响哈尔滨关与瑷珲关两地税收汇率的因素相同,且哈尔滨关已与海关总税务司署通信,说明瑷珲关亟待提高税收汇率的需要,本署遂提议瑷珲关应使用与当日市场汇率更为接近的税收汇率。

4. 卢布与海关两之间的汇率似乎自哈尔滨关开设之日起就一直使用固定汇率（早期记录已不完整）,直到俄国大革命结束后,才开始使用当日市场汇率。1919 年末,鉴于卢布与海关两之间的兑换汇率已低至 30000 卢布兑换 100 海关两,海关遂决定令商人使用哈大洋来支付税款。当时海关与中国银行签订协议,指定中国银行为海关的合作银行,并由海关与中国银行共同商议哈大洋与海关两之间的固定汇率。1920 年 1 月 3 日,双方宣布固定汇率为 100 海关两兑换 154 哈大洋,至 1921 年 4 月 1 日,固定汇率提高至 100 海关两兑换 156.65 哈大洋,该汇率至今仍为瑷珲关所沿用。由此可见,按照当日市场汇率制定固定汇率之做法,着实早有先例。

5. 瑷珲关银圆、日元及上海规银的汇款汇率与哈尔滨关所定汇率相同,哈尔滨银行每日都以电报形式将当日汇率告知其分行。瑷珲关向哈尔滨关以哈大洋汇款时,按平价兑换。一月份,经哈尔滨关汇至江海关的银圆汇率平均为 100 海关两兑换 188 银圆。而瑷珲关由于目前所有盈余都被纳入办公经费,因此尚未汇款至江海关。

6. 兹认为,哈尔滨关与瑷珲关既已使用相同的汇率,则亦可使用相同的税收汇率。哈尔滨关每月根据前三个月的平均汇率制定下个月的汇率,并于当月 23 日公布。所以若哈尔滨关每月制定汇率后,即发电报告知瑷珲关,那么瑷珲关便可以将此汇率作为其税收汇率执行。

7. 瑷珲关的主要税收项目为江捐,因该项税收是使用银圆支付而非海关两,故不受汇率影响。除江捐与附加税外,去年实际税收仅达11700海关两,其中约有5700海关两均为外国商行支付的皮草税。由此可见,提高汇率对中国民众不会有太大影响。

8. 在薪俸方面,瑷珲关自1922年开始,对拥有上海规银账户的华、洋职员,均以规银发放薪俸,但这部分薪俸在薪俸发放总额中所占的比例很小。况且随着满洲纸币的贬值,生活成本大幅增加。因此本署建议,若要提高税收汇率,则也应同时提高薪俸发放的汇率,望贵署酌情考量。

9. 瑷珲关目前的薪俸发放汇率为100海关两兑换156.56哈大洋。在此情况下,若海关总税务司署向瑷珲关在上海的海关账户拨款6000海关两用于办公经费,那么以预计市场汇率即100海关两兑换180哈大洋计算,瑷珲关转账后可得10800哈大洋。但由于该笔款项主要用于发放薪俸,所以就要按照瑷珲关薪俸发放的汇率——100海关两兑换156.56哈大洋来计算,如此,海关可获收益为1400哈大洋上下,然而职员亦将相应地损失约1400哈大洋。

本署已与哈尔滨关税务司联系,对其在建立现行变动税收汇率系统过程中所遇到的困难以及所做的努力表示理解和感激。目前,既然哈尔滨关、奉天政府及相关商会已经协商妥当,相信瑷珲关的海关监督与商会也将会欣然接受这一汇率系统。但是,由于本署想先询问贵署的意见及指令,故而还未向地方政府问询。

您忠诚的仆人

铎博赉（R. M. Talbot）

瑷珲关署理税务司

致瑷珲关第 333/111451 号令　　　　海关总税务司署（北京）1927 年 3 月 1 日

尊敬的瑷珲关税务司：

第 303 号呈收悉：

"建议修改海关征税汇率，按照当前市场上银圆与海关两的兑换比率，取代之前
156.65 银圆兑换 100 海关两的固定汇率。与哈尔滨关新规则保持一致。"

现批复如下：兹告知，原则上批准贵署提议，但是贵署须先与海关监督达成同意更改的书
面协定。

在与海关监督的通信中，贵署可以不参考以往征税汇率，而是解释瑷珲与哈尔滨同一
币种不同汇率的异常，说明将采用的汇率与哈尔滨关规定采用的汇率相同，且哈尔滨关税
务司将发送电报告知贵署。

如海关监督对贵署所提议的会晤无异议，则授权贵署向公众发布告示，对规程作出了
修改，且无须再次提交申请。须至少提前两周发布告示。

敬请正式报告与海关监督的协商结果，且贵署须知征税汇率更改生效后，当地经费及
当地发放薪酬按届时新规定汇率计算。

您忠诚的仆人

易纨士（A. H. F. Edwardes）

代理总税务司

3. 为汇报海关监督同意基于哈大洋市价来计算税收汇率的提议事

REVENUE COLLECTION RATE: proposal to base on
market value of local dollar approved by Supt:
new rate be introduced from 15th April,
reporting.

308 X.

I.C.

Registered

308
—
I.G

Aigun   1st   April, 1927

Sir,

With reference to I. G. despatch No.

333/111,451 (in reply to Aigun despatch No. 303);

approving in principle the
recommendation that the Revenue
Collection Rate for Aigun be
based on the market value of
the local dollar, directing that
the approval of the Superintendent
be first received and issuing
instructions as to the procedure
to be followed with regard to
Office Allowance and salaries in
case the Superintendent's approval
is given;

I now have the honour to inform you that, in

accordance with your instructions, I addressed the

Superintendent on the 21st ultimo pointing out the

low value of the local dollar, referring to the

practice that had been introduced in Harbin whereby

the Collection Rate was calculated according to the

average

Officiating Inspector General of Customs,

P E K I N G.

average of remittance rates based on the cost of the remittance of Shanghai Taels from Harbin to Shanghai, and proposing that in the interests of uniformity the Aigun Collection Rate be the same as that of Harbin in the future. A copy of my despatch to the Superintendent is enclosed.

On the 26th ultimo I received the Superintendent's reply approving this proposal and saying that he had notified the Aigun and Taheiho Chambers of Commerce accordingly. I acknowledged the receipt of this despatch on the 30th ultimo informing him that the new rate would be introduced as from the 15th April. Copies of these two despatches are also enclosed.

In response to a wire from myself the Harbin Commissioner informed me that the rate for April will be 175 and I have issued a notification to the effect that this rate would come into force as from the 15th April and that, hereafter,

hereafter, the rate would be changed monthly to conform to the Harbin rate, seven days notice first being given the public of such a change. I added that the payment of River Dues would still be in dollars and would not be effected by this new procedure.

The middle of the month is not the most convenient time for making a change in rates but the alternative is to wait until the first of May which would mean a possible loss to the Staff in the payment of salaries. I propose to write down all Revenue and Official Haikwan Tael balances in Taheiho on 15th April from 156,65 to 175. The Office Allowance for June Quarter will remain in Shanghai for the time being and will not be effected.

I have the honour to be,

Sir,

Your obedient Servant,

Acting Commissioner.

345   COMMRS.   INSPECTORATE GENERAL OF CUSTOMS.

Aigun   No. 112,314.   PEKING,   28th April 1927.

    Sir,

      I have to acknowledge receipt of your

  despatch No. 308 :

        reporting that the Superintendent has

        raised no objection to the raising

        of the Aigun revenue collecting rate

        to correspond to that ruling at

        Harbin; that you had accordingly

        notified the public that the rate

        for April would be $ 175 = Hk.Tls. 100

        which would come into force as from

        the 15th of that month, but that

        river dues would still be payable

        in dollars and consequently would not

        be affected by the new procedure; and

        that you proposed to write down all

        Revenue and Official Haikwan tael

        balances on 15th April from $156.65

        to $ 175 = Hk. Tls. 100 :

    and, in reply, to say that adjustment should

    be made in your Haikwan tael balances at

    each change in the dollar collecting rate,

              and

The Commissioner of Customs,

  A I G U N.

and the gain or loss on each occasion clearly shown on the voucher.

With regard to the arguments you advance in your letter to the Superintendent, I have to remark that time may possibly show the unwisdom of your references to the cost of remittance to Shanghai and to the depreciated condition of Manchurian currency. Duties are not payable in currency but in the commodity silver, and currencies are merely accepted in lieu of silver as a convenience to merchants. When bank notes are no longer convertible into silver they no longer represent silver and the Customs may collect less in duty than it should in accordance with Treaty stipulations unless the actual value of the local dollar (notes) in relation to silver can be accurately determined. Owing to the difficulties which the Harbin Commissioner experienced in ascertaining the relative values of commodity silver and bank notes, he was compelled to base his

calculations

calculations on the demand rate for Shanghai taels, allowing 1½% as the cost of remittance, which cost is a legitimate charge on the revenue and may in no circumstances be transferred to duty-payers. Experience at other ports has shown that, when any question arises regarding an inadequacy of the collecting rate, any reference to the cost of remittance is liable to be adduced by merchants as evidence of the Customs intention to throw such cost upon duty-payers, complicating considerably the further negotiations on the subject.

I have, further, to request you to note that though for purposes of practical convenience and policy from the time that the change in the rate was authorised at Harbin such changes have so far been made monthly, yet what was authorised was not a monthly collecting rate, but a rate based upon the market value of the local dollar (notes) vis-à-vis the Haikwan tael

tael and subject to more frequent changes if

necessary. You should, therefore, be prepared

to act accordingly: it would appear from your

despatch now under reply that you are under

the impression the rate is definitely a monthly

one.

I am,

Sir,

Your obedient Servant,

Officiating Inspector General.

呈海关总税务司署 <u>308</u> 号文　　　　　　　　璦珲关 1927 年 4 月 1 日

尊敬的代理海关总税务司（北京）：

根据海关总税务司署第 333/111451 号令（回复璦珲关第 303 号呈）：

"原则上批准璦珲关按哈大洋市值确定税收汇率，但应先取得海关监督批准，海关监督同意后，再发布海关经费及薪俸相关发放办法的指令。"

兹汇报根据海关总税务司署指令，璦珲关已于 3 月 21 日向海关监督发送函件，指出哈大洋市值偏低，哈尔滨关的惯例为按照哈尔滨关汇至江海关的上海规银汇率计算出平均兑换汇率，再根据此平均汇款汇率计算出税收汇率，建议今后璦珲关的税收汇率与哈尔滨关保持一致。兹附璦珲关致海关监督函件的副本。

海关监督已于 3 月 26 日回信，表示支持本署提议，且已将此事告知璦珲及大黑河商会。本署于 3 月 30 日呈文告知海关监督新汇率将自 4 月 15 日起开始施行。兹附该两份函文。

哈尔滨关税务司回复璦珲关电报时告知本署，4 月的汇率为 175 哈大洋兑换 100 海关两。璦珲关已正式宣布，该汇率自 4 月 15 日起生效，此后每月更改一次，与哈尔滨关的汇率保持一致，且每次更改均提前七天公布。此外，江捐不受此新规定影响，仍须使用银圆缴纳。

本月中旬并不是更改汇率的最佳时机，但如果等到 5 月 1 日再行更改，职员的薪俸发放便会减少。兹提议，划销大黑河 4 月 15 日的税款兑换海关两时在汇率 156.65（156.65 哈大洋 =100 海关两）至 175（175 哈大洋 =100 海关两）之间的差额。第二季度海关经费暂时仍存于上海账户之中，且不受汇率变更影响。

您忠诚的仆人

铎博赉（R. M. Talbot）

璦珲关署理税务司

致瑷珲关第 <u>345/112314</u> 号令　　　　海关总税务司署（北京）1927 年 4 月 28 日

尊敬的瑷珲关税务司：

第 308 号呈收悉：

"为与哈尔滨关现行汇率保持一致，提议上涨瑷珲关征税汇率，海关监督对此无异议；贵署已告知公众 4 月汇率为 175 银圆 =100 海关两，自 4 月 15 日起生效，但是江捐仍用银圆支付，且之后也不受新规程影响；贵署提议划销 4 月 15 日（从 156.65 银圆 =100 海关两至 175 银圆 =100 海关两），所有税收与海关两之间的差额。"现批复如下，兹告知，每次征收的银圆汇率更改时，须调整贵署海关两差额，且在传票上清楚标识每次损益。

至于贵署致海关监督的信件，我提出几点问题。贵署提及汇款至上海的费用及满洲流通的货币（哈大洋券）贬值情况并不明智。征收税款只接受银子，而不是哈大洋券，且商人为使用方便，几乎不用银子，而是哈大洋券。当银行发行的纸币（哈大洋券）不再兑换成银子的时候，也就不再能体现银子的价值了。而这时，海关的税收也会比协定的要少，除非哈大洋券兑换银子的实际价值能准确地确定下来。由于哈尔滨关税务司难以确定银子与哈大洋券的相对价值，其需根据上海规银即期汇率计算，其中允许有 1.5% 的汇款费用，此费用在税收中属于合法费用，且绝不会向缴税人征收。从其他口岸事例得知，当因征税汇率过低而引起的任何争议时，商人们都会拿海关汇款成本来做文章，说海关意图把这些汇款成本转嫁到纳税人头上，使问题的协商复杂化。

此外，贵署须知，哈尔滨关自授权变更汇率时起，因需适当的调整及政策的变化，截至目前每月都会变更汇率。所批准的汇率并非每月的税收汇率，而是海关两兑换哈大洋券的市价而确定的汇率，且在需要时会频繁更改，因此，贵署需参照哈尔滨关做好相应的准备。从贵署第 308 号呈得知，贵署对汇率的理解可能还停留在一个月须有一个固定汇率的阶段。

您忠诚的仆人

易纨士（A. H. F. Edwardes）

代理总税务司

4. 为使用海关金的海关案件解决惯例事

[1—29]

COMMRS. No. 127,101

Aigun No. 522

No.

SHANGHAI OFFICE OF THE
INSPECTORATE GENERAL OF CUSTOMS, 1st April, 1930.

SIR,

I append for your information and guidance an advance summary of Practice Questions Settled in connection with the introduction of the Customs Gold Unit system.

I am,

Sir,

Your obedient Servant,

Inspector General.

Appendix.

The Commissioner of Customs,

AIGUN.

A P P E N D I X.

Subject.	Rule.	Reference.
No ... Customs Gold Unit: (1) Inquiring whether cargo arriving before, but paying duty on and after 16th March is to be levied duty on a 1.50 or 1.75 basis	Such cargo is to pay duty on a 1.50 basis.	Telegrams of 24th February, 1930 from, of 27th February, 1930 to, Canton.
(2) Cargo bonded between 1st February and 15th March and withdrawn from Bond after 15th March: to pay on 1.50 or 1.75 basis?	Such cargo is to pay duty on a 1.75 basis	Same.
No. ... Customs Gold Units: Transit Dues Inwards: Inquiring whether such dues are to be levied strictly in conformity with the instructions of Circular No. 4025 § 6 or whether the practice reported adopted elsewhere of allowing Transit Dues Inwards to continue to be collected on the Haikuan Tael basis in the case of cargo imported into China before the 1st February may be followed?	The Circular instructions regarding this question are quite distinct, and were so drawn up, in accordance with the Government's instructions, in order to obviate fraud. The ruling is that all Inward Transit Dues, whether for goods which have paid on Hk. Tls. basis or not, are to be levied on the old 5% Import Tariff (of 1922) on the Gold Unit basis, both for specific and ad valorem rates	Despatch No. 5,640 from Chinkiang. I.G. Airmail reply of 27th February, 1930

Subject.	Rule.	Reference.
No. ... Customs Gold Units: Ruling requested regarding Transhipment and "To Pay" cargo.	(1) For Transhipment cargo the date of entry of the importing vessel at the port of transhipment is to determine which tariff basis is applicable, and (2) for goods marked "To Pay" it is to be noted that they are subject to the new tariff if the importing vessel cleared from a Chinese port of origin on or after the 1st February.	Despatches Nos. 9,064 and 5,723/126,180 from and to Hankow, respectively.

致瑷珲关第 <u>522/127101</u> 号令　　　　海关总税务司署（上海）1930 年 4 月 1 日

尊敬的瑷珲关税务司：

　　兹附关于使用海关金的海关案件解决惯例，作为参考。

您忠诚的仆人

华善（P. R. Walsham）

总务科税务司

附录

案件	惯例	参考文件
No.... 海关金：		
（1）询问货物于 3 月 16 日之前到达，但是在 3 月 16 日当天或之后交税以 1.50 还是 1.75 海关金征税？	这样的货物需按一海关两合 1.50 海关金征税。	粤海关 1930 年 2 月 24 日到 1930 年 2 月 27 日电报
（2）2 月 1 日至 3 月 15 日期间的保税货物于 3 月 15 日后撤销保税：以 1.50 还是 1.75 海关金征税？	这样的货物需按一海关两合 1.75 海关金征税。	相同
No.... 海关金：内地子口税：询问此类税金是否应该按照第 4025 号通令第 6 章指示严格征收；还是 2 月 1 日之前进口到中国的货物会参照在其他地方实行的惯例继续以海关两征收？	关于此问题的通令发布得比较早，且为防止欺诈，依据政府指示起草。规定所有内地子口税，无论之前是否以海关两征收，均按 5% 旧进口税率（1922）以海关金单位征收，不仅按照特定税率，也按照从价税率。	镇江海关致海关总税务司署航空信件第 5640 号呈，于 1930 年 2 月 27 日回复。江汉关致海关总税务司署第 9064 号呈及海关总税务司署致江汉关第 5723/126180 号令。
No.... 海关金：关于转船货物及待付货物的惯例。	（1）　对于转船货，根据进口轮船进入转船口岸的日期来决定采用哪种税率征收； （2）　2 月 1 日以后结关的进口货船，标记为"待付"的货物遵循新的海关税率。	

专题七

征税总况

1. 1921 年征税总况

N.G.

Aigun / Taleiho 25th February, 22

Sir,

    In conformity with your instructions, I have the honour to report that the total collection of this Port for the year 1921 has been as follows:

	Foreign Flags.	Chinese Flag.	Total.
	Hk. Tls.	Hk. Tls.	Hk. Tls.
Import Duty	1,676.250	.690.864	5,367.114
Export Duty	4,788.786	65,211.364	70,000.150
Coast Trade Duty	...	...	...
Tonnage Dues	...	...	...
Total: Hk.Tls.	6,465.016	98,902.248	105,367.264

Transit Dues { Inwards	Hk.Tls. ... }		...
{ Outwards	" ... }		
Surtax Duty			6,524.260

    Total Collection: Hk.Tls.111,891.524

    I regret that this despatch was not sent earlier by a misinterpretation of your instructions; the Aigun Collection being embodied in the Harbin District Collection to the end of 1921, a separate report was thought unnecessary.

    I have the honour to be,

Inspector General of Customs.   Sir,

PEKING.   Your obedient Servant,

     Acting Commissioner.

呈海关总税务司署 <u>30</u> 号文　　　　　瑷珲关 / 大黑河 1922 年 2 月 25 日

尊敬的海关总税务司（北京）：

　　兹照海关总税务司署指令汇报瑷珲关 1921 年年度征税总况：

	挂外国旗轮船	挂中国旗轮船	总计
	海关两（两）	海关两（两）	海关两（两）
进口税	1676.230	33690.884	35367.114
出口税	4788.786	65211.354	70000.150
土货复进口半税	……	……	……
船钞	……	……	……
总海关两	6465.016	98902.248	105367.264
子口税	出口 海关两 ……	……	
	进口 海关两 ……	……	
附加税	……	……	6524.260
总征税额	……	……	111891.52

　　本署此前对贵署指令有所误解，以为瑷珲关 1921 年年度征税情况将由哈尔滨关一并汇报，故未能早日呈送此报告，特此致歉。

您忠诚的仆人

包安济（G. Boezi）

瑷珲关署理税务司

2. 1922 年征税总况

88.

I. G.   Aigun/Taheiho 5th January, 23.

Sir,

  In accordance with the instructions of Circular No. 12 of 1875 :

   Total Annual Collection to be reported by despatch ;

I have the honour to report that the total Aigun collection for the year 1922 was as follows :

	Foreign Flag	Chinese Flag	Total
	Hk.Tls.	Hk.Tls.	Hk.Tls.
Import Duty	5,475.330	19,392.415	24,867.745
Export Duty	29,400.526	32,213.481	61,614.007
Coast T.D.	.....	948.854	948.854
River Dues*	8,555.580	12,202.550	20,758.130
Total Hk.Tls.	43,431.436	64,757.300	108.188.736

Transit Dues { Inwards Hk. Tls. ..... } ....

     { Outwards " " ..... } ,....

Famine Relief Surtax   1,283.647

  Total Collection Hk. Tls. 109,472.383

* applied locally to Aids-to-Navigation.

  I have the honour to be, Sir,

    Your obedient Servant,

The Inspector General of Customs,

  PEKING.   Acting Commissioner.

呈海关总税务司署 <u>88</u> 号文　　　　　瑷珲关 / 大黑河 1923 年 1 月 5 日

尊敬的海关总税务司（北京）：

　　　　根据海关总税务司署 1875 年第 12 号通令：

　　　　"请呈报年度征税总况；"

　　　兹汇报，瑷珲关 1922 年年度征税总况如下：

	挂外国旗轮船	挂中国旗轮船	总计
	海关两（两）	海关两（两）	海关两（两）
进口税	5475.330	19392.415	24867.745
出口税	29400.526	32213.481	61614007
土货复进口半税	……	948.854	948.854
江捐 *	8555.580	12202.550	20753.130
总海关两（两）	43431.436	64757.300	108108.736
子口税	进口	海关两……	……
	出口	海关两……	
附征赈捐			1283.647
总征税额：			109472.383

　　* 适用于地方航务

您忠诚的仆人

包安济（G. Boezi）

瑷珲关署理税务司

3. 1923 年征税总况

No. 147.

I. .

Aigun/Taheiho   4th. January, 1924.

Sir,

In accordance with the instructions of Circular No. 12 of 1875 :

Total Annual Collection to be reported by despatch :

I have the honour to report that the total Aigun collection for the year 1923 was as follows :

	Foreign Flags	Chinese Flag	Total
	Hk. Tls.	Hk. Tls.	Hk. Tls.
Import Duty	785.684	8,463.357	9,249.041
Export Duty	78.057	15,097.702	15,175.759
Coast Trade Duty	...	553.678	553.678
River Dues*	2,990.420	12,856.180	15,846.600
Total Hk. Tls.	3,854.171	36,970.917	40,825.088

Transit Dues   Inwards   Hk. Tls. . .... }
                Outwards   "   "   . .... }   . ....

Total Collection Hk. Tls.   40,825.088

* applied locally to Aids-to-Navigation.

I have the honour to be,

Sir,

Your obedient Servant,

The Inspector General of Customs,

P E K I N G.

R. F. Chengelunk

Commissioner.

呈海关总税务司署 <u>147</u> 号文　　　　　瑷珲关／大黑河 1924 年 1 月 4 日

尊敬的海关总税务司（北京）：

　　根据海关总税务司署 1875 年第 12 号通令：

　　"请呈报年度征税总况。"

　　兹汇报，瑷珲关 1923 年年度征税总况如下：

	挂外国旗轮船	挂中国旗轮船	总计
	海关两（两）	海关两（两）	海关两（两）
进口税	785.684	8463.357	9249.041
出口税	78.067	15097.702	15175.769
土货复进口半税	……	553.678	553.678
江捐 *	2990.420	12856.180	15846.600
总海关两（两）	3854.171	36970.917	40825.088
子口税	进口	海关两两……	……
	出口	海关两两……	……
总征税额：			40825.088

　　* 用于本地助航事务

您忠诚的仆人

贺智兰（R. F. C. Hedgeland）

瑷珲关税务司

4.1924 年征税总况

AIGUN CUSTOMS TOTAL COLLECTION FOR 1924:reporting.

204

I. G.   Aigun/Taheiho   10th January, 1925.

Entered in Card-Index.

Sir,

In accordance with the instructions of Circular No. 12 of 1875 :

Total Annual Collection to be reported by despatch :

I have the honour to report that the total Aigun collection for the year 1924 was as follows :-

	Foreign Flags.	Chinese Flag.	Total.
	Hk. Tls.	Hk. Tls.	Hk. Tls.
Import Duty	320.293	9,986.171	10,306.464
Export Duty	...	9,689.952	9,689.952
Coast Trade Duty	...	528.141	528.141
River Dues*	8.290	11,519.210	11,527.500
Total Hk. Tls.	328.583	31,723.474	32,052.057

Transit Dues	Inwards Hk. Tls. ... Outwards " " ...	...
	Total Collection Hk.Tls.	32,052.057

* applied locally to Aids to Navigation.

I have the honour to be,

Sir,

Your obedient Servant,

[signature]

Commissioner.

The Inspector General of Customs,

PEKING.

呈海关总税务司署第 204 号文　　　　瑷珲关／大黑河 1925 年 1 月 10 日

尊敬的海关总税务司（北京）：

　　根据海关总税务司署 1875 年第 12 号通令：

　　"请呈报年度征税总况。"

　　兹汇报，瑷珲关 1924 年年度征税总况如下：

	挂外国旗轮船 海关两（两）	挂中国旗轮船 海关两（两）	总计 海关两（两）
进口税	320.293	9986.171	10306.464
出口税	……	9689.952	9689.952
土货复进口半税	……	528.141	528.141
江捐 *	8.290	11519.210	11527.500
总海关两（两）	328583	31723.474	32052.057
子口税　进口		……	……
子口税　出口		……	……
总征税额			32052.57

　　＊用于本地助航事务。

您忠诚的仆人

贺智兰（R. F. C. Hedgeland）

瑷珲关税务司

5. 1925 年征税总况

AIGUN CUSTOMS TOTAL COLLECTION FOR 1925:
reporting.

252   Registered.

I.G.

                              Aigun, 4th January, 1926.

              Sir,   INDEXED

              In accordance with the instructions of Circular
No. 12 of 1875 :

              Total Annual Collection to be reported by
              despatch ;

I have the honour to report that the total Aigun

collection for the year 1925 was as follows :-

	Foreign Flags.	Chinese Flags.	Total.
	Hk. Tls.	Hk. Tls.	Hk. Tls.
Import Duty	. ...	1,800.338	1,800.338
Export Duty	. ...	10,231.445	10,231.445
Coast Trade Duty	. ...	259.291	259.291
River Dues*	. ...	19,213.070	19,213.070
Total Hk. Tls.	. ...	31,504.144	31,504.144
Transit Dues	Inwards Hk. Tls. . ...) Outwards ,, ,, ...)		. ...
Surtax Duty	. ...	28.123	28.123
Total Collection	. ...	31,532.267	31,532.267

* applied locally to Aids to Navigation.

              I have the honour to be,

                        Sir,

                 Your obedient Servant.

                 Asst.-in-Charge, temporarily.

The Inspector General of Customs,
              Peking.

呈海关总税务司署 252 号文　　　　　　　瑷珲关 1926 年 1 月 4 日

尊敬的海关总税务司（北京）：

　　根据海关总税务司署 1875 年第 12 号通令：

　　"请呈报年度总征税总况。"

　　兹汇报，瑷珲关 1925 年年度征税总况如下：

	挂外国旗轮船	挂中国旗轮船	总计
	海关两（两）	海关两（两）	海关两（两）
进口税	……	1800.338	1800.338
出口税	……	10231.445	10231.445
土货复进口半税	……	259.291	259.291
江捐 *	……	19213.070	19213.070
总海关两（两）	……	31504.144	31504.144
子口税　出口	……	……	……
子口税　进口	……	……	……
附加税	……	28.123	28.123
总征税额	……	31532.267	31532.267

　　* 用于本地助航事务

您忠诚的仆人

派特森（C.M.Petterson）

瑷珲关暂行代理税务司

6. 1926 年征税总况

AIGUN CUSTOMS TOTAL COLLECTION FOR 1926,   296
reporting.   I.G.

296.

I.G.   Aigun,   3rd January, 1927.

Sir,

     In accordance with the instructions of Circular
No. 12 of 1875:

       Total Annual Collection to be reported by
       despatch;

I have the honour to report that the total Aigun
collection for the year 1926 was as follows :-

	Foreign Flags.	Chinese Flags.	Total.
	Hk. Tls.	Hk. Tls.	Hk. Tls.
Import Duty	...	6,646.378	6,646.378
Export Duty	...	4,821.573	4,821.573
Coast Trade Duty	...	291.230	291.230
River Dues*	...	23,646.270	23,646.270
Total Hk. Tls.	...	35,405.451	35,405.451
Transit Dues Inwards Hk. Tls. ...) Outwards " " ...)			...
Surtax Duty	...	414.840	414.840
Total Collection:	...	35,820.291	35,820.291

* applied locally to Aids to Navigation.

     I have the honour to be,

         Sir,

       Your obedient Servant,

         Acting Commissioner.

The Inspector General of Customs,
     Peking.

呈海关总税务司署 <u>296</u> 号文　　　　　　瑷珲关 1927 年 1 月 3 日

尊敬的海关总税务司（北京）：

根据海关总税务司署 1875 年第 12 号通令：

"请呈报年度征税总况。"

兹汇报，瑷珲关 1926 年年度总征税总况如下：

	挂外国旗轮船	挂中国旗轮船	总计
	海关两（两）	海关两（两）	海关两（两）
进口税	……	6646.378	6646.378
出口税	……	4821.573	4821.573
土货复进口半税	……	291.230	291.230
江捐 *	……	23646.270	23646.270
总海关两（两）	……	35405.451	35405.451
子口税　进口	……	……	……
子口税　出口	……	……	……
附加税	……	414.840	414.840
总征税额	……	35820.291	35820.291

＊用于本地助航事务

您忠诚的仆人

铎博赉（R. M. Talbot）

瑷珲关署理税务司

7. 1927 年征税总况

347.

I.G.

Aigun   5th January, 1928.

Sir,

In accordance with the instructions of Circular
No. 12 of 1875:

Total Annual Collection to be reported
by despatch:

I have the honour to report that the total Aigun
collection for the year 1927 was as follows:-

	Foreign Flags.	Chinese Flags.	Total.
	Hk. Tls.	Hk. Tls.	Hk. Tls.
Import Duty	. ...	5,634.462	5,634.462
Export Duty	. ...	8,230.413	8,230.413
Coast Trade Duty	. ...	240.671	240.671
River Dues*	. ...	33,618.360	33,618.360
Total Hk. Tls.	. ...	47,723.906	47,723.906
Transit Dues Inwards Hk. Tls.	. ...)		. ...
Outwards Hk. Tls.	. ...)		
Surtax Duty	. ...	31.970	31.970
Total Collection:	. ...	47,755.876	47,755.876

*Applied locally to Aids to Navigation.

I have the honour to be,

Sir,

Your obedient Servant,

Acting Commissioner.

The Inspector General of Customs,

Peking.

呈海关总税务司署 <u>347</u> 号文　　　　　　　　瑷珲关 1928 年 1 月 5 日

尊敬的海关总税务司（北京）：

　　根据第海关总税务司署 1875 年第 12 号通令：

　　"请呈报年度征税总况。"

　　兹汇报，瑷珲关 1927 年年度征税总况如下：

	挂外国旗轮船	挂中国旗轮船	总计
	海关两（两）	海关两（两）	海关两（两）
进口税	……	5634.462	5634.462
出口税	……	8230.413	8230.413
土货复进口半税	……	240.671	240.671
江捐	……	33618.360	33618.360
总海关两（两）	……	47723.906	47723.906
子口税 进口	……	……	……
子口税 出口	……	……	……
附加税	……	31.970	31.970
总征税额	……	47755.876	47755.876

　　＊用于本地助航事务

您忠诚的仆人

铎博赉（R. M. Talbot）

瑷珲关署理税务司

8. 1928 年征税总况

AIGUN CUSTOMS TOTAL COLLECTION FOR 1928, reporting.

402.

I. G.   Aigun   5th January 1929.

Sir,

In accordance with the instructions of Circular No. 12 of 1875:

          Total Annual Collection to be reported by despatch:

I have the honour to report that the total Aigun collection for the year 1928 was as follows:-

	Foreign Flags.	Chinese Flag.	Total.
	Hk.Tls.	Hk.Tls.	Hk.Tls.
Import Duty	...	5,502.253	5,502.253
Export Duty	6,295.800	5,861.294	12,157.094
Coast Trade Duty	...	58.436	58.436
River Dues*	2,255.490	34,066.620	36,322.110
Total Hk.Tls.	8,551.290	45,488.603	54,039.893
Transit Dues	Inwards Hk.Tls. ...) Outwards Hk.Tls. ...)		....
Total Collection:	8,551.290	45,488.603	54,039.893

*Applied locally to Aids to Navigation.

I have the honour to be,

Sir,

Your obedient Servant,

Acting Commissioner.

THE INSPECTOR GENERAL OF CUSTOMS.

SHANGHAI.

呈海关总税务司署 <u>402</u> 号文　　　　　　　瑷珲关 1929 年 1 月 5 日

尊敬的海关总税务司（上海）：

　　根据海关总税务司署 1875 年第 12 号通令：

　　"请呈报年度征税总况。"

　　兹汇报，瑷珲关 1928 年年度征税总况如下：

	挂外国旗轮船	挂中国旗轮船	总计
	海关两（两）	海关两（两）	海关两（两）
进口税	……	5502.253	5502.253
出口税	6295.800	5861.294	12157.094
土货复进口半税	……	58.436	58.436
江捐 *	2255.490	34066.620	36322.110
总海关两（两）	8551.290	45488.603	54039.893
子口税　进口	……	……	……
出口	……	……	……
总征税额	8551.290	45488.603	54039.893

　　* 用于本地助航事务

您忠诚的仆人

铎博赉（R. M. Talbot）

瑷珲关署理税务司

9. 1929 年征税总况

AIGUN CUSTOMS TOTAL COLLECTION FOR 1929, REPORTING.

463.

I. G.   Aigun (Harbin) 4th January, 1930.

Sir,

In accordance with the instructions of Circular No. 12 of 1875:

Total Annual Collection to be reported by despatch:

I have the honour to report that the total Aigun collection for the year 1929 was as follows:-

Foreign Revenue.

	Foreign Flags.	Chinese Flags.	Total.
	Hk. Tls.	Hk. Tls.	Hk. Tls.
Import Duty	. ...	992.423	992.423
Export Duty	. ...	1,457.311	1,457.311
Coast Trade Duty	. ...	43.826	43.826
Transit Dues:			
Inwards		16.571)	
Outwards		42.428)	58.999
Total Foreign Revenue	. ...	2,552.559	2,552.559

Additional Duty and Surtax.

Import	. ...	787.862	787.862
Export	. ...	710.909	710.909
Coast trade	. ...	16.924	16.924
Total Add. Duty & Surtax	. ...	1,515.695	1,515.695
River Dues			14,697.380
Total Collection for 1929:			18,765.634

* Applied

THE INSPECTOR GENERAL OF CUSTOMS,
    SHANGHAI.

329

* Applied locally to Aids to Navigation.

I have the honour to be,

Sir,

Your obedient Servant,

Acting Commissioner.

呈海关总税务司署 <u>463</u> 号文　　　　瑷珲关（哈尔滨）1930 年 1 月 4 日

尊敬的海关总税务司（上海）

　　根据海关总税务司署 1875 年第 12 号通令：

　　"要求瑷珲关呈报年度总征税情况。"

　　兹呈报瑷珲关 1929 年度总征税情况如下：

外贸税收

	挂外国旗轮船	挂中国旗轮船	总计
	海关两（两）	海关两（两）	海关两（两）
进口税		992.423	992.423
出口税		1457.311	1457.311
沿岸贸易税		43.826	43.826
子口税			
入境		16.571	
出境		42.428	58.999
总计税收		2552.559	2552.559

附加税

进口		787.862	787.862
出口		710.909	710.909
沿岸贸易		16.924	16.924
共计关税及附加税		1515.695	1515.695

江捐

			14697.380
1929 年总征税额：			18765.634

　　＊用于本地助航事务

您忠诚的仆人

富乐嘉（H. G. Fletcher）

瑷珲关署理税务司

10. 1930 年征税总况

531

$\frac{531}{I\ G}$

I.G.　　　　　　　　　　　A I G U N　　31st December 1930.

Sir,

　　　　In accordance with the instructions of Circular No. 12 of 1875 :

　　　　　　Total Annual Collection to be reported by despatch :

I have the honour to report that the total Aigun collection for the year 1930 was as follows :

Old Tariff Revenue:

	C.G.U.	Hk. Tls.
5% Import Duty	721.555	684.811
Export Duty		4,270.026
Coast Trade Duty		106.881
Transit Dues: Inward		. ....
" 　 " Outward		. ....
Total Old Tariff Revenue		5,061.718

Additional Duty and Surtaxes:

Additional Import Duty	929.851	879.298
Export Surtax		2,134.566
Coast Trade Surtax		53.592
Total Additional Duty & Surtaxes		3,067.456
Total Collection for 1930		8,129.174
River Dues Collection for 1930 (applied locally to Aids to Navigation)		29,047.170
Grand Total		37,176.344

　　　　I have the honour to be, Sir,

　　　　　　Your obedient Servant,

　　　　　　　(Signed) C. B. Joly

　　　　　　　　(C. H. B. Joly)

　　　　　　　Acting Commissioner.

The Inspector General of Customs,　checked & found correct:

S H A N G H A I.　　　　　Dawson
　　　　　　　　1st Clerk B
　　　　　　In charge of General office.

呈海关总税务司署 <u>531</u> 号文　　　　　　　瑷珲关 1930 年 12 月 31 日

尊敬的海关总税务司（上海）：

根据海关总税务司署 1875 年第 12 号通令：

"请呈报年度征税总况。"

兹汇报，瑷珲关 1930 年年度征税总况如下：

按旧税则所征税收：		海关金（两）	海关两（两）
5% 进口税		721.555	684.811
出口税			4270.026
土货复进口半税			106.881
子口税	进口		...
	出口		...
按旧税则所征税收总计：			5061.718
新增关税及附加税：			
新增进口税			879.298
出口附加税			2134.566
复进口半税附加税			53.592
新增关税及附加税总计：			3067.456
1930 年税收总计：			8129.174
1930 年江捐税收 *			29047.170
税捐共计：			37176.344

＊用于本地助航事务

您忠诚的仆人

周骊（C. H. B. Joly）

瑷珲关署理税务司

11. 1931 年征税总况

AIGUN CUSTOMS TOTAL COLLECTION FOR 1931: reporting.

594
I.G.

594

I.G.   A I G U N   30th December 1931.

Sir,

In accordance with the instructions of
Circular No. 12 of 1875 :

Total Annual Collection to be reported by
despatch :

I have the honour to report that the total Aigun
collection for the year 1931 was as follows :

Foreign Revenue Account:

	C.G.U.	Hk.Tls.
5% Import Duty	1,340.998	1,567.953
Export Duty		1,535.476
Interport Duty		3,904.966
Total		7,008.395

Additional Duty and Surtax:

	C.G.U.	Hk.Tls.
Additional Import Duty	3,502.402	4,086.018
Export Surtax		513.040
Interport Surtax		1,952.580
Total:		6,551.638
Total Collection for 1931:		13,560.033
Navigation Fees(applied locally to Aids to Navigation)		71,247.770
Grand Total:		84,807.803
Flood Relief Surtax on Foreign Revenue(December only)	15,539	17.953
Flood Relief Surtax on Additional Duty(December only)	69.721	80.517

I have the honour to be,

Sir,

Your obedient Servant,

(Signed) C. H. B. Joly
(C. H. B. Joly)
Acting Commissioner.

The Inspector General of Customs,

S H A N G H A I.

呈海关总税务司署 <u>594</u> 号文　　　　　　　　瑷珲关 1931 年 12 月 30 日

尊敬的海关总税务司（上海）：

根据海关总税务司署 1875 年第 12 号通令：

"请呈报年度征税总况。"

兹汇报，瑷珲关 1931 年年度征税总况如下：

进出口贸易：

		海关金（两）	海关两（两）
5% 进口税		1340.998	1567.953
出口税			1535.476
土货复进口半税			3904.966
子口税	进口		……
	出口		……
外币税收账户总计：			7008.395
附加税：			
新增进口税			4086.18
出口附加税			513.040
转口附加税			1952.580
总计：			6551.638
1931 年税收总计：			13560.033
江捐 *			71247.770
税捐共计：			84807.803

水灾附加税（仅 12 月）	海关金（两）	海关两（两）
进出口贸易	15.539	17.953
附加税	69.721	80.517

　* 仅用于地方航务

您忠诚的仆人

周骊（C. H. B. Joly）

瑷珲关署理税务司

专题八

海关与税捐局、报关行

1. 为东省银行请海关接受以其纸币支付关税事

12.

I. G.   Aigun/Tahtiho   3rd December, 1921.

Sir,

I have the honour to report that on 4th August I received a letter from the newly opened Branch of the Eastern Provincial Bank (or Bank of Manchuria — 东三省银行, informing me that they were going to circulate their own Bank Notes on the Market, and asking that these be accepted by the Customs in payment of Duties. — On the 8th I replied in writing that the terms of the Agreement between the Harbin Commissioner of Customs and the Bank of China prevented me from taking their demand into consideration.

Copy of the correspondence is enclosed.

Knowing that the Bank would not be satisfied, and would certainly approach Harbin on the

subject,

Inspector General of Customs,

        P E K I N G.

339

subject, I wrote semi-officially to the Commissioner referring the case, asking for his instructions, and expressing the advice that no Notes besides those of the Bank of China and Bank of Communications be accepted.

The Commissioner replied that he had received a similar application through the Superintendent ; he had answered that if the Bank of China agreed to accept these notes he would be satisfied, but this should be a private matter between the Banks, and not the matter of public notification. I had in the meantime warned the Staff to accept only Banknotes of the two Government Banks in payment of Special Permit Fees, Examination Fees, Fines, etc.

Later on, in October, I was again approached especially by the Acting Manager of the Bank of China, who pointed out to the impossibility for him, of refusing Banknotes of Chang Tso-lin's Bank, and said that all the Banks had a system of daily clearance of their Banknotes, a fact which was already well known to me. - My reply to him was

exactly

exactly in the terms suggested by the Harbin Commissioner.

I now have the honour to solicit your approval of my action. I think we run no special risk in following this course : officially our revenue is collected in Silver or in Bank Notes of the Bank of China and Bank of Communication, so far as they are circulated at par; on the other hand, the Bank of China is obliged to accept the Notes of the Eastern Provincial Bank in ordinary business intercourse, and our Revenue will not weigh for much in the amount of Notes accepted. If, eventually, Notes of the Bank of China become depreciated through accepting Notes of other Banks, we can always claim our collection in silver or Notes of the two Government Banks at market rate, according to our Agreement.

The Kuang Hsin Lung-ssu (廣信公司) have also started circulating locally their Tsitsihar Notes, but they have asked no privileged treatment from the Customs.

I have the honour to be,

Sir,

Your obedient Servant,

Acting Commissioner.

呈海关总税务司署 <u>12</u> 号文　　　　　　瑷珲关／大黑河 1921 年 12 月 3 日

尊敬的海关总税务司（北京）：

　　兹报告，东省银行（或东三省银行）新开分行于 8 月 4 日来函告知，其将于本地市场发行自制纸币，请瑷珲关接受商人以该纸币支付关税。本署于 8 日回函说明，因哈尔滨关税务司早与中国银行签订相关协议，本署无法应允。

　　随呈附上本署与该行往来信函抄件。

　　考虑该行不会就此罢休，必然会与哈尔滨关联系，本署已就此事向哈尔滨关税务司发送半官函征询意见，并建议只接受中国银行和交通银行两家银行之纸币。

　　哈尔滨关税务司回函称，其已通过海关监督收到类似请求，业已告知该分行，若中国银行接受其纸币，哈尔滨关亦可接受，但说明此事应由其私下与中国银行协定，无须公示。

　　与此同时，本署已告诫瑷珲关职员，仅接受商人以两家政府银行所发行之纸币支付特别执照费、海关检验费及罚金等款项。

　　10 月，中国银行代理经理来函称已接受张作霖银行所发行之纸币，且所有银行皆有其纸币每日清算系统（本署早已知悉此事）。本署已照哈尔滨关税务司之建议予以回复。

　　特此申请批准上述行动，相信按照当前安排，海关应不会有何风险，因为按照规定，只要银圆及中国银行和交通银行所发行之纸币仍按票面价值流通，海关关税便须使用此等货币支付；另一方面，中国银行被迫于常规业务往来中接受东省银行纸币后，在其所收纸币的总金额数中，海关税收所占比例亦不会太多。而且根据协议，即使最终中国银行因接受他行纸币而使自己的纸币贬值，海关亦有权要求银行按照市场汇率以银圆或两家政府银行的纸币支付税款。

　　广信公司亦已于当地发行齐齐哈尔纸币，然并未要求海关予以特权对待。

您忠诚的仆人

包安济（G. Boezi）

瑷珲关署理税务司

2. 为理清瑷珲关与税捐局管辖范围事

25.

I. G.   Aigun/Taheiho 26th January, 1922.

Sir,

1.   I have the honour to acknowledge the receipt of your despatch No. 17 / 87,500 :

concerning the possible closing of the Liangchiat'un Barrier, and the relations between the Customs and the Local Tax Office.

The two questions being distinct, and the reply to each requiring considerable development, I shall deal in the present despatch with the Local Tax Office, making the Liangchiat'un Barrier the object of a separate report.

2.   The Local Tax Office or Shui Chüan Chü (税捐局) has been long established in Aigun and at Taheiho. The list of goods subject to taxes, and the amount to be paid, vary from time to time : when merchants object too strongly to a certain tax, it is generally abolished, or the rate lowered, and another tax introduced. The rates are considerably

higher

The Inspector General of Customs,

PEKING

higher than the Customs duties, and there is reason
to believe that they are more than a trifle
elastic. Cargo arriving overland has the option of
paying at Tsitsihar or here, but it appears that
sometimes collection takes place at both ends.

At present, according to the Director, taxes
are levied on certain classes of native goods,
notably those imported from other Provinces, and on
foreign goods imported from abroad. In practice duties are sometimes collected on foreign goods exported to Siberia as well.

3.   In collecting duties the Chü follows several methods :

Goods imported by River : they are caught
in the streets or the shops, after having
been released by the Customs;
Goods imported overland from Tsitsihar are
similarly taxed on arrival, after having passed
the C. M. Customs;
Goods exported overland are dealt with generally before they are reported to the Customs.
Goods exported across the River :
a) In Winter : the topography is such,
that cargo can only pass through the Kuan Tu
Lu ; the Tax Office station their watchers at
the corner of that street with the Ta Ksing.
Chieh,

Chieh, so that all the cargo must necessarily pass through their hands before being reported to our winter Bond Office;

  b) __In Summer__ the traffic goes by Ferry, and access to the stretch of land opposite our Ferry Office, where examination takes place most of the time, can be gained from three different roads, the Ying An lu, Ying Yuan lu and Shi Hsing lu; besides, re-export cargo is examined by us on the Bund, in front of the Custom House, wherefrom it proceeds to the Ferry, following the Bund. In order, therefore, to have an efficient control over this traffic, the Chü maintain an Office (Chien Ch'a ch'u – 檢查處)just near our Ferry Office, right on the foreshore, so located as to block the access to the Ferry Barge, which carries merchandise. Whenever cargo is not covered by the proper documents, the watchers stop it, and pretend to bring to the Tax Office in town for examination and levy of duty, regardless of the fact that it is export or re-export cargo already passed by the Customs. With passengers the Chü does not interfere.

Enclosure No. 1.

  The enclosed sketch of the Taheiho Bund and foreshore, and of the roads leading to them, gives an idea of the situation of the Customs' and Shui Chüan Chü's Offices and ways of controlling cargo, to or from Blagovestchensk.

4. There is nothing that we can object to

     in

in the methods adopted by the Tax Office in dealing with cargo moved overland and with imported
goods ; nor concerning exports over the Winter Road,
except that they may stop goods especially examined
by us in godown. But such large lots do not try
to escape payment of local Taxes, and no complaints
have been heard on this account . - It may be a
question whether the Chü is right in collecting
certain duties, namely on foreign goods, especially
in Aigun, which is a Treaty Port ; however, the
point need not, in my opinion, be raised by the
Customs, but by the Merchants and their Consuls.

5.　　　What closely regards the Customs is the
encroachment on our jurisdiction by the Tax Office,
when, at the Ferry, they examine, detain, and otherwise tamper with, export and re-export cargo which
has been examined and passed by the Customs, and
which should be handled solely by the Customs
until definitely exported. - Complaints have been
lodged several times, and each time the Chü has
promised to be careful not to interfere with our
work ; encroachments having continued, I tried to

settle

settle the question for good.

6.   The opportunity for a test case presented
itself on 6th July, 1921, when a watcher of the
Shui Küan Chü stopped a foreign carriage and horse
belonging to a Russian, on their way to Blagovestchensk ; the goods had been passed by the Customs,
as evidenced by a receipt duly endorsed by the
General Office, in the possession of the owner. The
Russian, on being led to the Town Office of the
Chü, stopped in front of the Customs House, where
he reported matters to the senior Officer. I was
summoned, and enquired of the watcher by what right
did he stop goods already passed by the Customs
for export. — I then wrote to the Tax Office, com-
plaining of their encroachment and asking for explana-
tions. A reply came, which, on the whole, admitted
the fault of the Chü, and said that orders would
be given to the underlings to avoid the recurrence
of similar mistakes. Copy of the correspondence is
enclosed. —

      It is interesting to note, _en passant_, that
notwithstanding the Chü's declaration to the contrary,

                       foreign

foreign goods are sometimes taxed on exportation.

I reported officially the facts to the Harbin Commissioner, who approved my action.

7.   Again, on 1st August, I was informed by the local agent of Messrs. Zilgalv & Co. of Vladivostock that the Chü wanted to levy duty on foreign hides re-exported to Blagovestchensk, which had been examined by the Customs and passed duty-free. With the Senior Out-Door Officer I then proceeded to the Ferry, enquired personally from the representative of the Tax Office, and satisfied myself that he was detaining the goods in question, and asked payment of duty on them. I told the merchant, however, that I had no right to interfere with the doings of the Chü, except insofar as they encroached on the Customs, but that it was opened to him to make a formal complaint to the Commissioner.

8.   The question had reached a point, where I felt I should ask the Commissioner for further and definite instructions before taking action with the Shui Chüan Chü. In reply to my queries, the Commissioner wrote that the stand to take was to

tolerate

tolerate no interference with vessels or their cargo
within Harbour limits afloat, along the foreshore,
and in registered godowns ; that cargo under Customs
Documents, or cargo once reported at Liangchiat'un
for Aigun or Tahsiho under our Barrier passes,
should not be interfered with by the Tax Office
until finally released.

I then wrote to the Taoyin the letter
which is reported in the communication of the
Shui Wu Ch'u enclosed in your despatch under reply.
In it I set forth our grievances and our conten-
tions, and asked the Taoyin to take up the matter
with the Tax Office ; I insisted mainly on the
exclusive rights of the Customs on the foreshore
and Bund — the latter because most of our examination of export and re-export cargo is carried on
the Bund, and also because, at exceptionally high
waters, the foreshore is entirely covered up, leaving
nothing but the Bund for us to work on.

9.   The Taoyin informed me after a while that
the matter could not be settled without reference
to the Provincial Authorities, and I waited for a

definite

definite reply. - I only quite recently learned,
from your despatch and from a Superintendent's letter,
that the case had been submitted to the Shui Wu
Ch'u, which Body could form no impartial view of
the facts, the Customs' point of view not having
been represented.

10.   I decided to have a direct verbal explanation with the Director of the Shui Chuan Chü,
Mr. Liu Pao-chin (劉 保 搢), and I asked the
Superintendent to arrange a meeting, which took place
on the 18th of this month. - I clearly told my
reasons for not allowing anybody to interfere with
goods, as long as they are under Customs jurisdiction ; Mr. Liu readily agreed with me on the principles, and confirmed that no difficulty exists in
practice for overland traffic, for imports by River,
and for exports to Blagovestchensk in winter, as
well as for cargo covered by Inward or Outward
Transit Pass, or other Customs Documents. - But he
did not know of a way of controlling native exports
unless he had a check on them when they are actually sent across in summer. I suggested that it
would be easy for him to post watchers at the

roads

roads leading to the Bund, so as to catch goods before they come under our jurisdiction ; he objected that he had strict orders not to increase expenses, and, consequently, staff, a fact which was confirmed by the Taoyin. -

This reply, which may be an argument, but is not a reason, reduced the question to one of means and expedients. I then made another suggestion, namely that he collect duty according to the Books of the Merchants, which are opened to him for the collection of the Tax on Retail Sales. He said this may be done, except for travelling merchants, which are the most likely smugglers, and which escape his control most easily. After some discussion (which was very friendly from beginning to end) the Superintendent suggested that he may, as Taoyin, issue a joint notification with the Shu, making resident merchants responsible for travelling merchants whom they may lodge, and adjoining upon everybody to report goods intended for export to the Shui Chüan Chü before declaring them at the Custom House, under penalty of heavy fines.

Mr.

Mr Liu contended that his Office on the foreshore should anyhow be retained, for the purpose of seeing which cargo and by which merchants is passed without documents by the Tax Office; he guaranteed that his watchers would not search or detain cargo in case of attempted fraud, but that the Chü would fall back on the merchants (which are all well known to his Staff), and collect duty and/or fines from the shops.

11.   We parted on the agreement that Mr. Liu would draft a short Memorandum defining our respective jurisdictions, to be corrected by me if necessary, and then submitted to our respective Superiors. But the next day, when he came with his draft, there was a hitch : it appeared that, in a few cases, when the packing is not sufficiently indicative of the contents, and the receipts of the Chü are not in order, or no receipts are presented, the Chü has to open the packages to ascertain the value of the contents, for the purpose of levying duty and fines. - This opened the question again, although he assured me that there have been only

two

two such cases last year.

12.   After more discussion and another meeting at the Superintendent's, it was suggested that, should such a case occur, the Chü may notify the Customs, so that one of our Officers be present during the examination, and until the cargo is finally shipped.

13.   The enclosed correspondence shows the _modus operandi_ which has been tentatively proposed. By it the Shui Ch'üan Chü recognises our contention that imported cargo must be dealt by the Customs first, and export cargo must be taxed by the Chü before it comes under our jurisdiction – neither party being however responsible for the collection of the other party – ; the Chü would be allowed to retain the Office on the Bund, under the conditions and guarantees specified above, i.e., one of our Officer being present, if and whenever the Chü has to deal with export cargo already passed by the Customs.

14.   This arrangement is open to criticism. It would be infinitely better to have **nobody** exercise any functions within the legal and **territorial** limits of our jurisdiction : if we had **exclusive**

control

control of the Bund and foreshore, and the Shui Chüan Chü removed their Chien Ch'a Ch'u, there would be cause for friction, no chance of encroachments.

Besides, if we come to a compromise, we may one day be in the uncomfortable position of helping, however indirectly, in the collection of local duty contrary to Treaty.

15. On the whole, we could with justice put up a fight for our exclusive rights. But we would have heavy odds against us. The Tax Office have carried on their work on the foreshore for a long time, and it will be difficult to oust them from their positions; the Provincial authorities are backing the Shui Chüan Chü, from which they derive no small profit, and they won't be easily persuaded to yield to our reasons; the merchants are less opposed to the Chü, with whom they can come to terms, than to us - besides the former is an organ of the Province, while we represent the far away Central Government ; finally, the Superintendent himself is above all the Taoyin, as such responsible to

the

the Provincial Authorities and partaking of the
Provincial Revenues.

Besides, the peaceful solution of this
case is likely to go a long way towards promo-
ting good feelings and smoothing matters generally,
and eventually in solving other important problems.

16.   I took the step of discussing matters
in details with the Director of the Tax Office
in order to ascertain the views of his Administration, and in the hope of finding out an
acceptable common ground ; unluckily we could only
outline a _modus operandi_ which is not entirely
satisfactory, and the matter must be gone over
again in Peking.

I have made it clear during the procee-
dings that the negotiations were entirely of my
own initiative, that the suggested procedure is
not even strictly in accordance with Customs principles, - and that, as far as the Customs are concerned, a decision can only come from you.

17.   At Aigu the question does not exist for
the present; the ferry is some five **li** away from

the

the Custom House, and there being very little
traffic going across. - At Taheiho itself, the
Tax Office has never interfered with cargo shipped
by steamers other than the Ferry.

I have the honour to be,

Sir,

Your obedient Servant,

Acting Commissioner.

G.

55.

I. G.   Aigun / Taheiho 15th June, 1922.

Sir,

In reply to your despatch No. 42/89,154,

paragraph 7 :

> Working Agreement with Local Tax Office
> for the delimitation of the respective
> jurisdictions, submitted in Aigun despatch
> No. 25, is fundamentally wrong and can-
> not be sanctioned; the Local Tax
> Office is to be asked to regularize
> their position, and to remove outside
> certain limits of exclusive Customs
> jurisdiction :

I have the honour to append copy of the corres-

pondence exchanged with the Taoyin-Superintendent in

this connection.

In his despatch No. 156, of 14th April, he

informed me that the Shui Wu Ch'u had approved the

modus operandi; in the absence of your instructions,

                                                    I

Inspector General of Customs,

P E K I N G.

I did not reply at the time.

On receipt of your despatch under reply, I wrote and explained your decision (despatch No. 27 of 1st June) and asked that your demands be complied with.

The Superintendent wrote on 7th June (his despatch No. 176) saying that the Shui Wu Ch'u having already ruled in favour of the working Agreement, it would be difficult for you to repudiate it.

I replied (despatch No. 39 of 16th June) that, from the text of his communication, it appears that the modus vivendi has been wrongly reported to the Shui Wu Ch'u as agreed to locally, while I always made the most explicit reserves, both verbally and in writing; that, therefore, the Ch'u has ruled without exact knowledge of the case; that the circumstances and the Customs point of view having been fully reported to you, the Ch'u had better consult with you; and that I would follow the decision transmitted through yourself.

I think that the question, as it is now,

cannot

cannot be settled locally; I am sorry if the discussions which I have carried on locally have in any way prejudiced the issue : I never thought that the case would be thus misrepresented, nor that the Ch'u would decide, apparently, without having consulted with you, without communicating their decision to you. The Ch'u ought to know, with special regard to this question, that the Superintendent at this Port derives nearly all his Revenue and prestige from his Taoyinship, and that he cannot be expected therefore, in his reports, to go against Provincial interests, in favour of the Customs.

I have the honour to be,

Sir,

Your obedient Servant,

Acting Commissioner.

[L—18]

58   Commrs.   INSPECTORATE GENERAL OF CUSTOMS,

Aigun   No.90,437   PEKING, 25th July 1922.

Sir,

With reference to your despatch No. 55:

stating that the Superintendent has been notified of the Inspector General's disapproval of the Working Agreement with the Local Tax Office and has been asked to again submit the question to the Shui-wu Ch'u:

I am directed by the Inspector General to say that you are to inform the Superintendent that the Ch'u has not communicated to the Inspector General any approval of the Working Agreement, that the Inspector General does not approve of it, and that pending instructions from him you are not authorised to give effect to it.

I am,

Sir,

Your obedient Servant,

Audit Secretary
for
Chief Secretary.

The Commissioner of Customs,

AIGUN.

9.   Aigun/Taheiho   28th May, 1923.

Sir,

1.   In continuation of former correspondence

concerning the Shui Chüan Chü (local Tax Office)

in Taheiho, and with special regard to your despatch

No. 81/91,319 :

> informing that the Shui-wu Ch'u has at your
> request, withdrawn its approval of the pro-
> posed agreement between the C. M. Customs and
> the local Tax Office submitted by the Aigun
> Superintendent ;

I have the honour to report that, when the Super-

intendent returned to his post in November 1922,

after a two months' absence in Mukden and Tsitsihar,

I appraised him, verbally, of the contents of your

Despatch, and asked him to help the Customs in

having the Office at the Ferry of the local Tax

Office removed. The Superintendent then asked me

to wait until the Board's instructions be communic-

ated to him. I waited in vain several months,

until,

The Inspector General of Customs,

        P E K I N G.

until, on 5th April 1923, I wrote to the Superintendent (despatch No. 127) enclosing the text of the
Shui-wu Ch'u's despatch, and requesting him to give
instructions accordingly to the local Tax Office.

2.   The Director of the local Tax Office,
accompanied by the Superintendent's Secretary came to
see me shortly afterwards, wishing to discuss the
question anew. The discussion disclosed nothing of
interest, nothing that had not been said before.
I made clear once more the exclusive Customs right
to control of the foreshore and Bund, and my contention could not be seriously challenged by the
Director of local Tax Office. The only excuse he
could make for maintaining his Office at the Ferry
is the facility for checking traffic, and the large
expense which would be rendered necessary by the
removal of that Office, and the establishment of a
control at the three roads leading to the Bund.
I insisted that the local Tax Office should regu-
larise their position vis-à-vis the Customs, even
if this should entail a slight increase in expenses,
in the same way as the Customs had given up

                                        taxation

taxation of Native Goods at Liangchiat'un, thereby losing considerable revenue and increasing the expenditure in the establishment of patrols. The Director of local Tax Office however said that he could not increase expenditure nor take any steps without authority from the Ts'ai Chêng T'ing, to whom this question must be referred again. I then asked him to represent to the Provincial Treasurer the urgency of the C. M. Customs and the local Tax Office operating each within its own sphere of jurisdiction, and to solicit authority for a slightly larger expenditure, by which the question could most satisfactorily be settled.

3.   A few days after this interview, the Superintendent informed me, in his despatch No. 402, that the Director of the Shui Chüan Chü was reporting the matter to the Ts'ai Chêng T'ing, being unable to come to a decision locally.

4.   The reply from the Provincial Treasurer was not long in coming, and was communicated to me by the Superintendent in his despatch No. 419 of 14 May 1923. — The despatch shows that the Shui Chüan Chü

Chü tried to demonstrate that their Office at the
Ferry was not encroaching on the rights of the
Customs; and the Ts'ai Chêng T'ing in reply, as
rules that
each Office is working on its own account, the
Office of the Shui Chüan Chü on the Bund is to
remain, and the Superintendent should ask the
Customs not to interfere any longer.

5.   I have replied to the Superintendent (desp.
No. 139) that the question concerns the Customs
very much and the encroachments are very actual;
that I have no other course left but to report
the circumstances to the I. G.; and I have asked
him to report to the Shui-wu Ch'ü, on one side,
and on the other to further insist on the Provincial Treasurer conforming to the decisions of
the Board.

6.   Copy of the correspondence with the Superintendent is appended. It is interesting to note
that this Official, who is supposed to represent
the Shui-wu Ch'u, never communicated to the Customs
the Shui-wu Ch'u's despatch adopting your reasons
for disapproving the Agreement proposed between the

Customs

監束字第一百二十七號
監束字第四百二號
監束字第四百九號
監束字第一百三十九號

Customs and the local Tax Office; and that he never even mentioned the authority of the Shui-wu Ch'u in his correspondence with the Provincial Authorities.

7.   I am afraid that for the time being, unless the Shui-wu Ch'u is ready to take further steps in order to ensure compliance with its decisions by the Local Authorities and the Superintendent himself, nothing more can be done by the Customs except lodging a protest against the unlawful action of the Provincial Authority, and fresh protests in every instance of actual encroachment on our jurisdiction by the local Tax Office.

I have the honour to be,

Sir,

Your obedient servant,

Acting Commissioner.

呈海关总税务司署 <u>23</u> 号文　　　　　　　瑷珲关／大黑河 1922 年 1 月 26 日

尊敬的海关总税务司（北京）：

1. 根据海关总税务司署第 17/87300 号令：

　　"为梁家屯分卡关闭事及瑷珲关与税捐局关系事。"

兹汇报，鉴于该两事并不相干，且皆须详细汇报，故本呈文仅述税捐局一事，梁家屯分卡事宜将另呈汇报。

2. 瑷珲与大黑河两地早已设有税捐局，但其征税对象及征税金额向来不定。比如，若有税项遭到商人强烈抵制，通常会被废止，或降低税率，继而引入新税项。税捐局所定税率远高于海关所征税率，故可推断其税率波动绝非小幅弹性变动。经陆路运输抵达之货物可选择于齐齐哈尔或本埠交税，然亦有两处均须交税之例。

税捐局局长称，目前其征税对象仅限某类土货（主要为外省进口之土货）以及自国外进口之洋货，偶尔亦有对出口至西伯利亚之洋货征税之情况。

3. 税捐局征税办法如下：

经水路进口之货物：海关放行后，在街道或商铺对之征税。

经陆路自齐齐哈尔进口之货物：海关放行后，在街道或商铺对之征税。

经陆路出口之货物：通常于货物报关前对之征税。

跨江出口之货物：

（1）冬季：因货物须经由官渡路抵达海关冬令过江检查处，故税捐局于大兴街和官渡路交叉口设卡，以便在货物至海关冬令过江检查处报关前对之征税；

（2）夏季：海关通常于横江码头检查处对由渡船运输之货物进行查验，但对复出口之货物会先于海关办公楼前的堤岸上进行查验，货物被放行后再运往渡船处；共有三条路可通往横江码头检查处对面的空地，分别为迎恩路、迎源路和西兴路；税捐局遂于前滩靠近横江码头检查处之地设立检查处，以拦截运往轮渡驳船之货物。若遇有缺少相应凭证之货物，税捐局检查处的巡役便会将之扣押并送至镇中税捐局接受检查并交税，全然不顾该出口或复出口之货物是否已由海关放行；但税捐局之检查并不涉及乘客。

兹附大黑河堤岸与前滩草图（附件 1），图上已将通往堤岸与前滩的各条道路、瑷珲关及税捐局各自设立之检查处的位置以及对布拉戈维申斯克（Blagovestchensk）往来货物进行检查之处悉数标出。

4. 对于税捐局的各项征税办法，除拦截已由海关于关栈进行查验并放行之货物一项外,海关并无可反对之处。然目前,此类货物并无逃避向税捐局交税之企图,且此事亦未收到任何投诉。不过,税捐局是否有权对洋货收税,尤其是于瑷珲此等通商口岸之内,仍有待商榷,但兹以为,即使有何质疑,亦应由洋商及其领事提出,而非海关。

5. 然而,税捐局屡屡侵犯瑷珲关之管辖权,于渡船处对已由海关查验放行之出口及复出口货物进行检查,甚至扣押,擅自处置,而此等货物于出口前应完全由海关处置。为此,瑷珲关已多次向税捐局控诉,然皆仅收到保证不再干预之回复,可侵犯管辖权之现象仍在。

6. 1921 年 7 月 6 日,一名俄商在驱马车前往布拉戈维申斯克的途中被税捐局的巡役拦下,但该俄商手中分明持有征税汇办处开具的完税证明,足以证实其货物已由海关放行。该俄商在被带往镇中税捐局的途中,于海关办公楼前停下,向超等外班关员报告了此事,随后又向本署提出,该巡役有何权力拦截已由海关放行之出口货物。本署遂致信税捐局,请其对此越权行为做出解释。税捐局回信承认此过失,并称已命下属职员不得再有类似之过。随附信函抄件（附件 2——来字第五百八十七号）。

目前,税捐局虽已声明不会再有越权之行为,但偶尔依然会有对出口洋货征税之情况。

此事已呈报哈尔滨关税务司,其亦赞同本署之行动。

7. 8 月 1 日,符拉迪沃斯托克某商行大黑河代理前来汇报称,税捐局要向已由海关查验并免税放行之复出口至布拉戈维申斯克的洋货征税。随后,本署便与超等外班关员一同前往渡船处查看,发现税捐局代表确实已将其所述货物扣押,意欲征税,于是向该商人说明,本署无权干预税捐局行为,除非瑷珲关管辖权受到侵犯,但已告知该商人可正式向哈尔滨关税务司投诉税捐局。

8. 鉴于事情发展至此,本署决定向哈尔滨关税务司申请进一步明确指示,以便与税捐局进行交涉。哈尔滨关税务司回复,凡轮船或货物于港口界限以内前滩一带或已登记的关栈之中者,税捐局均不得干涉；凡货物持有海关凭证或曾于梁家屯分卡报明并获分卡完税凭证前往瑷珲或大黑河口岸者,最终放行前,税捐局均不得干涉。

本署随后致信道尹（参阅海关总税务司署第 17/87300 号令所附税务处文）,说明海关之不满及主张,指出因海关通常须于堤岸对出口及复出口货物进行检查,尤其是水位较高时,前滩完全被淹没,唯有堤岸可用,故前滩及堤岸应供海关专用。

9. 道尹随后回复称,此事须提请省政府裁夺。如此本署便只能静候佳音,直到最近方从贵署令文及海关监督信函中得知此事已提交至税务处,然因海关之观点未能被如实转达,恐怕该机构无法做出公正判断。

10. 于是，本署决定与税捐局局长刘保掯先生当面说明此事，并请海关监督安排会面，最终于本月18日完成会谈。会谈中，本署申明凡货物于海关管辖范围内者，均不应受到干涉，并阐明有此规定之原因，对此刘保掯先生表示赞同，并坦承在对经陆路进出口之货物、经水路进口之货物、冬季跨江出口至布拉戈维申斯克之货物以及持有进出口过境单或其他海关凭证之货物的管控上，税捐局并无难处，但对于夏季跨江出口之土货，税捐局若不予检查，实难以管控。对此，本署建议其在通往堤岸的道路上安设巡役，以便在货物进入海关管辖范围前对之进行检查；但其表示已有严令不得增加开销及人员（此事已得道尹确认）。

若如刘保掯先生所言，此事便无法可解，兹以为其言论只是一种托辞，并非客观之原因，遂又建议其根据商人名册对零散销售之货物征税。对此，其表示可行，但认为对于极易走私之行商依然难以管控。最后，经过多番讨论（气氛始终融洽），海关监督提议由其以道尹之身份与税捐局发布联合声明，由当地商户为所收留之行商负责，凡出口之货物，均须于向海关报明前，向税捐局报检，违者将处以高额罚款。

刘保掯先生坚持保留税捐局于前滩所设检查处，认为唯有如此，方可确保未持海关凭证之货物能够接受税捐局之检查，同时亦承诺其巡役绝不会以防止欺诈之名而搜查或扣押货物，但会依靠商人（商人皆与其职员熟识）对商铺征税或罚款。

11. 双方最终协定，由刘保掯先生起草一份备忘录，确定双方各自的管辖权，如有必要，再由本署修正，最后提交双方各自上级裁夺。然次日，刘保掯先生携其备忘录草案前来时，提出有时仅凭包装不足以判断货物，而货主所持凭证又属无效文件，或根本未持凭证，每每此时，税捐局只得打开包装，确认货物价值，以便征税或处以罚款。但如此一来，便又引起越权之问题，尽管刘保掯先生一再强调，去年此类事件仅有两起。

12. 于是，我们再次于海关监督处进行讨论，最终商定若此类事件再次出现，则由税捐局通知瑷珲关，以便海关关员可于检查时从旁监督，直至货物最终运出。

13. 兹附暂定办法相关函件（附件3——总字十八号）。其中规定，凡进口货物，均须由海关先行处置，凡出口货物，均须于进入海关管辖范围前，由税捐局收税，双方均不得越权征税；税捐局于堤岸所设检查处可以保留，但须于处置已由海关放行之出口货物时，通知海关关员从旁监督。

14. 当然，该暂定办法或将引来争议，毕竟在海关合法管辖范围之内，最好无其他机构行使职能，然若由瑷珲关独占堤岸和前滩，让税捐局撤除其检查处，虽不会再有侵权之事，但必然会引发矛盾。

不过,此次若妥协,海关日后或许会被迫协助征收地方税,处境难免会有些尴尬,亦会有违条约之规定。

15. 总体来说,海关依然可以争取独占前滩和堤岸之权,但胜算确实不大,毕竟税捐局于前滩所设检查处已运营多年,不会轻易撤出,而且省政府通过税捐局受益颇丰,必会予以支持,不会轻易倒向海关,另外,商人方面对税捐局的反对情绪亦低于对海关的抵触,因为他们可与税捐局达成协议,但与海关无法达成,此外,税捐局隶属省政府,海关直属远在北京的中央政府,而海关监督亦有道尹之身份,须对省政府负责,其俸禄亦来自省内税收。

如此,唯有和平解决此事,方能促进双方关系友好发展,促使问题得以顺利解决,其他重要事项亦会因此而得到妥善处置。

16. 本署与税捐局局长详谈此事,主要是为了明确其管理意图,力求双方能够达成一致观点,无奈最终仅得出一套未能尽善的暂定办法,具体如何解决还须由北京方面重新定夺。

不过,本署已于交谈中说明,此次会谈完全为本署一人之主张,拟议办法亦未能严格遵循海关原则,且凡涉及海关之事,终须由总税务司裁定。

17. 目前,瑷珲口岸尚未出现越权之事,因为渡船处与海关办公楼仅相距 5 里,且往来货物运输极少。而大黑河口岸,税捐局亦仅是在渡船运输之货物上存在越权行为,对于轮船运输之货物,从未加以干涉。

您忠诚的仆人

包安济（G. Boezi）

瑷珲关署理税务司

呈海关总税务司署 55 号文　　　　　　瑷珲关 / 大黑河 1922 年 6 月 15 日

尊敬的海关总税务司（北京）：

　　根据海关总税务司署第 42/89154 号令：

　　　　"瑷珲关第 23 号呈所提交之与税捐局界定各自管辖权拟定办法有根本性错误，不予批准；请税捐局摆正位置，退至海关专有管辖权界限以外。"

　　兹附与道尹（兼海关监督）就此事来往信函抄件。

　　兹报告，道尹（兼海关监督）于其 4 月 16 日第 136 号信函中告知税务处已批准拟定办法；但因未收到贵署指令，本署未立即回复。

　　收到海关总税务司署第 42/89154 号令后，本署当即致信道尹（兼海关监督）（6 月 1 日第 37 号信函），说明贵署决定，并请其遵照执行。

　　道尹（兼海关监督）于其 6 月 7 日第 176 号信函中回复称，税务处已规定照拟定办法行事，总税务司恐怕难以驳斥。

　　本署于 6 月 13 日（第 39 号信函）回复说明，据其信函内容可知，其向税务处汇报拟定办法时言辞有误，未照地方协定内容——说明，然本署皆为明朗措辞，无论口头或书面；因此，税务处是在未完全了解之情况下有此决定，而本署业已将地方形势及海关意见据实呈报海关总税务司，税务处亦会向总税务司询问意见，所以本署将谨遵总税务司传达之决定行事。

　　兹认为，此事已无法于地方解决，若本署于此协商之事对整件事情之发展有何不利影响，本署深感抱歉，但的确从未想过此事会出现误解，亦未料到税务处会在未询问贵署意见之情况下做出决定，甚至未将决定告知贵署。税务处理应知晓，本口岸海关监督所获收益及威望皆源自于其道尹之身份，因此涉及此等问题时，其必不会于报告中违背政府之利益，支持海关。

您忠诚的仆人

包安济（G. Boezi）

瑷珲关署理税务司

致瑷珲关第 <u>68/90437</u> 号令 　　　　　海关总税务司署 1922 年 7 月 25 日北京

尊敬的瑷珲关税务司：

根据第 55 号呈：

"海关监督已知晓海关总税务司不同意与黑河税捐局商量的拟订办法六条，已向税务处申请复议。"

奉总税务司之命，兹通知贵署，请转告海关监督，税务处未就任何拟订办法与海关总税务司进行沟通审批，且海关总税务司并未批准该办法，在等待总税务司指示之时，贵署无权使该办法生效。

您忠诚的仆人

贝乐业（J. H. Berruyer）

会计科税务司受总务科税务司委托签发

呈海关总税务司署 <u>120</u> 号文　　　　瑷珲关 / 大黑河 1923 年 5 月 28 日

尊敬的海关总税务司（北京）：

1. 根据此前与大黑河税捐局相关信函及海关总税务司署第 81/91319 号令：

　　"应海关总税务司要求，税务处已撤回对瑷珲关海关监督呈送之中国海关与税捐局共同拟定之暂定办法的批准。"

兹报告，海关监督于 1922 年 11 月自奉天及齐齐哈尔出差两月返回后，本署便向其说明了海关总税务司署第 81/91319 号令之指示，并请其协助将税捐局于渡船处设立之检查处撤除，但其表示尚未接到税务处指令，希望本署可耐心等待。然本署静待数月，杳无音信，无奈于 1923 年 4 月 5 日向海关监督（监去字第一百二十七号）致函并附税务处令，请其向税捐局下发相应指令。

2. 不久之后，税捐局局长同海关监督秘书前来会晤，以期重新商讨此事。但此次讨论之内容与此前并无二致，亦未涉及任何利益问题。本署再次声明，前滩及码头应为海关专用，税捐局局长亦无可辩驳，但认为其于渡船处所设检查处应予保留，以便检查货物运输，而且若将之拆除，另于通往码头的三条道路上新设检查处，所需费用未免太大。对此，本署指出，税捐局应使其与海关相对应之地位合法化，虽然费用会因此而有所增加，但海关同样因放弃对经由梁家屯分卡之土货征税而损失巨大，而且还增加了巡缉的相关开支。税捐局局长表示，其须向财政厅汇报此事，在得到批准之前，无法擅自增加经费支出，或采取任何行动。本署遂请其向省财政厅说明中国海关与税捐局须于各自管辖范围内行事，并申请支出更多经费，以便妥善解决此事。

3. 数日后，海关监督来函（监来字第四百零二号）告知，税捐局已向财政厅报告此事。

4. 1923 年 5 月 14 日，海关监督来函（监来字第四百一十九号）传达省财政厅之回复。从中可知，税捐局试图说明其于渡船处所设检查处并未侵犯海关权利，财政厅于回信中表示，既然双方各司其职，税捐局于渡船处所设检查处则应保留，并请海关监督转告海关，不得再次介入此事。

5. 本署随后致函海关监督（监去字第一百三十九号），说明此事于海关而言关系重大，且侵权属实，现已别无他法，只得将此事呈报海关总税务司；另请其向税务处报告此事，并强调省财政厅应遵照税务处之决定。

6. 随呈附上与海关监督往来信函抄件。值得指出的是，海关监督本应代表税务处，但却从未将税务处应贵署要求撤回对中国海关与税捐局共同拟定之暂定办法的批准一事传达与本署，亦从未在与省政府的通信中提及税务处之决定。

7. 于目前而言，除非税务处愿意进一步采取措施，保证地方政府与海关监督遵照其决定行事，否则海关现阶段除抗议省政府不法行为以及税捐局所有侵权行为外，再无他计可施。

您忠诚的仆人

包安济（G. Boezi）

瑷珲关署理税务司

3. 为汇报东三省前巡阅使张作霖将军企图挪用海关税收盈余事

51

I. G.

Aigun / Taheiho 27th May, 1922.

Sir,

1.　　　I have the honour to report that on the evening of the 16th instant I received an urgent message from Harbin, conveying the information that Chang Tso-lin was about to declare the independence of the Three Eastern Provinces and to appropriate the surplus Revenue of the Manchurian Ports.　The following day I transferred the balance in the Revenue Account to Account D, according to the instructions of your Despatch No. 40/89,064, in partial repayment of cost of lands and Buildings recently purchased; and, fearing that the money may be in danger even in Service Account, I made a telegraphic transfer of $ 11,000 to the Hongkong and Shanghai Bank in Harbin.　The reason for not remitting to Shanghai was that the minimum quotation was 11 per cent., while I only paid 6 per mille

on

The Inspector General of Customs,

PEKING.

on the remittance to Harbin; when rates become
more reasonable, I will remit from my Account D
to your Service Account in Shanghai through the
Hongkong and Shanghai Bank in Harbin.

2.   On the 17th I received your telegram of
the 16th, enjoining not to retain a large Revenue
balance in the Chinese Bank, but to remit
frequently.   In reply, I informed you the same
day of the steps I had just taken.

3.   On the 19th, as I went to see the
Taoyin-Superintendent, he started talking about the
amount of Collection and Expenditure in this Port,
and what the surplus would be.   I saw at once
what he was driving at, and told him that I
could not give exact figures, but that he knew
that an appropriation of $ 29,400 has been
sanctioned by the Shui-wu Ch'u, and that therefore
no surplus of any kind is to be looked for, for
quite a time.   Then he said he had received
a telegram
~~acct telegram~~ from the former Inspector General of
the Three Eastern Provinces, General Chang Tso-lin,
instructing him to remit the Customs surplus to

                                        Mukden

Mukden instead of Peking. I replied that my duty is to remit any available Revenue to yourself in Shanghai, or as directed by you; that I would never ask your authority to do otherwise; that it may be a very dangerous course for Chang Tso-lin to try and confiscate the Customs Revenue which guarantees foreign loans and Indemnities.

On coming back to Office, I found that the Taoyin-Superintendent had already sent copy of Chang's telegram; which states that the Peking Government is now under oppression and unable to exercise its functions; therefore the surplus of Customs and Salt Revenue, after deducting payments on account of foreign indebtedness, should, from 1st May, be remitted to the Fengtien Treasury instead of Peking; severe punishment is threatened in case of disobedience. The Taoyin added of his own that he would like to know the amount of the surplus and the place where the Revenue is deposited.

I

I replied at once with two despatches: in one, to the Taoyin, I stated that according to instructions, the available Revenue is to be remitted to the Inspector General; also that the payments towards foreign indebtedness are ~~also~~ made by you, so that the amount of surplus can in no case be ascertained by this Office. In another despatch addressed to the Superintendent, I informed him that, very likely, for some time, the Revenue would entirely be absorbed by ordinary expenses and by the cost of the land and building recently purchased. Copy of the correspondence is appended (No. 1).

4. On the 20th the Bank of China sent copy of a communication from the Taoyin-Superintendent, which apprised the Bank of the orders received from Mukden and forbade for the future any remittance for the Customs without knowledge and sanction of his own office. Copy of the letter is appended (No. 2). I went at once to see the Acting Manager; I pointed out that the Bank would lose all credit if they allowed

anybody

anybody but myself to interfere with Customs Moneys and he agreed that the Bank holds the Revenue to the order of the Commissioner and nobody else; asked me to take no notice of their letter, which they were bound to write, as the information concerned the Customs; and sent a reply to the Taoyin stating that they cannot comply with his orders.

5.   The same day the Taoyin came to see me, and asked what solution could be found to the problem. I replied that the only one was to drop any pretence at confiscating the surplus of the Revenue; that my position was very clear, and I could not recede from it. He was very much worried; he said that already he had advised the Fengtien Government against such a course, but had again been ordered to go on as directed; he asked if I could state in writing that for two or three months there would be no remittance to either Peking, Shanghai or Mukden, in the hope that Chang Tso-lin might be satisfied with the guarantee that no money would go to his enemies.

Of

Of course I refused to enter into any such engagement and said that I had already gone far enough in writing to him, as Superintendent, and in order to help him out of trouble, that the Revenue is likely to be entirely used for Service purposes for some time to come. There the matter rests for the present.

6.   I cannot say whether there will be difficulties in future.   But the position taken by the local Authorities is generally one of prudent neutrality; the General, who has been asked to proceed to the front, has again excused himself alleging the unsettled state of the Siberian border, and the threat of Hunghutze; the local Chamber of Commerce is supporting him, and the Taoyin has rallied to this policy. Consequently, I do not think there will be any violence against the Customs; should new developments occur, I shall report; if necessary, and before taking any important step, I shall ask for your instructions by wire.

I have the honour to be, Sir,

Your obedient Servant,

Acting Commissioner.

呈海关总税务司署 <u>51</u> 号文　　　　　　瑷珲关 / 大黑河 1922 年 5 月 27 日

尊敬的海关总税务司（北京）：

　　1. 兹报告，本署于 5 月 16 日晚收到哈尔滨关发来紧急信件，告知张作霖将宣布东三省独立，并将挪用满洲各口岸税收盈余。根据海关总税务司署第 40/89064 号令指示，本署已于 17 日将税收账户余额转入 D 账户，部分用于支付最近购置地产及房屋之费用；然款项即便存于海关账户中，本署仍担心其安全性，遂向汇丰银行哈尔滨分行电汇 11000 银圆。未汇至上海分行皆因汇至上海之汇费最低为每百元十一元，而汇至哈尔滨分行仅为每千元六元；待汇率恢复正常后，本署将通过汇丰银行哈尔滨分行将瑷珲关 D 账户款项汇至海关总税务司于汇丰银行上海分行的海关账户。

　　2. 5 月 17 日，本署收到贵署 5 月 16 日关于不得将大笔税收余额存放于华籍银行而须经常汇出之电报后，便于当日汇报了瑷珲关所采取之措施。

　　3. 5 月 19 日，本署前去面见道尹（兼海关监督），当其开始谈及本口岸税收与开支金额，以及盈余金额时，本署便马上了解其意图，并告知目前无法给出确切数额，但如其所知税务处此前已批准为瑷珲关拨款 29400 银圆，因此近期之内应不会有何盈余。随后道尹扬言已收到东三省前巡阅使张作霖将军之电报，命令其将海关盈余汇至奉天而非北京。本署回复称，本署之职责乃是将可用税收汇至海关总税务司于上海之账户，或依海关总税务司命令行事，断不可做出其他请示，而且税收乃为中国外债及赔偿之担保，张作霖若欲挪用，着实危险。

　　本署回至瑷珲关后，发现道尹（兼海关监督）已将张作霖电报抄件发来；电报中说明，北京政府已遭受压制，无法行使职责，故于支付外债后，关税及盐税余额应自 5 月 1 日起汇至奉天国库而非北京，并威胁若不从令必以严惩。道尹另于电报抄件中提出欲知瑷珲关税收盈余金额及储存之处。

　　本署立即向道尹（兼海关监督）发送两封回函；其一至其道尹之身份，说明，根据指令可用税收均汇至海关总税务司，并由总税务司支付外债，因此瑷珲关无法确定盈余金额。另一至其海关监督之身份，告知其税收或将完全用于常规经费支出及近期所购土地及房屋之开销。随呈附上信函抄件（附件 1）。

　　4. 5 月 20 日，中国银行发来道尹（兼海关监督）信函抄件一份，函中通知中国银行奉天方面所下达之命令，命中国银行今后不得于道尹公署不知情及不批准的情况下为海关汇款。随呈附上该信函抄件（附件 2）。收到该函后，本署立即与中国银行大黑河支行代理行长会面,并指出银行若允许税务司以外之人干涉海关钱款,信誉必将受损,代理行长于是同意仅照本署之命令保存税款,并说明此前致信皆因事关瑷珲关,不必挂怀,之后便向道尹回函表明中国银行无法遵照其指令行事。

5. 5月20日,道尹前来询问如何解决此事。本署向其表明立场,告知唯有政府不再利用任何借口没收税收盈余方为解决之道。道尹十分担忧,表示早已建议奉天政府放弃此做法,但再次收到命令要求继续如此行事,随后又询问本署可否书面声明,今后两至三个月内不会再向北京、上海或奉天汇款,以此作为不向张作霖敌方提供钱款之保证,希望张作霖可满意此做法。本署固然拒绝达成任何此类约定,并表示此前向其海关监督之身份致信,告知未来一段时间税收或全部为海关所用,已是在尽最大努力助其摆脱困难。此事已暂且搁置。

6. 虽然将来是否会有何麻烦,目前仍难以确定,但是当地政府十分谨慎,基本采取中立态度;而张作霖将军因西伯利亚边境局势动荡及土匪(红胡子)横行已赴前线;商会对其十分拥护,道尹亦紧随其方针行事。因此,本署认为海关暂不会遭遇任何暴力,待有何进展,再行呈报,如有必要采取重要措施,本署亦会提前发送电报请求指示。

您忠诚的仆人

包安济(G. Boezi)

瑷珲关署理税务司

4. 为同海关监督商议对报关行进行管理事

79

I. G.   Aigun / Taheiho 17th November, 1922.

Sir,

In conformity with the instructions of Chinese Secretary's Memorandum of 20th October :

Particulars of Case No. 21 of Aigun Confiscation Report for the June quarter, 1922, to be reported by despatch ;

I have the honour to report that on 8th May last, a Chinese Merchant by the name of T'sui Fu (崔福) called at the General Office to make enquiries about certain cargo of his. He proved to be the owner of 2 c/s Hemp Skin, weight 1 picul, and 4 c/s brooms, value Hk. Tls. 5.50, which were imported and passed through the Customs by Broker Kwang Chü Kung (廣聚公), on 24th April, under Liangchiat'u cargo memo. No. 546 of 22nd April.

T'sui

The Inspector General of Customs,

P E K I N G.

Ts'ui Fu then produced a Bill, duly stamped by the
Broker, showing beyond doubt that a charge had been
made, for Customs Duty, of $ 7.57, while the
Broker actually paid Hk. Tls. 0.800 = $ 1.25. -

The representative of the Broker, summoned in
the Office, could offer no explanation, admitted the
fault and asked for leniency. There are at this
Port no Regulations concerning Customs Brokers, but
I felt that such an abuse of confidence perpetrated
in the name of the Customs was calculated, in the
words of Circular No. 2680, to "bring the Customs
"Administration into ill repute with Chinese traders";
and, accordingly, gave the culprit the choice
between being for ever debarred from acting as Broker to the Customs, and the refund of the amount
overcharged, a fine of Hk. Tls 50, and a close watch
on his doings afterwards. He preferred the latter
course; and I informed the Chamber of Commerce, so
that merchants be on their guard against unscrupu-
lous brokers.

I take this opportunity to ask whether I
can approach the Superintendent in view of establishing a control on Brokers at this Port, on the

lines

lines suggested by Circular No. 2680. Firms have never been registered at this Port; but I think such course unnecessary in Taheiho and Aigun, where most of the firms and their representatives are personally known to our Staff - neither have Brokers ever been subjected to any Regulations; and a certain control would, on the contrary, prove beneficial to the Customs and the Public.

In Tahsiho there are three large firms doing Brokers' work with the Customs : the Wu T'ung S. S. Co (戊通公司), Kung Ho Chan (共合栈) and Kung Chi Chan (公济栈), and they deal mostly with steamer-borne cargo. In addition, some twelve Inns act as Customs Brokers, pparticularly for overland cargo, and for travelling merchants: these bring their goods from Tsitsihar or other places in Manchuria, and entrust the Innkeeper not only with Customs operations, but, against a small percentage, with the task of finding a buyer.

In Aigun there are only about 10 Inns acting as Customs Brokers.

I am to add that only steamer-borne goods

are

are at times entrusted, before completion of all

Customs formalities, to the custody of the three

principal Brokers, in their capacity as Steamer

Agents; otherwise, no goods are released, no guarantee

ever cancelled, until all Customs requirements have

been complied with.

      I have the honour to be,

        Sir,

      Your obedient Servant,

       Acting Commissioner.

[l—27c]

No. 95   COMMRS.   **Inspectorate General of Customs,**

Aigun   No. 92,186   *PEKING,* 1st December 19̃22.

SIR,

I am directed by the Inspector General to acknowledge receipt of your Despatch No. 79:

reporting your action in inflicting a fine on a Customs Broker for exacting from a Merchant duties in excess of those charged by the Customs and requesting permission to approach the Superintendent with a view to establishing control over Customs Brokers on the lines suggested in Circular No. 2680:

and, in reply, to say that the case was clearly one calling for protection of the trader from the rapacity of the Broker and for punishment of the latter, but while the Commissioner can act as prosecutor it will be best for him to abstain from acting as Magistrate and such cases should not be entered in the Confiscation Reports.

You may approach the Superintendent with a view to establishing control over Customs

Brokers

THE COMMISSIONER OF CUSTOMS,

     A I G U N.

Brokers at your port, submitting the arrangements arrived at for the Inspector General's approval before putting them into force.

    I am,

     Sir,

    Your obedient Servant,

      Chief Secretary.

呈海关总税务司署 <u>79</u> 号文　　　　　　　瑷珲关 / 大黑河 1922 年 11 月 17 日

尊敬的海关总税务司 (北京):

根据 1922 年 10 月 20 日汉文秘书科税务司通函：

"请详细汇报瑷珲关 1922 年第二季度没收货物报单第 21 号案件。"

兹报告，1921 年 5 月 8 日，华商崔福来至瑷珲关征税汇办处，询问其货物相关事宜。经查，此前广聚公（报关行）持梁家屯分卡 4 月 22 日第 546 号货物单于 4 月 24 日至大黑河报关并已获放行之货物，包括 2 箱麻皮（重 1 担）及 4 箱金雀花麻（价值 6.50 海关两），均为崔福所有。崔福随后出具了一份由广聚公盖章之提单，据提单所示，海关征收关税金额为 7.57 银圆，但报关行实付金额为 0.800 海关两，即 1.25 银圆。

广聚公代表随后被传唤至征税汇办处，但其无以辩解，只得予以承认，并请求宽大处理。本口岸虽无与海关事务代办人有关之章程，但本署认为此等以海关名义滥用职权之行为，正如海关总税务司署第 2680 号通令所述，"令海关于中国商界之名誉受损"，故令其选择或不再充任报关行，或退还索取之超额费用，并缴纳罚款 50 海关两，今后亦会受到海关的密切监视。广聚公代表最终选择后者；本署已告知商会，让商人提高警惕。

借此机会，兹请示可否照海关总税务司署第 2680 号通令指示方针与海关监督商议本口岸报关行（或海关事务代办人）的管理事宜。虽然各商行从未于本口岸注册，但大黑河与瑷珲两地的商行及其代表均为瑷珲关职员所熟知，故本署以为不必行注册之事，只是报关行（或海关事务代办人）从未受过任何章程之约束，若可稍加监管，于海关及公众而言，势必更为有利。

大黑河共有三家代办海关事务的大商行，分别为戊通公司、共合栈和公济栈，三家商行主要针对由轮船运输之货物。此外另有 12 家客栈在从事海关事务代办之事，主要针对经陆路运输之货物及行商；行商自齐齐哈尔或满洲其他地方将货物运至本地后，通常都会委托店户办理报关事宜，亦有委托店户寻找买家者。

瑷珲仅有 10 家客栈在从事海关事务代办之事。

此外，唯轮船运输之货物有时可在未完成所有海关手续前委托三家大商行以航业公司之名代为监管；余者只有在遵照海关要求将所有手续办理妥当后，方可获准放行，取消担保。

您忠诚的仆人

包安济（G. Boezi）

瑷珲关署理税务司

致瑷珲关第 <u>95/92186</u> 号令　　　　海关总税务司署（北京）1922 年 12 月 1 日

尊敬的瑷珲关税务司：

第 79 号呈收悉：

　　"汇报某报关行向商人强行征收远高于海关规定的税款,已对其处以罚款;并请求批准联络海关监督,以第 2680 号通令为准则,建立对报关行的管控。"

奉总税务司命令,现批复如下：显然,该案件充分表明商人欲寻求保护,免受报关行贪婪的剥削并寻求对其进行处罚。税务司虽可以如检察官一般行事,但最好还是不要越俎代庖行使法官的权力。此类案件不应出现在"没收货物报单"中。

贵署可以会同海关监督,建立对贵口岸报关行的管控,请将达成的办法呈交海关总税务司批准,然后方能照章执行。

您忠诚的仆人

包罗（C. A. Bowra）

总务科税务司

5. 为具报各口岸报关行之组成及营业手续以及海关如何管理之详细方法事

<u>CUSTOMS BROKERS</u>: report on, called for by I.G.
Circular No.4214, forwarded.

556

$\frac{556}{I\ G}$

I.G.

A I G U N　12th May 1931.

Sir,

1.　　　　I have the honour to acknowledge receipt of
Circular No. 4214 :

calling for a report on Customs brokers and
on the measures taken for their control :
and to report that there are at this port no special
regulations for the registration and control of brokers
and that, under present abnormal conditions and trade
restrictions, none would appear necessary. Authority
was received in December 1922 from the Inspector
General, in despatch No. 95/92,186, to approach the
Superintendent with a view to establishing control over
brokers, but the necessity for such action disappeared
with the closure of the Sino-Soviet frontier in the
summer of 1923, since when trade has been confined
almost entirely to goods moved from and to Harbin and
other Sungari ports, and to goods moved along the
Chinese side of the Amur. In the case of the former,
the carrying vessels belong to one shipping concern,
the Harbin Shipping Syndicate (哈尔滨官商航业联合局), which
acts as broker. Goods of the latter category are
conveyed by junk and by steamer and are, by local
regulation, entitled to duty-free treatment. The
steamers engaged in this trade also belong to the
Harbin Syndicate, which attends to the Customs
formalities, and for cargo carried by junks the necessary
formalities are attended to by the junk masters.

2.

The Inspector General of Customs,

S H A N G H A I.

2.　　　　The following is a summary of the local practice : -

(a) Trans-frontier trade: Very limited. All cargo passed through the Customs by the Soviet Far Eastern Trading Bureau (Dalgostorg) under special permission from the Heilungkiang authorities;

(b) Cargo moved by steamer along the Chinese side of the Amur and from and to Sungari Ports: The steamers all belong to the Harbin Shipping Syndicate, which acts as broker. A few odd shipments are applied for by the owners of the goods; and

(c) Goods moved along the Chinese side of the Amur by junk: The junk master acts as broker.

3.　　　　There is one Chinese firm at Taheiho which is prepared to undertake business as Customs broker, but the amount of cargo entrusted to its care is negligible.

4.　　　　A Chinese version, in duplicate, of this report is forwarded enclosed herewith.

I have the honour to be,

Sir,

Your obedient Servant,

(Signed) C. B. Joly

(C. H. B. Joly)

Acting Commissioner.

呈海关总税务司署 <u>556</u> 号文　　　　　　　　瑷珲关 1931 年 5 月 12 日

尊敬的海关总税务司（上海）：

　　1. 根据海关总税务司署第 4214 号通令：

　　　　"请将各口报关行之组成及营业手续以及海关如何管理之方法详细具报。"

　　兹报告，瑷珲关未曾订立报关行注册及管理章程，且按现时贸易衰落情况而论，此等章程似乎亦并无订立施行之必要。

　　案查 1922 年 12 月间海关总税务司署第 95/92186 号令曾指示，海关管理报关行事宜，应与本关监督磋商办法。然此事迄今仍未进行，且自 1923 年夏季中俄采取封锁边境政策以来，贸易已然停滞，此事似无办理之必要。

　　现今，本口贸易仅限于往来哈尔滨或松花江沿岸各地，及黑龙江华岸各处往来运输之货物而已。前项往来松黑两江各处之货物，一概均由哈尔滨官商航业总联合局轮船运输，该局亦同时代理一切报关事宜；后一项在黑龙江华岸各处往来之货物，照章概不完纳关税，运输时，亦由该局轮船装载，其报关事宜仍归该局代理。由民船载运者，则向来由民船船主报关。

　　2. 本口惯例概括如下：

　　（1）跨境贸易：中俄国际间之贸易为数极微，概由苏联远东贸易公司管理一切进出口货物，且须现行呈请黑河市政筹备处转请黑龙江省政府核准后，方能起运。

　　（2）轮船运输沿黑龙江华岸各处及往来哈尔滨或松花江各地货物：均由哈尔滨官商航业总联合局轮船运输，并由该局办理报关事项；有时亦归货主自行报关，但并不多见。

　　（3）民船运输沿黑龙江华岸各处往来之货物：由民船船主自理报关事宜。

　　3. 此外，大黑河仅有华商一家有时亦办理报关事项，唯所经手之货物数量极少，似无关重要。

　　4. 兹附此报告之汉文译本，一式两份。

您忠诚的仆人

周骊（C. H. B. Joly）

瑷珲关署理税务司